Linking the Formal and Informa

UNU WORLD INSTITUTE FOR DEVELOPMENT ECONOMICS RESEARCH (UNU-WIDER) was established by the United Nations University as its first research and training centre and started work in Helsinki, Finland in 1985. The purpose of the institute is to undertake applied research and policy analysis on structural changes affecting developing and transitional economies, to provide a forum for the advocacy of policies leading to robust, equitable, and environmentally sustainable growth, and to promote capacity strengthening and training in the field of economic and social policymaking. Its work is carried out by staff researchers and visiting scholars in Helsinki and via networks of collaborating scholars and institutions around the world.

World Institute for Development Economics Research (UNU-WIDER)
Katajanokanlaituri 6 B, FIN-00160 Helsinki, Finland
www.wider.unu.edu

THE EXPERT GROUP ON DEVELOPMENT ISSUES (EGDI) consists of a number of international experts in development-related academic fields along with Swedish policymakers. The main task of EGDI is to contribute to an increased understanding of global development and an improved effectiveness of development policies. The group initiates and produces studies of importance for the international development debate. EGDI is funded by the Swedish Ministry for Foreign Affairs. The research interests of the group, as well as approaches taken in EGDI studies, provide important perspectives on the Swedish policy for global development.

EGDI Secretariat, Ministry for Foreign Affairs
SE-103 39 Stockholm, Sweden
www.egdi.gov.se

Linking the Formal and Informal Economy

Concepts and Policies

Edited by

Basudeb Guha-Khasnobis, Ravi Kanbur,
and Elinor Ostrom

UNU-WIDER Studies in Development Economics

OXFORD
UNIVERSITY PRESS

Great Clarendon Street, Oxford OX2 6DP

Oxford University Press is a department of the University of Oxford.
It furthers the University's objective of excellence in research, scholarship,
and education by publishing worldwide in

Oxford New York

Auckland Cape Town Dar es Salaam Hong Kong Karachi
Kuala Lumpur Madrid Melbourne Mexico City Nairobi
New Delhi Shanghai Taipei Toronto

With offices in

Argentina Austria Brazil Chile Czech Republic France Greece
Guatemala Hungary Italy Japan Poland Portugal Singapore
South Korea Switzerland Thailand Turkey Ukraine Vietnam

Oxford is a registered trade mark of Oxford University Press
in the UK and in certain other countries

Published in the United States
by Oxford University Press Inc., New York

First published 2006
First published in paperback 2007

British Library Cataloguing in Publication Data
Data available

Library of Congress Cataloging in Publication Data
Data available

Typeset by SPI Publisher Services, Pondicherry, India
Printed in Great Britain
by Ashford Colour Press Ltd., Gosport, Hampshire

ISBN 978–0–19–920476–2 (Hbk.) 978–0–19–923729–6 (Pbk.)

10 9 8 7 6 5 4 3 2 1

Foreword

The distinction between formal and informal organizations remains central to the theory and practice of development more than half a century after the concepts of formality and informality were first defined and discussed. The distinction influences the way that statistical services collect data on developing countries, the development of theoretical and empirical analyses and, most important, the formulation and implementation of policies.

This volume brings together a major new collection of studies on formality and informality in developing countries. The contributions were originally presented at a conference organized in Helsinki in September 2004 by the World Institute for Development Economics Research of the United Nations University (UNU-WIDER) in collaboration with the Expert Group on Development Issues (EGDI) at the Swedish Ministry for Foreign Affairs. The volume includes chapters from some of the very best analysts in development studies and is multidisciplinary in nature, with contributions from anthropologists, economists, sociologists, and political scientists.

Between them the chapters argue for moving beyond the formal–informal dichotomy. Useful as it has proven to be, a more nuanced approach is needed in light of conceptual and empirical advances, and in light of the policy failures brought about by a characterization of 'informal' as 'disorganized'. The wealth of empirical information contained in these chapters, and in the literature more widely, can be used to develop guiding principles for intervention that are based on ground level reality.

Anthony Shorrocks
Director, UNU-WIDER
Finland

Annika Söder
Chairperson, EGDI
State Secretary for International Development Cooperation, Sweden

Contents

List of Figures

List of Tables

List of Abbreviations

ADB	Asian Development Bank
AEs	agricultural enterprises
DC-SSI	Development Commissioner for Small Scale Industries
DEs	Directory Establishments
EGDI	Expert Group on Development Issues
FDI	foreign direct investment
FEDITAPUL	United Front of Informal Workers of the District of Pueblo Libre
FLCs	financial lease companies
GDP	gross domestic product
GNI	gross national income
GSO	General Statistical Office
IFLS	Indonesian Family Life Survey
ILO	International Labour Organization
IMF	International Monetary Fund
INDECOPI	National Institute for the Defense of Competition and Protection of Intellectual Property
INGOs	International Non-Governmental Organizations
JSBs	joint-stock banks
JVBs	joint-venture banks
LED	local economic development
MCC	Maputo Corridor Company
MCDT	Mozal Community Development Trust
MCLI	Maputo Corridor Logistics Initiative
MDC	Maputo Development Corridor
MFIs	microfinance institutions
MISP	Maputo Iron and Steel Project
NAEs	non-agricultural enterprises

NAIS	National Agricultural Insurance Scheme
NDEs	Non-Directory Establishments
NGOs	Non-Governmental Organizations
OAEs	Own Account Enterprises
PPPs	public–private partnerships
ROSCA	rotating savings and credit associations
SBV	State Bank of Vietnam
SDI	Spatial Development Initiative
SEMP	strategic environmental management plan
Sida	Swedish International Development Cooperation Agency
SIDO	Small Industries Development Organisation
SMEs	small and medium enterprises
SOCBs	state-owned commercial banks
SOEs	state-owned enterprises
SSEs	small scale enterprises
SSIs	small scale industries
SSSBEs	small scale service and business enterprises
UNDP	United Nations Development Programme
UNOCHA	United Nations Office for the Coordination of Humanitarian Assistance
UNU	United Nations University
VBP	Vietnam Bank for the Poor
VBSP	Vietnam Bank for Social Policy
VLSS	Vietnam Living Standard Surveys
WIDER	World Institute for Development Economics Research of the UNU
WIEGO	Women in Informal Employment: Globalizing and Organizing

List of Contributors

Rajeev Ahuja is a health finance specialist in the World Bank, Delhi Office. His recent work has been focused on health insurance, especially for the low-income people.

Krister Andersson is Assistant Professor of Political Science and Environmental Studies at the University of Colorado, Boulder, and an affiliated research fellow at the Workshop in Political Theory and Policy Analysis at Indiana University. He studies the politics of international development and environmental governance in nonindustrial societies, and is published in *Public Administration and Development, World Development,* and the *Journal of Environment and Development.*

Martha Alter Chen is a Lecturer in Public Policy at the Kennedy School of Government and Coordinator of the global research-policy network—Women in Informal Employment: Globalizing and Organizing (WIEGO). Her areas of specialization are gender and poverty alleviation, with a focus on issues of employment and livelihoods.

Robert K. Christensen is Assistant Professor of Public Administration in the University of North Carolina at Charlotte's Department of Political Science. His research focuses on the legal aspects of globalization, public and nonprofit administration, and public policy.

Basudeb Guha-Khasnobis is a Research Fellow at UNU-WIDER. His main areas of research include trade and development, role of financial sector in growth, informal sectors, food security, and gender issues.

Keith Hart lives in Paris and teaches anthropology part-time at Goldsmiths College, London. He is currently writing a book on Africa and is the author of *Money in an Unequal World* (2001) and *The Hit Man's Dilemma* (2005).

Ravi Kanbur is the T.H. Lee Professor of World Affairs, International Professor of Applied Economics and Management, professor of economics at Cornell University, and a member of the Expert Group on Development Issues (EGDI) of the Swedish Ministry for Foreign Affairs.

He has taught previously at Oxford, Cambridge, Princeton, Essex and Warwick Universities, and has served on the staff of the World Bank, including as Chief Economist for Africa.

Robert Lensink is Professor in Finance and Financial Markets at the Faculty of Economics, University of Groningen, The Netherlands. His main interest relates to international and development finance.

Norman Loayza is currently lead economist in the research department of the World Bank. He has studied several areas related to economic and social development, including economic growth, private saving, financial depth, monetary policy, trade openness, poverty alleviation, and crime prevention.

Mark McGillivray is a Senior Research Fellow at UNU-WIDER. His research is mainly on the allocation and impact of development aid and on measuring human well-being achievement.

M. R. Narayana is a Professor of Economics at the Institute for Social and Economic Change in Bangalore, India. His current research areas include economics of unorganized, informal, and small-scale enterprises in India.

Jeffrey B. Nugent is Professor of Economics at the University of Southern California where he teaches Development Economics. His research focuses on New Institutional Economics, Income Inequality, Education and Growth, the Political Economy of Reforms, and the Determinants and Effects of Different Property Rights Regimes.

Elinor Ostrom is Arthur F. Bentley Professor of Political Science; Co-Director, Workshop in Political Theory and Policy Analysis; Co-Director, Center for the Study of Institutions, Population and Environmental Change (CIPEC), Indiana University; and, a former member of the Expert Group on Development Issues (EGDI) of the Swedish Ministry for Foreign Affairs.

Ana María Oviedo is a Ph.D. candidate in Economics at the University of Maryland, College Park. Her research focuses on the empirical and theoretical study of the effects of regulation and institutional quality on firm dynamics, productivity, and macroeconomic outcomes; and on the measurement of technological progress.

Diego Pacheco is a Ph.D. candidate in Public Policy and an assistant researcher at the Center for Institutions, Population and Environmental Change (CIPEC) at Indiana University. He has published several books and articles regarding rural development, decentralization, environmental policies, and indigenous populations.

Sally Roever is Visiting Professor in the Department of Public Administration at Leiden University (The Netherlands). Her research fields are Latin American politics, comparative politics, and research methods.

Amos Sawyer is Co-Director and research scholar at the Workshop in Political Theory and Policy Analysis at Indiana University. He is a former Dean of the College of Social Sciences at the University of Liberia, and has published extensively on governance and post-conflict challenges in Africa.

Luis Servén manages the World Bank's research programme on macroeconomics and growth. He has taught at the Universidad Complutense of Madrid, MIT, and CEMFI. His recent research focuses on open economy macroeconomics, fiscal policy and growth, international portfolio diversification, and microeconomic regulation and growth.

Alice Sindzingre is a Research Fellow currently posted at the French public agency for research, the Centre National de la Recherche Scientifique (Paris) and affiliated to the University Paris-X (Research Center Economic). She has conducted research on development economics and political economy mostly in West Africa and has published in academic journals on a wide range of topics, including poverty and the theory of institutions in relation with development.

Fredrik Söderbaum is Associate Professor at the Department of Peace and Development Research at Göteborg University, Sweden and Associate Research Fellow at the United Nations University—Comparative Regional Integration Studies (UNU-CRIS), Bruges, Belgium.

Shailender Swaminathan is an Assistant Professor in the School of Public Health at the University of Alabama, Birmingham. His research areas include the Effects of Social and Economic Context on Human Health, the Long Term Benefits of Early Investments in Children, and Applied Econometrics.

Pham Thi Thu Trà is currently doing her Ph.D. in Finance at the Faculty of Economics, University of Groningen. Her research deals with Economics of Information, Financial Contracting, and the related empirical issues on Vietnam.

Liz Alden Wily works as an independent land tenure adviser to governments and donors, with specialties in common property and decentralized rural land administration. She is currently working in both Sudan and Afghanistan.

Acknowledgements

The editors are grateful to Adam Swallow and Janis Vehmaan-Kreula of UNU-WIDER for their tireless commitment in preparing the final manuscript. They would also like to thank the staff of the Expert Group on Development Issues (EGDI) at the Swedish Ministry for Foreign Affairs, especially Ingrid Widlund and Torgny Holmgren. They would also like to thank Patricia Lezotte at the Workshop in Political Theory and Policy Analysis for her useful contributions at various stages of the development of this volume.

UNU-WIDER acknowledges the financial contributions to the research programme by the governments of Denmark (Royal Ministry of Foreign Affairs), Finland (Ministry for Foreign Affairs), Norway (Royal Ministry of Foreign Affairs), Sweden (Swedish International Development Cooperation Agency—Sida) and the United Kingdom (Department for International Development).

Basudeb Guha-Khasnobis, Helsinki
Ravi Kanbur, Ithaca
Elinor Ostrom, Indiana

1

Beyond formality and informality

Basudeb Guha-Khasnobis, Ravi Kanbur, and Elinor Ostrom

1.1 Introduction

The constructed opposites of formality and informality have been a constant of the development discourse for more than half a century. They have anchored theoretical, empirical, and policy discussions in many disciplines as they have studied the development process. In the 1940s, the Dutch anthropologist Boeke (1942) developed a vision of a developing economy as a 'dual' economy, comprised of the market economy part of the world and a part which lay outside. In the 1950s, Arthur Lewis (1954) conceptualized an influential two-sector model of development in which one sector had modern capitalist firms that maximized profit, while the other sector was comprised of peasant households where the rules for sharing output were different. In the 1970s, the Harris and Todaro (1970) model in development economics brought the dual economy into the standard two-sector framework of equilibrium economics. In development studies more generally, however, the paper by Keith Hart (1973) and the International Labour Office (ILO) mission to Kenya (ILO 1972) established the importance of the dichotomy, and led to an outpouring of research and policy focus. It has helped to organize thinking, served to structure official statistics, and generated a series of policy measures to 'help' the informal sector.

Despite this pedigree, the usefulness of the formal–informal dichotomy has constantly been debated in the literature. Early critiques include those by Bromley (1978). Lipton (1984) defends the usefulness of the concept of the informal sector, but argues for care and nuance in application. Over the past 30 years, this 'to and fro' has continued as new evidence from new areas has been brought to bear on the debate. For example, detailed work, in the 1980s and the 1990s, on the management of common property regimes has shed new light on what were once considered to be 'informal' arrangements (McCay and Acheson 1987; Ostrom 1990; Bromley *et al.* 1992). Policies introduced to 'formalize' these arrangements have been criticized in light of their sometimes counterproductive consequences (Platteau and Gaspart 2003; Platteau 2004; Agrawal and Gupta 2005). In the last few years, the idea of extending formal legal property rights to the 'informal' sector has taken hold as a possible powerful policy tool to help the poor make the best of their assets (de Soto 1989, 2003; Alden Wily, chapter 15, this volume). In light of these developments, it is appropriate to consider once again the conceptual and empirical basis of the formal–informal divide, and to assess carefully its policy implications.

This chapter introduces a significant new collection of studies on formality and informality in developing countries. The chapters were originally presented at a major conference organized in Helsinki in September 2004 by the Expert Group on Development Issues (EGDI) at the Swedish Ministry for Foreign Affairs and the World Institute for Development Economics Research (UNU-WIDER). All of the chapters use the terminology of formal and informal, and some make use of the conceptual dichotomy to begin the discussion. Most of the chapters, however, highlight the basic thesis of this chapter—that we need to move beyond formality and informality to make progress in understanding the realities of economic activities in poor countries, and to design policies to benefit the poor. These chapters, as well as the broader literature, form the basis of the arguments advanced in this introduction to the volume.

The plan of this chapter is as follows. Section 1.2 addresses the conceptualization of formal versus informal. Section 1.3 begins the discussion of policy by specifying the objectives of interventions in this area. Section 1.4 continues the policy analysis by examining some of the lessons learnt and deriving recommendations for successful policy intervention, based on experiences in a range of countries and situations. Section 1.5 concludes by renewing the call for the development discourse to go beyond formality and informality.

1.2 Conceptualizing Formal and Informal

Given the prominence of the formal–informal dichotomy in the development discourse, one might expect to see a clear definition of the concepts, consistently applied across the whole range of theoretical, empirical, and policy analyses. We find no such thing. Instead, it turns out that formal and informal are better thought of as metaphors that conjure up a mental picture of whatever the user has in mind at that particular time.

In his early defence of the informal sector (IS) concept, Lipton (1984: 196) set out the problem as follows: 'The IS concept has become discredited on account of three alleged deficiencies: misplaced dualism, misplaced isolation and confusion'. He then goes on to specify each critique and to mount a defence against it. Misplaced dualism refers to the fact that in practice there is no clear split between formal and informal; rather, there is a continuum. The defence is that a dichotomy can nevertheless prove useful in analytical terms. Misplaced isolation is the neglect of the fact that the relationships of the informal sector to the rest of the economy are not investigated. While this is a valid critique of some of the literature, as Lipton also notes, we agree with Lipton that this is not an inherent weakness of the dichotomy, but rather of the uses to which it is put.

Under the third critique, that of confusion, is the idea that the characteristics of this sector are not well spelt out. Nor, relatedly, are the entities that would fall into this sector. So we come to a situation where Harriss (1978: 1,077, quoted in Lipton 1984) says, 'It is for the initiates to spot IS and they know it when they see it'. Lipton's (1984) defence is that in standard sources (such as ILO 1972; Sethuraman 1976; Souza and Tokman 1976), only three key characteristics are used to define IS. These are: (1) 'substantial overlap between providers of capital and providers of labour in each enterprise' (pp. 198–200); (2) 'prevalence of perfect, or rather... near-perfect, competition' (p. 200); and (3) 'IS consists largely of "unorganised," unicorporated enterprises, to which legal restrictions on employment (wage minima, regulations affecting working conditions, etc.) and on acquisitions of non-labour inputs (licences, quotas, etc.) do not apply... ' (pp. 200–201).

However, in the literature since Lipton (1984), the tendency to use many different characterizations has persisted. A bewildering range of (often only implicit) definitions are used to discuss the formal and the informal. Reviews since Lipton (1984) have concluded that there are competing perspectives rather than a single dichotomy (Portes and Schauffler 1993; Cross 1998), and this view is supported by the most recent examinations of the literature (Christensen, chapter 3, this volume; Sindzingre, chapter 4, this volume). And discussions of the formal and the informal have been enriched considerably by the literature of the past two decades on (self) organization of common property regimes (Ostrom 2005), and by the push in some policy circles to extend property rights to groups of individuals who do not currently 'enjoy' such rights (de Soto 2003).

Not surprisingly, the views on the entities that comprise the informal sector also differ greatly. Lipton (1984) argued strongly for the 'Family Mode of Production' as a general category that fell naturally into this category. In official statistics, different countries use the terms differently in detail even when they might mean the same thing in a general sense (Muller and Esselaar 2004; Narayana, chapter 6, this volume; Sindzingre, chapter 4, this volume). The international official definitions, for example as codified by the ILO, have been expanding. The current official definition of 'informal sector' was adopted by the 1993 International Conference of Labour Statisticians based on characterizing an enterprise as informal. In 2003, guidelines were introduced to expand the definition to include informal employment outside informal enterprises, with an appropriate definition of the former (Chen, chapter 5, this volume).

From this mass of alternative uses of the terms and alternative characterizations, we would like to highlight two strands that are particularly relevant for the current policy dialogue. The first strand is the notion of informal as being outside the reach of different levels and mechanisms of official governance and formal as being reachable by these mechanisms. This notion underlies many official definitions of 'informal enterprises' as those that are not registered and are legally outside the tax net. It also underlies many analytical investigations of enterprises and activities that operate illegally, in violation of formal state rules and regulations, even though informality and illegality are not considered to be equivalent in this notion. The notion also animates the lively policy debate on the extent to which the informal sector owes its existence to 'overly constraining' official regulations which lead to economic activity taking place outside this net, either by organizing so that the regulations do not formally apply, or operating in contravention of the regulations. And, of course, this is also the dimension that best captures different views on the benefits or otherwise of extending the reach of official structures to where they currently do not reach (e.g. legal property rights), or of reducing this reach (e.g. labour regulations).

The second strand that can be discerned in the discourse, and which we believe to be important in shaping policy responses, has to do with the nature of organization. The informal is often identified with 'lacking structure' and the formal with 'structured'—the term 'unorganized sector' is often used. Other cross-cutting themes one finds are 'simple' versus 'complex' or 'irregular' versus 'predictable' (Hart, chapter 2, this volume). In the policy discourse, the association of the informal with unstructured has been a powerful impetus for interventions that have often led to disaster. A striking illustration of this is the attempt to nationalize forests in Nepal, based on the analysis that deforestation was being caused by the inability of small local communities to prevent environmental degradation (Ives and Messerli 1989). In fact, as we now know, the local communities had better structures in place to deal with the deforestation that was the result of population and other pressures (Arnold 1993; Varughese and Ostrom 2001). These structures were not recognized, and were replaced by the formal state structures which proved to be ineffective and corrupt, leading to even faster deforestation (Gilmour and Fisher 1991; Waltner-Toews *et al.* 2003). Now, the government of Nepal is trying to reverse its earlier policy and is turning many forests over to Forest User Groups that it organizes (Nagendra and Ostrom, forthcoming).

Exactly the opposite is true of the software industry of India, now recognized as a world leader. It flourished under the entrepreneurship of some highly skilled and far-sighted individuals, quickly becoming the fastest growing export sector of India. Its current reforms notwithstanding, India still remains a fairly regulated economy, but the government was surprisingly non-interfering as far as the software sector was concerned. Even until very recently, the industry's output and exports were categorized as 'miscellaneous' in India's national accounts (as opposed to being called 'manufacturing' or 'services'), such was the degree of informality. The initial abstinence of the government was indeed a blessing in disguise.

These two dimensions—the reach of official governance and the degree of structuring—need to be further specified and made precise,[1] but they provide an initial entry to a framework for capturing the many definitions that abound in the literature. In this conception, an economic activity can be characterized along two dimensions. The first is the extent to which it interacts with, or comes into the net of, the structures of official governance at the national or local levels.[2] The question of whether an employer is registered or not with a governmental unit would be a simple illustration of this dimension (see chapters 2–6 in Part I of this volume).

[1] Loayza *et al.* (chapter 7, this volume), for example, note that there are at least seven areas of a firm's activity that are potentially subject to regulation: entry, exit, labour market relationship, fiscal burden, international trade, financial markets, and contract enforcement.

[2] Christensen (chapter 3, this volume) points out the importance of the international level as well.

The second dimension is the extent to which an activity and the interactions among its constituent individuals are structured according to a predictable framework (not necessarily one that is written down). Muller and Esselaar (2004), for example, refer to the casualization of employment as involving employees of both registered and unregistered firms who lack a written contract or any form of employee benefits. They find that a significant number of employees have a casual (e.g. unstructured) relationship with employers in South Africa.

The distinction between the two dimensions is not redundant. This is illustrated, for example, by the detailed empirical work showing the highly structured interactions within groups that manage common-pool resources, far removed from any interaction with official governance (Tucker and Ostrom 2005; Ostrom 2005). Moreover, for similar levels of connection with the state tax system, we see enterprises with very different types and complexities of internal structure.

The two dimensions do, however, interact. On the one hand, attempts by official governance to extend its reach, for example, by widening a regulation to an area where it was not previously applied, will in general lead to a response that may move some activities outside the reach of the regulation (legally or illegally). In so doing, it may well change the structuring of the activities that escape the official net. It has been observed, for example, that relationships within illegal activities are often very highly structured, sometimes more so than in legal activities, as a response to the risks of the activity in question (Gambetta 1996). By the same token, some types of (re)structuring of activities make official intervention easier, or may even be predicated by the nature of the official governance frameworks. For example, as an enterprise expands, it can be monitored and taxed more easily. As another example, if an enterprise wants to become a publicly held company, it can only do so within the framework of existing company law, by definition.

Thus, both dimensions are needed to adequately characterize activities and to analyse interventions. And it is not helpful to say that activities to one extreme of both dimensions—for example with high official intervention and highly structured interactions—are 'formal' while those at the other end are 'informal'.

On the policy front, as the chapters in this collection make clear, the policy issue is not one of 'greater' or 'lesser' reach of government being better in general, as it is so often characterized, but one of the 'right' reach of government (Söderbaum, chapter 9, this volume; Shuaib 2004). This right reach has to take into account (1) the objectives of intervention, (2) the implementation of the intervention, and (3) the response of the structuring of activities to this intervention—it being recognized that 'more' or 'less' structured does not necessarily correlate with 'good' or 'bad' (Nugent and Swaminathan, chapter 12, this volume).

What then are we to do with the terms *formal* and *informal*? It seems clear that they cannot be suppressed—they are now too well ingrained in the academic and policy discourse. And, as Lipton (1984) argues, their continued use despite all the debates perhaps suggests a continued utility. We would propose, therefore, especially in light of official statistical conventions already adopted, that the formal–informal continuum apply strictly to the continuum between relatively high and relatively low levels of the reach of official governance mechanisms, suitably specified and measured in each context. This relates the terminology directly to the policy discourse on the nature and extent of government intervention in economic activity. This is our preferred option. However, even in this case, we would prescribe a healthy warning—informal does not mean unstructured and chaotic, and does not invite policy intervention on those grounds! More generally, we would keep the 'reach of government' as a purely descriptive term, leaving the issue of whether it is a good thing or a bad thing to be decided on a case by case basis, taking into account the self-organizing structures that communities are capable of producing, within or without the reach of official structures.

1.3 Objectives and Complexities of Interventions

At the broadest level, our objective is to understand diverse ways of improving the well-being of the poor in poor countries. We recognize that poor individuals interact with each other and with the rest of society through two primary channels—self-organized groups and markets. The objectives of intervention can then be seen under two broad headings: (1) Improving the well-being of the poor and of society at large by improving the capacity of individuals to self-organize and address their collective action problems by themselves, and (2) Improving the well-being of the poor and of society at large by addressing the problems that arise when individuals interact through markets.

These two objectives may be seen as addressing group failure and market failure through better operation of self-organized groups and through better operation of markets. Of course, it goes without saying that the two objectives interact, with outcomes in one influencing outcomes in the other. The myriad interventions that we actually see in practice can be assessed in the above framework. But why do some interventions achieve their objectives while others do not?

A key step is to focus on the goals of such efforts and the specificities of time and place. We have repeatedly learned from many studies of policy processes that no single institutional arrangement works across diverse policy areas or even diverse subtypes within a broad policy area (Korten 1980; Joshi 1998; NRC 2002). Copying interventions that worked well in one country may lead to a major failure in another (Webb 1991).

For example, trying to find the best property rights for allocation of forest resources (see Andersson and Pacheco, chapter 11, this volume) vary dramatically by the kind of specific forest problem one is trying to solve. Residual rights to a forest may be retained by individuals, private corporations, local indigenous communities, or local governments (Alden Wily, chapter 15, this volume). When there is pressure to move to commercial operations, local owners—whatever their form—may need to engage in contracting with a variety of professional organizations. Thus, not only are property rights to the residual income a major factor in sustaining resources or providing essential services to the poor, the type of non-governmental organization or for-profit entities that provide technical services is also a major factor. How their performance is monitored, what kind of contracting law can be used, and many other factors affect whether local users are able to devise sustainable forest management plans, gain income, or reduce their risks (Dietz *et al.* 2003). Guha-Khasnobis and Ahuja (chapter 10, this volume) also stress the role of NGOs and micro-credit organizations in effectively organizing the poor to obtain specialized insurance plans from either private-for-profit insurance companies as well as from governmental insurance providers.

At any one juncture in the history of a policy field, a need for an increased role of national, regional, or local government agencies, or an increased role of local NGOs and other kinds of non-governmental organizations, may exist. All of the organizations involved may be constituted under the laws of a country even though they may not themselves be governmental units. Thus, all of the organizational arrangements may be formal in the sense that they are registered, recognized, and predictable, but many of them may not be governmental in structure.

With a broad understanding of the goals of interventions discussed in this volume, and an eye for the complexities involved, we can try and synthesize the lessons of (positive and negative) experience with these interventions. The next section takes up this task.

1.4 Lessons Learned and Recommendations

The chapters in this volume, and many others in the literature beyond, provide a rich empirical account of the working, or not, of a range of interventions directed towards the 'informal sector'. Some of these interventions try to extend the net of government interventions into areas where they have not gone before. Others try to withdraw an intervention that already exists. Sometimes these movements are referred to as increasing or decreasing the degree of 'formalization'. The experiences indicate that no simple rule exists that increasing or decreasing 'formalization' necessarily improves or worsens the well-being of the poor or welfare of society at large. Three examples illustrate this basic point.

Söderbaum (chapter 9, this volume) describes the experience of the Maputo Development Corridor, which was created in 1995 by the Governments of South Africa and Mozambique to increase private investments in infrastructure and industry. The corridor has been, for years, a location where extensive informal trading, particularly by women, has flourished. Massive investments of private capital have been encouraged to build major physical infrastructure, without much concern for building the economic opportunities of those living in the area. The biggest of all investment projects under the MDC initiative is Mozal, which contributes around 5 per cent of the GDP of Mozambique and nearly half of its manufacturing output. Yet, Mozal's linkages with the domestic economy, in terms of creating additional employment in the region, are minimal. For other inputs too, most of Mozal's dealings are with foreign (South African) firms based in Mozambique, its purchases from domestic enterprises being restricted to water and energy, which have little spread effect. With Mozambique's development strategy showing an obsession with mega projects, the 'informal' sector is seen almost as a hindrance, rather than a potential contributor to growth.

Nugent and Swaminathan (chapter 12, this volume), on the other hand, analyse the impact of formal governmental assistance to local health centres—*posyandus*—on the level of volunteering by Indonesian women to these centres. They found positive effects on the level of volunteering, the level of usage of the health centre, and of governmental investments (in the form of number of visits from paid medical staff and the number of medical instruments purchased with governmental funds).

Sawyer (chapter 13, this volume) provides an entirely different view of the impact of more extensive government intervention when dealing with the problem of achieving peace after extended warfare. He finds that in the northwestern sections of Liberia, different ethnic groups rely on indigenous institutions, such as the *poro*, that are accepted across ethnic communities. These, and other evolved mechanisms for conflict resolution and for organizing collective action, are slowly achieving a positive level of peaceful coexistence if not even productive entrepreneurship and interchange. In other regions of post-warfare Liberia, diverse groups have relied more on linkages to Monrovia to settle inter group conflicts. Unfortunately, drawing on external relationships to the national capital has not enabled these communities to move ahead on the processes of reconciliation as rapidly as those communities building their own mechanisms based on indigenous ways of coping with conflict. Rival elite groups have turned frequently to the Ministry of Internal Affairs and have focused more on who is to be selected for local government office rather than how to build schools, roads, and water systems.

Thus, while specifics matter greatly and no general rules can be formulated, a number of themes run through the chapters of this book which can perhaps be brought together as a small number of lessons learnt to serve as recommendations for future work or evaluative criteria that could be applied. These include:

- *Subsidiarity in a multi-level system.* Place the intervention as close as possible (in terms of level of government and/or geographically) to where it is meant to influence markets or groups, but imbed it in a larger system that supports the autonomy of lower level governments and provides them essential back-up services including conflict resolution.
- *Balance between 'formal' interventions and 'informal' practices.* In other words, 'formal' interventions are more effective if they are not meant to replace or 'crowd out' 'informal' rules, but help fine-tune them instead.
- *Implementation capacity.* Design the intervention to be consistent with the implementation capacity of government, and the absorptive capacity of people it is meant to help.
- *Complementary interventions.* Interventions that work are usually in the form of a package. Complementary measures are needed to support the core intervention for it to work.

- *Use voting with their feet as an evaluation criteria.* If people try to move out of the net of an intervention in significant numbers, its presumed efficacy for their well-being must be questioned. If on the other hand people move into the net of an intervention (including when that intervention is reduced), this is a signal of its efficacy.

Let us briefly discuss each of these general lessons.

1.4.1 *Subsidiarity in a Multi-Level System*

For all too long, recommendations for structuring formal governmental structures have focused either on the need for greater centralization at the national level or for more decentralization at the local level. This should not be thought of as an either-or choice. Rather, future policies should address as to what responsibilities to place at which level of governance and how to design *multi-level* governance systems that work effectively to provide desired services, collect taxes, and resolve conflicts in a timely, transparent, and equitable manner. To improve the welfare of those facing poverty conditions, Di Gregorio *et al.* (2004) stress the importance of federal systems rather than highly centralized or fully decentralized systems. Tyrannical leaders can gain power at any level of governance. Accountable governance usually requires mechanisms at higher or lower levels that enable citizens to hold officials at any one level of government responsible for their actions. Sawyer (chapter 13, this volume) also stresses the importance of enhancing polycentricity in evolving governance systems in post-conflict settings of Africa. Local communities can undertake many forms of collective action more effectively by drawing on their own evolved institutions rather than demanding centralized solutions.

In a multi-level system, then, a key is devolving authority to the lowest level that can take effective action related to the scale of a particular collective action problem. With regard to the registration of land, for example, Alden Wily (chapter 15, this volume) reviews the land registration systems throughout most of Africa and finds that smaller units with considerable autonomy and more accessibility to landowners are cheaper, speedier, and more effective (i.e. they increase the proportion of land that is actually registered). Simply deconcentrating land registration is not, Alden Wiley finds, as effecting in achieving these benefits as moving the authority to undertake land registration to a semi-autonomous local unit of governance. The advice is: Go as close to the problem you are trying to solve as feasible.

In a globalizing economy, the principle of subsidiarity also recognizes that for some purposes the appropriate level is international rather than any governance mechanism within a particular nation. Christensen (chapter 3, this volume) urges scholars and policymakers to abandon the Westphalian paradigm that assumes that sovereign national states are the world's primary policy actors. He argues that participants in the 'non-sovereign/informal sector' organized at international, national, regional, and local levels are major actors that are ignored by policy that focuses entirely on the role of sovereign actors. NGOs organized at multiple levels are participants in the construction of soft law through the negotiation of treaties or the recognition of customary practices. Soft law, as Christensen explains it, would be called 'norms' by some scholars since it reflects the aversion of many national governments towards international law as such, but the recognition by the same national governments that agreements at the international level must be negotiated and followed. So for larger-scale problems, the principle of subsidiarity is that when the problem is genuinely international in scope, then one must go to the international level to try and solve it rather than remaining with an outdated concept of the sovereign state.

1.4.2 *Balance between 'Formal' Interventions and 'Informal' Practices*

Sometimes in their eagerness to solve problems on the ground, government officials keep imposing more and more formal legislation without recognizing how this impacts on informal practices, how multiple and rapid changes introduce confusion, and why those involved eventually ignore the pronouncements of governments and work out some kind of arrangements on the ground which may be entirely contrary to what policymakers prefer. Imposed rules can crowd out norms and rules evolved in self-organized groups (Frey and Jegen 2001).

Roever (chapter 14, this volume) graphically accounts how officials in Peru—the country where de Soto (1989) started his analysis of the impact of overly formalized rules on the 'informal' sector—continued their past practices of imposing more and more rules on street vendors. The definitions of who a street vendor is, differed across legislation, the nature of fee to be imposed differed, how the fees were to be collected and, more important, what services the fees were to support, changed often within a few years. The executive decrees issued after the election of Fujimori to the presidency involved more definitions of key terms and less coherence.

The end result has been a 'dizzying array of conflicting incentives' for the street vendors as well as for local officials.

Shuaib (2004) also looks at the inter-tie between government actions and the outcomes in regard to street vending in many developing countries. He specifically examines the features of the 'urban informal street food sector' (UISFS) in the urban landscape of many developing countries. Given the increasing volume of food sold by street vendors throughout the developing world, finding ways of increasing the safety of the food sold in this manner is a recognized challenge. Shuaib focuses on the selling of 'lunch packets' by street vendors in Colombo, Sri Lanka as an important case to illustrate these problems.

In contrast to the efforts of Peruvian officials, the Colombo Municipal Council has not, until recently, tried to adopt any formal rules (even though there are multiple legislative acts on the books that authorize regulation of food processes). Rather, the Municipal Council has only recently urged street vendors to stamp their names and addresses on the lunch packets they offer for sale. They have worked with local NGOs to increase their own capacity to monitor the quality of food sold, and have generally gained more information about the sector. Shuaib recommends that the Council formally recognize an organization of food street vendors, work directly with them to increase the facilities provided to them, reduce the multiplicity of definitions used and thus the lack of coherent and workable rules, and generate more effective information for all of those involved.

From these and related literature, the general advice is: Try not to replace or 'crowd out' informal rules that are generally understood and may potentially be relatively effective, but help to fine-tune them instead. Don't keep passing new legislation when past legislation is massively ignored on the ground (Alden Wiley, chapter 15, this volume). Find out what the problems on the ground are, and involve those who are to be regulated, in a real discussion of the sources of problems and how new formal rules might solve the problems being faced.

1.4.3 *Implementation Capacity*

The third lesson is to tailor the intervention to the capacity of the structure. This comes from some of the empirical work in the volume where it is shown that over-regulation while the regulatory units are very weak and incompetent is a terrible thing. The same level of regulation in a competent governance structure appears to have a positive macroeconomic effect. Try to avoid the natural tendency to create complex legislation. Where possible, build up the capacity of local regional units so that they can handle the desired regulation. The advice is: Tailor the intervention to the capacity that exists or help to build the capacity before you intervene.

Nugent and Swaminathan (chapter 12, this volume) illustrate a positive example of this lesson. When the government of Indonesia provided active backing for the capabilities of local health centres, this increased capacity helped to generate still further levels of volunteer labour by women served by the centres. Thus, modest investments in capacity building leveraged more active participation in the provision of health care in local villages.

Andersson and Pacheco (chapter 11, this volume) also illustrate the differential impact of a massive decentralization programme adopted in Bolivia on the actual policies adopted by municipalities. Simply assigning formal property rights is not a sufficient policy intervention to ensure that timber practices are improved and commercial income increased. Municipalities that were well connected to higher level government agencies, which helped to increase their capacity as well as link to local users, were able to utilize effectively the new property rights assigned to them. In none of the communities studied had local users acquired logging permits without substantial external technical support.

1.4.4 *Complementary Interventions*

The fourth lesson is that a successful intervention really needs multiple back-up services in terms of information, courts, larger-scale contexts, social capital, etc. Loayza *et al.* (chapter 7, this volume) conclude from their cross-country analyses that high levels of regulation of goods and factor markets are a major negative factor effecting macroeconomic performance. Many regulations act as barriers that disrupt the processes of private investment in new technologies that would lead to being more efficient and keeping up with dynamic processes. Their general finding is that governmental regulation tends to reduce economic growth. They find, however, that the quality of regulation—as measured by the institutional framework within which regulation is occurring—makes a big difference. In those countries where the broader institutions themselves are evaluated in World Bank studies as of high quality, the same regulations that produce bad outcomes in most countries are actually effective in the countries with high quality general institutions.

Guha-Khasnobis and Ahuja (chapter 10, this volume) provide a specific example of the effectiveness of a multi-organization package. In their study of the insurance for informal economy workers in India, they point out how difficult it has been in the past to offer insurance to those who are poor and earn irregular income. And yet, it is just such a population that is most in need of insurance. Insurance for low-income workers is feasible only when it can be provided in a very cost-effective manner that is designed specifically to meet the needs of those at risk. By working with 'nodal agencies' in the form of an NGO, a women's group, a trade union, a micro-finance organization, or an organization of micro-entrepreneurs, the transaction costs of delivering insurance, receiving payments, informing users of benefits, etc. are dramatically reduced.

1.4.5 *Use Voting With Their Feet as an Evaluation Criteria*

The fifth lesson has to do with a test of whether current formalizations are working or not. The test is the extent to which people are willing to be within the net. Basically, we can see street vendors, small businesses, and people who might gain formal ownership to their structures voting with their feet. If they decide to register, pay whatever taxes there are to, etc. they are voluntarily coming within the net and this is a good sign. Thus, if you change the structure to benefit group a, b, or c, one of the criteria is whether voluntary compliance is increasing or not. The advice is: A good test of whether an intervention is helpful or not is to know how many of the relevant population try to be outside of the net.

Lensink, McGillivray, and Thi Thu Trà (chapter 8, this volume) studied the effects of financial reforms in Vietnam. Traditionally, Vietnam always had a vibrant informal financial sector that fulfilled the credit needs of a large section of the population. Among other things, the reforms changed the composition of the formal and informal activities. However, they find that the relative importance of lending has gone up in what still remains as the 'informal' part of the financial sector.

The growing literature on informal trade (e.g. Pohit and Taneja 2004) provide examples where traders prefer to remain outside the ambit of official trade, because it is too costly and often beyond their logistical capacity to comprehend, and hence comply with 'rules'. A reflection of this is found in the current WTO negotiation on trade facilitation. In principle, the negotiation is meant to enhance trade. However, the uncertainty regarding the costs that developing and least developed countries will have to incur to implement the outcome of this negotiation has resulted in plenty of apprehension in such countries, who may simply decide to walk out of it.

1.5 Conclusion

The debate on what exactly constitutes informality and formality continues, more than half a century after the distinction was first introduced, and more than three decades after it took centre stage in the development policy discourse. We point to the multiple definitions and characterizations and come to two conclusions on the formal–informal divide—one negative and one positive. The negative conclusion is that the tendency to associate 'informal' with 'unstructured' and 'chaotic' must end. Such an association is conceptually unsound, empirically weak, and has led to policy disasters, as the state reached to provide 'structures' where it was presumed that none existed before. The positive conclusion is that we can fruitfully use the terminology, formal–informal to characterize a continuum of the reach of official intervention in different economic activities, especially since official statistics already use variants of such a criterion. However, it is to be clearly understood, as is made abundantly clear in the chapters in this volume, that 'more' or 'less' reach is not necessarily 'better' or 'worse'. Different types of intervention work better in different circumstances. The general principles outlined in this chapter, drawn from an array of detailed empirical investigations, suggest strongly that we should move beyond formality and informality and tackle directly the policy interventions that will help the poor to unlock their potential through groups and through markets.

References

Agrawal, A. and K. Gupta (2005). 'Decentralization and Participation: The Governance of Common Pool Resources in Nepal's Terai'. *World Development*, 33(7): 1101–14.

Arnold, J. E. M. (1993). 'Management of Forest Resources as Common Property'. *Commonwealth Forestry Review*, 72(3): 157–61.

Boeke, J. H. (1942). *Economies and Economic Policy in Dual Societies*. Haarlem: Tjeenk Willnik.

Bromley, R. (1978). 'Introduction: The Urban Informal Sector: Why is it Worth Discussing?' *World Development*, 6(9/10): 1034–5.

Bromley, D. W., D. Feeny, M. McKean, P. Peters, J. Gilles, R. Oakerson, C. F. Runge, and J. Thomson (eds) (1992). *Making the Commons Work: Theory, Practice, and Policy*. San Francisco, CA: ICS Press.

Cross, J. C. (1998). *Informal Politics: Street Vendors and the State in Mexico City*. Stanford, CA: Stanford University Press.

de Soto, H. (1989). *The Other Path: The Economic Answer to Terrorism*. New York: Basic Books.

de Soto, H. (2003). *The Mystery of Capital: Why Capitalism Triumphs in the West and Fails Everywhere Else*. New York: Basic Books.

Dietz, T., E. Ostrom, and P. Stern (2003). 'The Struggle to Govern the Commons'. *Science* 302(5652) (December 12): 1907–12.

Di Gregorio, M., K. Hagedorn, M. Kirk, B. Korf, N. McCarthy, R. Meinzen-Dick, and B. Swallow (2004). 'The Role of Property Rights and Collective Action for Poverty Reduction'. Paper presented at the EGDI-WIDER conference, 17–18 September.

Frey, B. S. and R. Jegen (2001). 'Motivation Crowding Theory: A Survey of Empirical Evidence'. *Journal of Economic Surveys*, 15(5): 589–611.

Gambetta, D. (1996). *The Sicilian Mafia: The Business of Private Protection*. Cambridge, MA: Harvard University Press.

Gilmour, D. and R. Fisher (1991). *Villagers, Forests, and Foresters: The Philosophy, Process and Practice of Community Forestry in Nepal*. Kathmandu: Sahayogi Press.

Harriss, B. (1978). 'Quasi-Formal Employment Structures and Behaviour in the Unorganized Urban Economy, and the Reverse: Some Evidence from South India'. *World Development*, 6(9/10): 1077–86.

Harris, J. and M. Todaro (1970). 'Migration, Unemployment and Development: A Two-Sector Analysis'. *American Economic Review*, 60: 126–42.

Hart, K. (1973). 'Informal Income Opportunities and Urban Employment in Ghana'. *Journal of Modern African Studies*, 11(1): 61–89.

ILO (International Labour Office) (1972). *Incomes, Employment and Equality in Kenya*. Geneva: International Labour Office.

Ives, J. D. and B. Messerli (1989). *The Himalayan Dilemma: Reconciling Development and Conservation*. London and New York: Routledge and United Nations University.

Joshi, A. (1998). 'Progressive Bureaucracy: An Oxymoron? The Case of Joint Forest Management in India'. *Rural Development Forestry Network*, Network paper 24a (Winter 1998/99): 1–20.

Korten, D. C. (1980). 'Community Organization and Rural Development: A Learning Process Approach'. *Public Administration Review*, 40(5): 480–511.

Lewis, A. (1954). 'Economic Development with Unlimited Supplies of Labour'. *Manchester School of Economic and Social Studies*, 22: 139–91.

Lipton, M. (1984). 'Family, Fungibility and Formality: Rural Advantages of Informal Non-Farm Enterprise versus the Urban-Formal State', in S. Amin (ed.), *Human Resources, Employment and Development*, vol. 5: Developing Countries. London: MacMillan, for International Economic Association, pp. 189–242.

McCay, B. J. and J. M. Acheson (1987). *The Question of the Commons: The Culture and Ecology of Communal Resources*. Tucson: University of Arizona Press.

Muller, C. and J. Esselaar (2004). 'The Changing Nature of Work in South Africa: Evidence from Recent National Household Surveys'. Paper presented at the EGDI-WIDER conference, 17–18 September.

Nagendra, H. and E. Ostrom (forthcoming). 'Institutions, Collective Action, and Effective Forest Management: Learning from Studies in Nepal', in J. N. Pretty, A. Ball, T. Benton, J. Guivant, D. Lee, D. Orr, M. Pfeffer, and H. Ward (eds), *Sage Handbook on Environment and Society*. London: Sage.

NRC (National Research Council) (2002). *The Drama of the Commons*. Washington, DC: National Academy Press.

Ostrom, E. (1990). *Governing the Commons*. New York: Cambridge University Press.

Ostrom, E. (2005). *Understanding Institutional Diversity*. Princeton, NJ: Princeton University Press.

Platteau, J.-P. (2004). 'Monitoring Elite Capture in Community-Driven Development'. *Development and Change*, 35(2): 223–46.

Platteau, J.-P. and F. Gaspart (2003). 'The Risk of Resource Misappropriation in Community-Driven Development'. *World Development*, 31(10): 1687–1703.

Pohit, S. and N. Taneja (2004). 'Formal and Informal Trading Between India and Nepal'. Paper presented at the EGDI-WIDER conference, 17–18 September.

Portes, A. and R. Schauffler (1993). 'Competing Perspectives on the Latin American Informal Sector'. *Population and Development Review*, 19(1): 33–60.

Sethuraman, S. V. (1976). 'The Informal Sector: Concept, Measurement, Policy'. *International Labour Review*, 114(1) (July–August): 69–81.

Shuaib, F. (2004). 'Linking the Formal and Informal Sectors Through a Supportive Institutional Policy Framework for Urban Local Authorities—The Case Study of Street Food Vendors in Colombo Municipal Council, Sri Lanka'. Paper presented at the EGDI-WIDER conference, 17–18 September.

Souza, P. R. and V. E. Tokman (1976). 'The Informal Urban Sector in Latin America'. *International Labour Review*, 114(3) (November–December): 395–406.

Tucker, C. M. and E. Ostrom (2005). 'Multidisciplinary Research Relating Institutions and Forest Transformations', in E. Moran and E. Ostrom (eds), *Seeing the Forest and the Trees: Human-Environment Interactions in Forest Ecosystems*. Cambridge, MA: MIT Press, pp. 81–104.

Varughese, G. and E. Ostrom (2001). 'The Contested Role of Heterogeneity in Collective Action: Some Evidence from Community Forestry in Nepal'. *World Development*, 29(5): 747–65.

Waltner-Toews, D., J. J. Kay, C. Neudoerffer, and T. Gitau (2003). 'Perspective Changes Everything: Managing Ecosystems from the Inside Out'. *Frontiers in Ecology and the Environment*, 1: 1–10.

Webb, P. (1991). 'When Projects Collapse: Irrigation Failure in the Gambia from a Household Perspective'. *Journal of International Development*, 3(4): 339–53.

Part I

Concepts and Measurement

2

Bureaucratic form and the informal economy

Keith Hart[1]

2.1 Introduction

Most readers of this book live substantially inside what we may call the formal economy. This is a world of salaries or fees paid on time, regular mortgage payments, clean credit ratings, fear of the tax authorities, regular meals, moderate use of stimulants, good health cover, pension contributions, school fees, driving the car to the commuter station, and summer holidays by the sea. Of course, households suffer economic crises from time to time and some people feel permanently vulnerable. But what makes this lifestyle 'formal' is the regularity of its order, a predictable rhythm and sense of control that we often take for granted. I discovered how much of this had become natural to me only when I went to live in a West African city slum 40 years ago.

I would ask questions that just did not make sense to my informants, for example concerning household budgets. How much do you spend on food a week? Households were in any case often unbounded and transient. Assuming that someone had a regular wage (which many did not), it was pitifully small; the wage-earner might live it up for a day or two and then was broke, relying on credit and help from family and friends or not eating at all. A married man might use his wage to buy a sack of rice and pay the rent, knowing that he would have to hustle outside work until the next paycheck. In the street economy people were moving everything,

[1] I have benefited from a long conversation on this topic with Knut Nustadt; thanks also to Massimiliano Mollona and Frances Pine.

from marijuana (*ganja*), to refrigerators, in deals marked more by flux than stable income. After completing a doctorate, I went to work in a development studies institute. There I saw my main task as trying to get this ethnographic experience across to development economists. My use of the conceptual pair formal/informal came out of those conversations. Now we have been brought together to examine how the poles might be linked more effectively in the context of development.

The formal and informal aspects of society are already linked of course, since the idea of an 'informal economy' is entailed by the institutional effort to organize society along formal lines. 'Form' is *the rule*, an idea of what ought to be universal in social life; and for most of the twentieth century the dominant forms have been those of bureaucracy, particularly of national bureaucracy, since society has become identified to a large extent with nation-states. This identity may now be weakening in the face of the neo-liberal world economy and a digital revolution in communications (Hart 2001a). Any initiatives combining public bureaucracy with informal popular practices need to be seen in this historical context.

The formal and informal appear to be separate entities because of the use of the term 'sector'. This gives the impression that the two are located in different places, like agriculture and manufacturing, whereas both the bureaucracy and its antithesis contain the formal/informal dialectic within themselves as well as between them. The need to link the sectors arises from a widespread perception that their relationship consists, at present, of a class war between the bureaucracy and the people. It was not supposed to be like this. Modern bureaucracy was invented as part of a democratic political project to give citizens equal access to what was theirs as a right (Weber 1978). It still has the ability to coordinate public services on a scale that is beyond the reach of individuals and most groups. So it is disheartening that bureaucracy (the power of public office) should normally be seen now as the negation of democracy (the power of the people) rather than its natural ally.

Forms are necessarily abstract and a lot of social life is left out as a result. This can lead to an attempt to reduce the gap by creating new abstractions that incorporate the informal practices of people into the formal model. Naming these practices as an 'informal sector' is one such device. They appear to be informal because their forms are largely invisible to the bureaucratic gaze. Mobilizing the informal economy will require a pluralistic approach based on at least acknowledgement of those forms. Equally, the formal sphere of society is not just abstract, but consists also of the people who staff bureaucracies and their informal practices. Somehow the human potential of both has to be unlocked together.

The remainder of this chapter has three sections. The first reviews the concept of an 'informal economy/sector' from its origin in discussions of the Third World urban poor to its present status as a universal feature of economy. The second asks how we might conceive of combining the formal/informal pair with a view to promoting development. In short concluding remarks I suggest how partnerships between bureaucracy and the people might be made more equal.

2.2 The Informal Economy in Retrospect

In the twentieth century, capitalism took the specific form of being organized through the nation-state. 'National capitalism' was the attempt to manage markets and money through central bureaucracy (Hart 2001a). Its antithesis is the informal economy, a term that originated in the early 1970s. Beginning as a way of conceptualizing the unregulated activities of the marginal poor in Third World cities, the informal sector has become recognized as a universal feature of the modern economy. Independence from the state's rules unites practices as diverse as home improvement, street trade, squatter settlements, open source software, the illegal drugs traffic, political corruption, and offshore banking. The issue of informal economy is thus intimately tied up with the question of how long national capitalism can continue as the world's dominant economic form.

Welfare-state democracy was sustained by macroeconomics, a term associated with Maynard Keynes (1936). Only the state could regenerate a damaged market economy, mainly by spending money it did not have to boost consumer demand. The economic boom of the 1950s and 1960s depended on the coordinated efforts of the leading industrial states to expand their public sectors. It all began to unravel in the stagflation of the 1970s. The neo-liberal conservatives who have dominated politics in the last quarter-century sought to counter inflation with sound money and to release the potential of the market by getting the state off its back. But their policies often combined privatization with a strengthening of state power. In the process they began to dismantle twentieth-century social democracy.

The idea of an informal economy has run as a submerged commentary on these developments. It came out of the lives of Third World city-dwellers, whose lack of money makes them about as conventionally poor as it is possible to be. By the 1970s it was becoming clear that development was a pipe-dream for Third World countries. Populations had exploded; cities were growing rapidly; mechanization was weak; productivity in predominantly agricultural economies remained low; and the gap between rich and poor was widening. The consensus was that the only institution capable of mobilizing economic resources was the state. Marxists and Keynesians agreed on this; free-market liberals had no effective voice at this time. The malaise was conceived of as 'urban unemployment'. Third World economies were supposed to deliver jobs, but, in the absence of machine-based industry, employment creation was left largely to the only economic agent of any significance, public bureaucracy. The number of corporate firms offering jobs was embarrassingly small. What then could all the other new inhabitants of the major cities be up to? They must be unemployed. Figures of 50 per cent unemployment and more were conjured up by economists. The spectre of the 1930s—broken men huddling on street corners (Buddy, can you spare a dime?) dominated development discourse.

Anyone who visited, not to mention lived, in these sprawling cities would get a rather different picture. Their streets were teeming with life, a constantly shifting crowd of hawkers, porters, taxi-drivers, beggars, pimps, pickpockets, hustlers—all of them getting by without the benefit of a real job. There was no shortage of names for this kind of early-modern street economy. Terms like underground, unregulated, hidden, black, and second economies abounded. The best account was Clifford Geertz's of the contrasting face of Indonesian entrepreneurship and especially of the *suq* or bazaar (1963). The majority of a Javanese town's inhabitants were occupied in a street economy that he labelled bazaar-type. The firm-type economy consisted largely of western corporations who benefited from the protection of state law. These had *form* in Weber's (1981) sense of rational enterprise, being based on calculation and the avoidance of risk. National bureaucracy lent these firms a measure of protection from competition, thereby allowing the systematic accumulation of capital. The bazaar, on the other hand, was individualistic and competitive, so that accumulation was well-nigh impossible. Geertz identified a group of reform muslim entrepreneurs who were rational and calculating enough; but they were denied the institutional protection of state bureaucracy granted to the existing corporations.

Here and in his later work on the Moroccan *suq* (Geertz *et al.* 1979), Geertz pointed out that modern economics uses the bazaar model to study the decisions of individuals in competitive markets, while treating as anomalous the dominant monopolies protected by state bureaucracy. The discipline found this model in the late nineteenth century, just when a bureaucratic revolution was transforming mass production and consumption along corporate lines. At the same time the more powerful states awarded new privileges to capitalist corporations and society took its centralized form as national bureaucracy. Perhaps because he was poking fun at the economists, Geertz's analytical vocabulary was not taken up by them. The antithesis of the state-made modern economy had not yet found its academic name. This came about through a paper I presented at a Sussex conference on 'Urban employment in Africa' in 1971.

The main message of the paper (Hart 1973) was that Accra's poor were not unemployed. They worked, often casually, for erratic and generally low returns; but they were definitely working. What distinguished these self-employed earnings from wage employment was the degree of *rationalization* of working conditions. Following Weber (1981), I argued that the ability to stabilize economic activity within a bureaucratic form made returns more calculable and regular for the workers as well as their bosses. That stability was in turn guaranteed by the state's laws, which only extended so far into the depths of Ghana's economy. Formal incomes came from regulated economic activities and informal incomes, both legal and illegal, lay beyond the scope of regulation. I did not identify the informal economy with a place or a class or even whole persons. Everyone in Accra, but especially the inhabitants of the slum where I lived, tried to combine the two sources of income. Informal opportunities ranged from market gardening and brewing through every kind of trade to gambling, theft, and political corruption. My analysis had its roots in what people generate out of the circumstances of their everyday lives. The laws and offices of state bureaucracy only made their search for self-preservation and improvement more difficult.

I hoped to interest economists by presenting my ethnography in a language they were familiar with. The idea of an informal sector was taken up quickly by some of them, so quickly indeed that a report by the International Labour Office (ILO 1972) applying the concept to Kenya came out before my own article had been published. The ILO report suggested that self-employed or informal incomes might reduce the gap between those with and without jobs and so could contribute to a more equitable income distribution. Following the growth or bust policies of the 1960s, they advocated growth with redistribution, that is, helping the poor out of the proceeds of economic expansion. This reflected a shift in

World Bank policy announced by its president, Robert McNamara, in Nairobi a year later. By now the Bretton Woods institutions were worried about potential social explosions; and they felt that more attention should be paid to peasants and the urban poor. A vogue for promoting the informal sector as a device for employment creation fitted in with this shift.

Most economists saw it in quantitative terms as a sector of small-scale, low-productivity, low-income activities without the benefit of advanced machines; whereas I stressed the reliability of income streams, the presence or absence of bureaucratic *form*. When the bureaucracy tried to promote the informal sector—by providing credit, government buildings or new technologies, for example—it killed the informality of the enterprises concerned and, moreover, exposed participants to taxation. The association of the idea with the sprawling slums of Third World cities was strong; but the commanding heights of the informal economy lay at the centres of political power itself, in the corrupt fortunes of public office-holders who often owned the taxis or the rented accommodation operated by the small fry.

The 1980s saw another major shift in world economy following the lead of Reagan and Thatcher. Now the state was no longer seen as the great provider. Its role became less visible in the leading exponents of 'national capitalism' and was actively undermined in the poor countries. Rather, 'the market', freed of as many encumbrances as possible, was taken to be the only engine of growth. The informal economy took on a new lease of life in the World Bank and similar institutions as a zone of free commerce, competitive, because it was unregulated. This coincided with the imposition on weak states of 'structural adjustment' policies that reduced public expenditures and threw responsibility onto the invisible self-help schemes of the people themselves. By now, the rhetoric and reality of development had been effectively abandoned as the Third World suffered the largest income drain in its history, in the form of repayment of debts incurred during the wild banking boom of the 1970s (George 1990).

So is it possible to assess the informal economy's role in Third World development? There has been an urban revolution there since 1945 with state economic power concentrated in a few cities. Rural–urban migration has vastly exceeded the growth of bureaucratic employment. Even those who have jobs often must supplement them with outside earnings. The growth of cities has not stimulated exchange between local agriculture and industry, since the subsidized farmers of the rich countries supply food imports, and cheap manufactures are available from Asia (Hart 2004).

This has only encouraged more of a stagnating peasantry to leave home for the city. The informal economy has in some cases been a source of economic dynamism, even capital accumulation. At the very least, it has allowed people to maintain themselves in the urban areas because of the concentration of market demand there.

The world economy has become increasingly informal in recent decades. Illegal drugs are the most valuable commodity traded internationally. Finance has been slipping its political shackles, by relocating offshore where money transactions can hardly be monitored or taxed. The armaments industry is a sea of corruption reaching the core of western governments. Grey markets for goods imitating well-known brands and unlicensed reproductions (especially videos, CDs, and tapes) have been labelled as 'piracy' (Hart 2005). The irrational borders of nation-states are riddled with smuggling. The informal economy is now considered to be a feature of the industrial countries, ranging from domestic do-it-yourself to the more criminalized economy of disaffected youth (Pahl 1984). Even before the collapse of Stalinist bureaucracy in the Soviet Union and its satellites, it was clear that the command economy had spawned a flourishing black market, antecedent of the criminal mafias and oligarchs who now dominate the Russian economy. In Europe, the dissident left has long had a slogan: 'Think red, work black, vote green'.

Meanwhile, the collapse of the state in many Third World countries has led to the whole economy becoming informal. President Mobutu and his successors have reduced the Congo region to shambles where soldiers loot at will and politicians fill foreign bank accounts (MacGaffey 1991). Mobutu boasted of being one of the richest men in the world and once hired a train for a lavish party in New York. Or take Jamaica, which in the 1970s was a model 'middle-income' developing economy. At one point the value of illegal marijuana sales was higher than the country's three leading legitimate industries (tourism, bauxite, and garments) taken together. No wonder politics was carried out by armed gangsters and youths left school early to learn hustling on the street. When most of the economy is 'informal', the usefulness of the category becomes questionable.

The term's original context was the stand-off of the Cold War (Hart 1992). The conflict between state socialism and the free market was frozen by the unthinkable prospect of a nuclear outcome. By the early 1970s national capitalism had taken on a timeless quality as a universal social form. The activities of little people in the cracks of a state-regulated economy were at best seen as a defensive reaction and aid to survival, and surely not as a basis for any serious alternative. It seemed unlikely then that the formal/informal pair contained much potential for movement; but now we know better.

The label 'informal' may be popular because it is both positive and negative. To act informally is to be free and flexible; but the term also says what people are not doing—not wearing conventional dress, not being regulated by the state. The informal sector allowed academics and bureaucrats to incorporate the teeming street life of exotic cities into their abstract models without having to confront the specificity of what people were really up to. To some extent, I sacrificed my own ethnographic encounter with real persons to the generalizing jargon of development economics. The 'velvet revolution' of Eastern Europe and the Soviet Union demonstrated that ordinary people could get rid of the most awesome bureaucratic states with remarkably little violence. Who can now think of the state as eternal when Stalin's successors were dispensed with so completely? And then, if the informal economy is a little people's alternative, would we want to live in a Moscow run by gangsters and the KGB?

West Africa's former colonies were among the last admitted to national capitalism and the first to leave. Ghana was already in an advanced condition of political and economic decay in the mid 1960s. Seen in that light, my fieldwork may be thought of as a harbinger of national capitalism's decline. After much of the Third World dropped out of the movement of the world economy, the communist bloc followed suit, leaving America, Western Europe, and a resurgent Asia to contemplate the consequences for their own societies. The informal economy was the self-organized energies of people excluded from participating in the benefits guaranteed by state rule. The question remains if those energies could be harnessed more effectively in partnership with bureaucracy.

2.3 Combining the Formal and Informal 'Sectors'

'Form' is an idea whose origin lies in the mind. Form is the rule, the invariant in the variable. It is predictable and easily recognized. For example, in a birdwatcher's guide, it would not do to illustrate each species with a photograph of a particular bird. It might be looking the wrong way or be missing a leg—so instead a caricature shows the distinctive beak, the wing markings, and so on. That is why idealist philosophers from Plato onwards thought that the general idea of something was more real than the thing itself. Words are forms, of course. In his *Science of Logic*,

Hegel shows the error of taking the idea for reality (James 1980). We all know the word 'house' and might think there is nothing more to owning one than saying 'my house'. But before long the roof will leak, the paint will peel, and we are forced to acknowledge that the house is a material thing, a process that requires attention. The formal sector is likewise an idea, a collection of people, things, and activities; but we should not mistake the category for the reality it identifies.

What makes something formal is its conformity with such an idea or rule. Thus formal dress in some societies means that the men will come dressed like penguins, but the women are free to wear something extravagant that suits them personally—they come as variegated butterflies. The men are supposed to look the same and so they adopt a uniform that cancels out their individuality. Formality endows a class of people with universal qualities, with being the same and equal. What makes dress informal is therefore the absence of such a shared code. But any observer of an informally dressed crowd will notice that the clothing styles are not random. We might ask what these informal forms are and how to account for them. The world's ruling elite is identified as 'the men in suits', because they choose to wear a style invented in the 1920s as an informal alternative to formal evening dress. The dialectic is infinitely recursive. No wonder that some economists find the conceptual dichotomy confusing and impossible to measure (Sindzingre, chapter 4, this volume).

There is a hierarchy of forms and this hierarchy is not fixed for ever. The twentieth century saw a general experiment in impersonal society whose forms were anchored in national bureaucracy, in centralized states, and laws carrying the threat of punishment. The dominant economic forms were also bureaucratic and closely linked to the state as the source of universal law. Conventionally these were divided according to principles of ownership into public and private sectors. This uneasy alliance of governments and corporations is now sometimes classified as the formal sector. What they share, at least on the surface, is conformity to the rule of law at the national and increasingly international levels. How then might non-conformist economic activities, 'the informal economy', relate to this formal order? They may be related in any of four ways: as *division, content, negation*, or as *residue*. This conceptualization should inform actions designed to improve the linkages between the two.

The moral economy of capitalist societies is based on an attempt to keep separate impersonal and personal spheres of social life (Hart 2001a; 2005). The establishment of a formal public sphere entailed another based on domestic privacy (Elias 1982). The latter was built up to constitute with the former complementary halves of a single whole. Most people, traditionally men more than women, divide themselves every day between production and consumption, paid and unpaid work, submission to impersonal rules in the office and the free play of personality at home. Money is the means whereby the two sides are brought together, so that their interaction is an endless process of separation and integration that I call division. The division of the sexes into male and female is the master metaphor for this dialectic of complementary unity. In Hegel's terms (James 1980), when the lines between the pair become blurred, we enter a phase of negative dialectic, from which a new idea may eventually emerge. Focusing on the informal practices that constitute a bureaucracy implies such a blurring at the expense of maintaining what was always only a utopian ideal.

For any rule to be translated into human action, something else must be brought into play, such as personal judgement. So, informality is built into bureaucratic forms as unspecified content. This is no trivial matter. Workable solutions to problems of administration invariably contain processes that are invisible to the formal order. For example, workers sometimes 'work-to-rule' (Scott 1998). They follow their job descriptions to the letter (the formal abstraction of what they actually do) without any of the informal practices that allow these abstractions to function. Everything grinds to a halt as a result. Or take a chain of commodities from their production by a transnational corporation to their final consumption in an African city. At several points invisible actors fill the gaps that the bureaucracy cannot handle directly, from the factories to the docks to the supermarkets and street traders who supply the cigarettes to smokers. Informal processes are indispensable to the trade, as variable content to the general form.

Of course, some of these activities may break the law, through a breach of health and safety regulations, tax evasion, smuggling, the use of child labour, selling without a licence, etc. The third way that informal activities relate to formal organization is thus as its negation. Rule-breaking takes place both within bureaucracy and outside it; and so the informal is often illegal. This compromises attempts to promote the informal sector as a legitimate sphere of the economy, since it is hard to draw a line between colourful women selling oranges on the street and the gangsters who exact tribute from them. When the rule of law is weak, the forms that emerge in its place are often criminal in character. A good part of modern society consists in protecting the public image of bureaucratic processes from a reality that mixes formal order with corruption and criminality.

We watch movies about cops and robbers, but we detach these fictions from the idea of the rule of law that helps us to sleep at night.

The fourth category is not so obviously related to the formal order as the rest. Some informal activities exist in parallel, as residue. They are just separate from the bureaucracy. It would be stretching the logic of the formal/informal pair to include peasant economy, traditional institutions, and much else within the rubric of the informal. Yet the social forms endemic to these often shape informal economic practices and *vice versa*. What is at stake here is whether society is just one thing—one state with its rule of law—or can tolerate a measure of legal pluralism, leaving some institutions to their own devices (Comaroff and Comaroff 2004). Communities exist to the extent that their members understand each other for practical purposes; and so they operate through culture. They use implicit rules (customs) rather than state-made laws and usually regulate their members informally, relying on the sanction of exclusion rather than punishment. European empires, faced with a shortage of administrative resources, turned to indirect rule as a way of incorporating subject peoples into their systems of government on a semi-autonomous basis. This legal pluralism delegated supervision of indigenous customary forms to appointed chiefs and headmen, reserving the key levers of power to the colonial regime. Anthropologists played their part in documenting how this might work out (Asad 1973). Any serious attempt to link the formal and the informal today requires a similar openness to plurality of form.

Take the case of South Africa (Marais 1998; Hart and Padayachee 2000). Even before the African National Congress (ANC) took power, they formulated an economic policy that would harness the energies of the black majority. It was called the Reconstruction and Development Programme (RDP). Redistribution from the white beneficiaries of apartheid could never meet the needs of 30 million poor Africans for income, jobs, education, health, housing, transport, etc. The government must contribute funds and coordination to self-help development projects mobilizing the labour contained in local communities. Two years after gaining power, the ANC replaced the RDP with GEAR (Growth, Employment, and Redistribution). Instead of helping communities to build their own houses, the government relied on foreign loans, imported materials, and development bureaucracy (Nustad 2004). The 'Rainbow Nation' joined the neo-liberal world economy with escalating economic inequality as the inevitable result. Why? Mobilizing communities sounds fine, but it is incompatible with running a strong state. The central bureaucracy found that it could not control projects at the periphery. Even worse, they were often empowering the ruling party's political opponents. GEAR recognized that, if the government could not enter partnership directly with the people, it would have to rely on international agencies and capital. So South Africa repeated the continent's post-colonial path towards dependence on outsiders. Cooperation with informal actors may require the central power to give up more than it is willing to.

A study of decentralized development in Scotland and three other European countries drew similar conclusions (Hart 2001b; Bryden and Hart 2004). Here too the aim was devolution from central government in the interest of self-organized rural development. Northern Scotland has been the target of regional development initiatives over a longer period than almost anywhere else. Yet we found that central government offered to release power to communities only to hold onto it subsequently, often frustrating any sense of local autonomy. They preferred government-appointed NGOs to elected bodies with popular legitimacy. Over and over again, local initiatives were thwarted by some fiat of a remote bureaucracy. The British government genuinely wanted to offload part of the tax burden by getting people to do some things themselves, but they just could not give up control. Even the creation of a new Scottish parliament was hamstrung by the retention of most economic power by the UK Treasury.

Might the multilateral agencies take the lead in establishing genuine partnership with individuals and groups located outside the bureaucracy? The World Bank has promoted the informal sector ever since it was coined. As the institution responsible for alleviating world poverty, the World Bank is acutely aware that it is a top-heavy bureaucracy remote from the people it would like to help. The informal sector stands for the people in some way, as does 'social capital', another of the concepts much in vogue there (McNeill 2003). How can the World Bank promote these ideas without killing them off? Would people be better-off being left alone by the bureaucracy? The excluded urban masses of the poor countries must play their own part in development; but a lasting solution should draw on the institutional resources locked up in international bureaucracies.

2.4 Conclusion

> General Forms have their vitality in Particulars, and every Particular is a Man.
>
> William Blake

The informal economy has been a brilliant success for over more than three decades. It lends the appearance of conceptual unity to whatever goes on outside the bureaucracy. Now, perhaps fearing its own isolation in a planet of slums (Davis 2004), the bureaucracy is offering partnership to the informals. The formal–informal dialectic is intrinsic to both the bureaucracy and the informal economy, as well as between them. We need to know how formal bureaucracy works in practice and, even more important, what social forms have emerged to organize the informal economy. If I once sought to translate my own ethnographic experience into 'economese', it is now time to reverse the process and examine the institutional particulars sustaining whatever takes place beyond the law.

The historians of comparative jurisprudence (Maine 1906; Maitland 1957) emphasized the concrete particularity of the customary legal institutions they studied in medieval England or Victorian India. For all their imperialist vision, they refused to sacrifice detail for the sake of generalization. Modern ethnographers have likewise documented in immense detail the kinship institutions and religious practices of local groups in Africa and the Pacific. This is no longer fashionable: anthropologists today are funded to study ethnicity, gender, AIDS and, of course, the informal economy. In my own research I focused on specific individuals and was obliged to study the contractual forms of their enterprises, their kinship ties and family organization, their friendship networks and voluntary associations, their religious affiliations, their relationship to criminal gangs and corrupt officials, their patronage systems, and political ties (Hart 1988). Only later did I join the rush to generalize about the population explosion of Third World cities. The issue of criminal organization inside and outside the formal bureaucracy cannot be wished away. Unlocking human potential by improving links between the 'formal and informal sectors' rests on confronting the cultural specificity of economic activities that cross the great divide.

Any attempt to divide an economy into complementary halves requires a massive cultural effort of both separation and integration. This idea of interdependent, but separate halves of a social whole is a powerful undercurrent in development discourse and should be subjected to criticism. The idea of informality as the content of abstract forms favours leaving more to people's imagination and accepting the legitimacy of most informal practices. When the informal is illegal, the obvious response is to crack down on rule-breakers; but such moves are often merely cosmetic—the biggest offenders escape and the law is made to appear an ass. The number of legal offences could often profitably be reduced. Finally, governments might adopt a genuinely hands-off approach towards semi-autonomous communities within their jurisdiction. If all of these modes of formal/informal linkage were considered, there might be some prospect of bureaucracy and the people entering a new partnership for development.

References

Asad, T. (ed.) (1973). *Anthropology and the Colonial Encounter*. London: Ithaca Press.

Bryden, J. and K. Hart (eds) (2004). *A New Approach to Rural Development in Europe: Germany, Greece, Scotland, Sweden*. Lampeter: Edwin Mellen Press.

Comaroff, J. and J. Comaroff (2004). 'Criminal Justice, Cultural Justice: The Limits of Liberalism and the Pragmatics of Difference in the New South Africa'. *American Ethnologist*, 31(2): 188–204.

Davis, M. (2004). 'Planet of Slums'. *New Left Review*, 23, March–April: 5–34.

Elias, N. (1982). *The Civilizing Process*. New York: Pantheon.

Geertz, C. (1963). *Peddlers and Princes*. Chicago: Chicago University Press.

Geertz, C., H. Geertz, and L. Rosen (1979). *Meaning and Order in Moroccan Society*. Cambridge: Cambridge University Press.

George, S. (1990). *A Fate Worse Than Debt*. London: Penguin.

Hart, K. (1973). 'Informal Income Opportunities and Urban Employment in Ghana'. *Journal of Modern African Studies*, 11(1): 61–89.

Hart, K. (1988). 'Kinship, Contract and Trust: The Economic Organization of Migrants in an African City Slum', in D. Gambetta (ed.), *Trust: Making and Breaking Co-operative Relations*. Oxford: Blackwell, pp. 176–93.

Hart, K. (1992). 'Market and State After the Cold War: The Informal Economy Reconsidered', in R. Dilley (ed.), *Contesting Markets*. Edinburgh: Edinburgh University Press, pp. 214–27.

Hart, K. (2001a [2000]). *Money in an Unequal World*. New York and London: Texere. (First published as *The Memory Bank: Money in an Unequal World*. London: Profile Books.)

Hart, K. (2001b) 'Decentralized Development in the Scottish Highlands and Islands'. *Progress in Development Studies*, 1(4): 337–42.

Hart, K. (2004). 'The Political Economy of Food in an Unequal World', in M. Lien and B. Nerlich (eds), *Politics of Food*. Oxford: Berg, pp. 199–220.

Hart, K. (2005). *The Hit Man's Dilemma: Or Business, Personal and Impersonal*. Chicago: Prickly Paradigm Press.

Hart, K. and V. Padayachee (2000). 'Indian Business in South Africa after Apartheid: New and Old Trajectories'. *Comparative Studies in Society and History*, 42(4): 683–712.

International Labour Office (1972). *Incomes, Employment and Equality in Kenya*. Geneva: ILO.

James, C. L. R. (1980 [1948]). *Notes on Dialectics: Hegel, Marx, Lenin*. London: Allison and Busby.

Keynes, J. M. (1936). *The General Theory of Employment, Interest and Money*. London: Macmillan.

MacGaffey, J. (1991). *The Real Economy of Zaire*. London: James Currey.

McNeill, D. (2003). 'Chapter 4: The Informal Sector: The Biography of an Idea'. 'Chapter 8: Social Capital and the World Bank', in M. Bøås and D. McNeill (eds), *Global Institutions and Development: Framing the World?* London: Routledge, pp. 46–60.

Maine, H. (1906 [1871]). *Ancient Law*. London: Murray.

Maitland, F. W. (1957). *Selected Historical Essays*. Cambridge: Cambridge University Press.

Marais, H. (1998). *South Africa, Limits to Change, The Political Economy of Transformation*. London and New York: Zed Books.

Nustad, K. G. (2004). 'The Right to Stay in Cato Crest: Formality and Informality in a South African Development Project', in K. Hansen and M. Vaa (eds), *Reconsidering Informality: Perspectives from Urban Africa*. Uppsala: Nordic African Institute, pp. 45–61.

Pahl, R. (1984). *Divisions of Labour*. Oxford: Blackwell.

Scott, J. (1998). *Seeing Like a State: How Certain Schemes for Improving the Human Condition have Failed*. New Haven: Yale University Press.

Weber, M. (1978). 'The City', in G. Roth and C. Wittich (eds), *Economy and Society*, Vol. 2. Berkeley and Los Angeles: University of California Press, 1212–1372.

Weber, M. (1981). *General Economic History*. New Brunswick, NJ: Transaction Books.

3

The global path: soft law and non-sovereigns formalizing the potency of the informal sector

Robert K. Christensen

3.1 Introduction

Scholarship and practice in economic and political development abounds with conceptual dichotomies. As simplifications of reality seeking to survey the existence of political and economic inequalities, an illustrative list might include: formal–informal institutions, sectors, and economies; rural–urban identities and economies; state–market mechanisms; legal certainty–uncertainty; regulated–unregulated activities; private–public sectors, institutions, and goods; and sovereign–non-sovereign powers. By unpacking the concepts of formality and informality, the editors and authors of this volume seek to transcend dichotomies to lay a theoretical and practical foundation to aid our understanding of how we might empower and grant 'citizens equal access to what was theirs as a right' (Hart, chapter 2, this volume).

Researchers have already clarified several possibilities, primarily rooted in local and state-based remedies, which challenge our thinking about development. Many scholars (e.g. Ostrom *et al.* 1978; V. Ostrom 1999; Ostrom 2005a; see Hart, chapter 2, this volume) have hypothesized and empirically demonstrated the power of localized, polycentric activity in addressing the often disempowering effect of policies that assign 'regional or national governments with the responsibility for local public goods and common-pool resources' (Ostrom 2005a). Hernando de Soto (1989: 181) in his book, *The Other Path*, recommends that states extend stable legal rights (a system including property rights, contracts, and extracontractual liability) to transcend the hurdles of legal uncertainty and dramatically increase the value of localized informal economic activity. In recommending more local, more state, more formal, or less formal *paths* to development, these scholars attend to tuning policies that would reduce the distinction between the empowered and disempowered. While many of this volume's contributors elaborate the importance of less central—particularly substate—remedies in grappling with these dichotomies, such approaches need not entrench a mutual exclusivity of state or local, formal or informal. For example, in demonstrating the pragmatic approach of the Self-Employed Women's Association (SEWA), Ravi Kanbur's recent work recommends transcending dichotomies when he observes that SEWA 'eschews ideological positions on state versus market' and is ultimately 'pro-poor' (2001: 1086).

My purpose in this chapter is to explore another *path*—a path through global civil society—to transcend some of the dichotomies of development. The importance of such a path has been identified in Ostrom's observation that 'to unlock human potential... we need to open the public sector to entrepreneurship and innovation at local, regional, national and *international* levels' (2005a, emphasis added). That civil society, in various forms, can play a role in development is also not new (Lipton 1991).

Just as unspecified and uncertain legal rights can be impediments to realizing the potential of informal economic activity in Peru, the concept of sovereignty often remains an obstacle to the empowerment of diverse polities—including informal ones. Sovereignty suggests the ability to act and govern, independent of external authority and control. In this sense, sovereignty is the most universal embodiment of formality.

In the context of policymaking, sovereign nation-states have traditionally constituted the primary policy actors. The tradition has had foundation since at least the mid-1600s, articulated in Hobbe's *De Cive* (1642) and when the Westphalian Peace Treaty (1648) recognized the concept of the sovereignty of nation-states (Delbruck 1997). The Westphalian paradigm is the notion that sovereign states constitute the world's principal, if not sole, policy actors (Benvenisti 1999). Under this paradigm, which legal realists argue to be relevant today (Nowrot 1999), sovereignty is the ultimate embodiment of policy potency.

In contrast, the non-sovereign/informal sector is oft-associated with the activities of non-sovereign/non-governmental organizations (NGOs), which can create, advocate, support, and train informal institutions seeking to empower the disenfranchised (e.g. Guha-Khasnobis and Ahuja, chapter 10, this volume; Thomas 2001: 6). While many NGOs might signal formality in many ways (e.g. state funding, political voice, etc.), under the traditional Westphalian paradigm, they lack the sovereignty to act independently (of the state) and are considered, for purposes of this piece, informal.

Nevertheless, reflecting upon evidence suggesting that non-sovereigns have the potential to do more than execute policy (e.g. Sikkink 2002; Christensen 2004)—but to actually prescribe, invoke, monitor, apply, and enforce policy—this piece utilizes the Institutional Analysis and Development (IAD) framework (Kiser and Ostrom 1982; Oakerson 1992; Ostrom *et al.* 1994) to articulate the legal authority of multiple governing units in a polycentric system that envisions a larger, more formal role for non-sovereigns—including NGOs—as well as local governments in the policy context. The IAD framework will be expounded in greater detail to follow, but is a conceptual apparatus to aid in understanding the way policy outcomes are affected by rules, community attributes, and physical conditions at various levels of analysis, for example, production/consumption, collective-choice, and constitutional levels (Gibson *et al.* 2005: ch. 2).

Many political scientists have argued that 'norms are becoming increasingly consequential... and that transnational nongovernmental actors are key instigators and promoters of new norms' (Sikkink 2002: 38). Soft law, as I discuss in greater length below, is an important mechanism by which non-sovereigns can influence the norms of international law, and ultimately the authority of nation-states—the external authority which may/may not encourage the development of humanity. While soft law lacks the binding force of hard law, it can serve as a 'way station to harder legalization... and has certain independent advantages of its own' (Abbott and Snidal 2000: 423).

Soft law's norms have direct implications for rules. For example, soft law allows non-sovereign policy actors to join, compete with, and complement sovereign policy actors in economic and political development policies. Relying on the IAD framework, I analyse how the legal innovation that is soft law might transform/create rules that elevate the informal sector, with a focus on NGOs, in gaining legal recognition and potency on the stage of global politics with derivatives of that power manifest nationally/locally. I specify how soft law can partially abrogate Westphalian sovereignty and potentially open the way for non-sovereigns to unlock human potential otherwise dependent on state-based intervention. In application, this analysis reveals some of the important dynamics underlying Hart's (chapter 2, this volume) observation that conceptualizing society in terms of nation-states may be increasingly unwarranted—at least empirically. I demonstrate here that conceptualizing economic and political development without considering global avenues to complement state and local approaches may also be undermining our full ability to unlock human potential.

3.2 Competing World Paradigms and Policy Processes

Orthodox views of policymaking may be one of the primary reasons that global paths to development are less frequently considered. In this section, I introduce the orthodoxy that inhibits full participation in development policy and an emerging paradigm that introduces avenues for great participation in development.

Scholars are more and more careful about the language used to describe global dynamics (Delbruck 1997); many are also questioning assumptions about governing processes and structures (e.g. Wise 1997; Kettl 2000). Two distinct concepts have emerged from the previously interchangeable words *internationalization* and *globalization*. Delbruck illustrates by noting that *internationalization* implies 'institutionalized cooperation between States with the aim to complement their national efforts to promote national power and welfare, [but that] "globalization" denotes a process of "denationalization" of the production or... the fulfillment of public tasks... that by their very nature and dimension transcend national capabilities' (1997: fn 3). International society, following the Westphalian tradition, features national policy actors and primarily reflects upon the interactions among those sovereign states.

Globalization, on the other hand, describes a society diversely populated and influenced by sovereign and non-sovereign actors (e.g. world corporations, NGOs, and individuals) 'characterized by a multitude of decentralized lawmaking processes in various sectors, independently of nation-states' (Nowrot 1999: 641). Whether referenced by using the term open constitutional state (Hobe 1997), world community (Seita 1997), transnational society (Slaughter 1995), or global society (Teubner 1997; Nowrot 1999), many of the policy actors suggested by globalization would find no influential home in a Westphalian world.

Policy studies affirm an applied context for these competing worldview models. Policy formulation has classically been conceptualized on a spectrum including synoptic processes, marked by comprehensive rationality, and incremental processes. Conceptualizing the policy process in terms of one or the other of these models would be short-sighted. For example, policy analysts have greatly benefited from complementing their synoptic notions about the policy process with incremental conceptions (Lindbloom 1959).

While the synoptic-incremental spectrum is typically used to illustrate policy as a process or product, the spectrum also intimates something about the actors involved in policy formulation. For example, in the decentralized setting of incrementalism, 'policy is made by many actors at many levels of government and indeed in society at large' (Diver 1981: 399). Diver's observation suggests a parallel between incrementalism as a policy paradigm and global society as a world paradigm. Likewise, the synoptic policy model would seem to affirm the Westphalian paradigm by identifying a finite and formalized list of policy actors and a more unified set of policy decision channels.

With this tension between synoptic and incremental, and international and global as a backdrop, I observe that sole acceptance/reliance upon the Westphalian paradigm handicaps utilization of other paradigms (e.g. a more global paradigm) relevant to development policy. Introducing globalization's impact on policy possibilities for development is similar to Graham Allison's classic analysis of the Cuban missile crisis, where Allison underscores the importance of exploring alternative frames of reference to understand more fully the policy. In trying to unite the often contentious approaches to development economics, Kanbur (2001: 1093) makes a similar argument. Kanbur implies that before we can construct a more complete intellectual apparatus to approach development issues we should first understand the nature of our implicit assumptions.

Such an approach reinforces Allison's first proposition, which is that policy actors 'think about [policymaking] in terms of largely implicit conceptual models that have significant consequences for the content of their thought' (Allison 1969: 689). Allison's second proposition is that most policy actors 'explain (and predict) the behavior of national governments in terms of various forms of one conceptual model . . . as the more or less purposive acts of unified *national* governments' (1969: 690, emphasis added). While most of Allison's readers focus on the purposive/unified part of his proposition, I highlight 'unified *national* governments' to suggest that most of us are limited by what I've discussed here as the Westphalian orthodoxy, with sovereign-centric solutions to development problems.

Allison's suggestion of over 30 years ago seems more relevant today: we should supplement our traditional frame of reference to reflect other policy actors and policy dynamics (1969: 690). Fortunately, Allison's suggestion has not lost potency over time. The validity of analysing policy only in relation to the unified acts of formal sovereignties is becoming suspect. O'Toole and Hanf (2002) observe that the success of government policy pursuits is a function of how well it adapts to changing institutional environments, making specific mention of the influence of transnational, non-sovereign institutions.

I reiterate here that under the traditional Westphalian paradigm, states have been the sole actors with power to initiate and direct policy, independent of external control. In this sense, they constitute the only actors with power to formalize policy—including development policy. Extra-Westphalian actors, such as NGOs, have been able to influence policy only with the consent of external, state control. Under this traditional view, NGOs (and all non-state actors) remain informal players at the policy table. Although there is now some suspicion shrouding the relevance of the Westphalian paradigm, little has been done to clarify the mechanisms that would empower non-sovereigns to integrate the informal with existing formal sectors. Using the IAD framework, the remainder of this piece begins the process of identification and clarification of the mechanism. A conceptual analysis is offered first, with evidence and discussion to follow. I argue that non-sovereigns and their use of soft law necessitate a non-Westphalian conceptual model that can be explained by their impact on institutional rules governing policymaking at various levels.

3.3 Institutional Analysis of Non-sovereigns as Policy Actors

At the outset of this analysis, it is important to note that the IAD framework is a meta-theoretical construct used simply to organize 'diagnosis, analysis, and prescription... provid[ing] a general compilation of the types of variables that should be used to analyze a relevant problem' (Gibson *et al.* 2005: 25). The framework is advantageous because of its ability to deal with multiple levels of analysis and to draw relationships among them. The present IAD analysis can be thought of in two related parts: (1) the variables (I focus on rules and action arenas, see Table 3.1 italicized) and (2) levels of the analysis where those variables might be relevant. To theorists and practictioners, this analysis facilitates an open-disciplinary structure in which to compare and contrast policy actors, sovereign and non-sovereign alike, and their influence in relation to rules or institutional environments, community attributes, and material and physical conditions (Ostrom *et al.* 1994). While the development of specific theories and models under this analysis with respect to non-sovereigns as policy actors will be left to future research, this conceptual foundation is an important preliminary step towards a fuller understanding of non-sovereigns in development policy. For example, for development analysts

Table 3.1. Primary components or variables of analysis and levels of action situations

Primary components or variables of analysis[a]	Levels of action situations[b]
Context • Physical/material conditions • Community attributes • *Rules* —*entry and exit rules (boundary), position rules, scope rules, authority rules, aggregation* rules, information rules, and payoff rules **Action arena** • *Action situation* —*participants, positions, actions,* outcomes, information, *control,* costs/benefits • *Actors* **Incentives** **Patterns of interaction** **Outcomes** **Evaluative criteria**	**Operational action situations** • Actions that directly affect variables in the world • Provision, production, distribution, appropriation, assignment, consumption **Collective-choice action situations** • Actions that directly affect rules of operational situations • Prescribing, invoking, monitoring, applying, enforcing **Constitutional action situations** • Actions that directly affect rules of collective-choice situations • Prescribing, invoking, monitoring, applying, enforcing **Meta-constitutional action situations** • Actions that directly affect rules of constitutional situations • Prescribing, invoking, monitoring, applying, enforcing

Notes:
[a] See Ostrom *et al.* 1994: 37 for relationships among components.
[b] See Figure 3A.1 for relationships among levels.

and policymakers, awareness of the variables below will alert *how* soft law empowers NGOs to influence policy. In short, this analysis is important to those seeking mechanisms by which informal organizations might engage in activities like poverty reduction.

Ostrom's work (1994: 37, and Figure 3A.1) depicts the relationships between the associated parts of the framework and the relationships between levels of analysis respectively, and will be helpful to the reader unfamiliar with the IAD framework.

3.3.1 *Components: Rules*

This analysis begins with a definitional focus on institutions and rules. Returning to O'Toole and Hanf's suggestion that domestic policy agendas should account for changing institutional environments, Scott and Meyer (1991: 123) appropriately define institutional environments as 'those characterized by the elaboration of rules and requirements to which individual organizations must conform if they are to receive support and legitimacy'. In the context of this piece, the legitimacy referred to would be credibility and authority to act as an authentic development policy actor. For example, the Westphalian paradigm as an institutional environment articulates rules and requirements affirming the legitimacy of nations as exclusive policy actors. Conversely, a global paradigm would be the enunciation of rules and requirements, opening the policy floor to non-state actors.

While Scott and Meyer's definition implies that rules and institutions can be used almost as interchangeable terms, the IAD framework would distinguish rules as 'shared understandings among those involved that refer to enforced prescriptions about what actions are required, prohibited, or permitted' (Gibson *et al.* 2005: 33). Institutions, on the other hand, frequently encompass rules (used both across and within organizations), as well as the organizations themselves (Gibson *et al.* 2005).

To articulate the role of rules beyond requiring, prohibiting, and permitting, authors have suggested that rules can be divided into seven categories related to the structure of a specific action situation: position, boundary (entry and exit), choice (authority), aggregation, information, payoff, and scope (Ostrom *et al.* 1994; Ostrom 2005b). Figure 3A.2 is an insightful illustration of how rules and action situations are related. Among the types of rules most relevant here are position, boundary (entry and exit), choice (authority), scope, and aggregation.

> Position rules create positions (e.g. member of a legislature, voter, etc.). Boundary [entry and exit] rules affect how individuals are assigned to or leave positions and how one situation is linked to other situations. Choice [authority] rules affect the assignment of particular action sets to positions. Scope rules affect which outcomes must, must not, or may be affected within a domain. Aggregation rules affect the level of control that individual participants exercise at a linkage within or across situations (Ostrom 2005b: 190).

Relevant to this analysis is the *entrance* of non-sovereigns in the global policy arena, the *positions* they may occupy within that arena (e.g. formulators, monitors, enforcers of policy), the understandings of the functional *scope* of non-state actors in the world policy arena, the *actions* non-sovereigns may take within a particular action situation in the policy arena, and whether those actions may be taken unilaterally or must be in conjunction or *aggregated* with some other actor (e.g. a contractor and subcontract bidder must agree on a price before a contract is completed).

3.3.2 *Components: Action Arena*

Shifting focus from the rules that influence an action situation to the situation itself allows identification of mechanisms, that would imbue non-state actors with legitimacy, traditionally held in monopoly by sovereign actors under the traditional Westphalian model. The action situation is used here to construct a conceptual model of the world policy arena and, as elaborated in the IAD framework, comprises the following seven generic elements: participants, positions, actions, outcomes, information, control, and costs/benefits (Ostrom *et al.* 1994: 29; again see Figure 3A.2 depicting the relationship between the seven types of rules and seven facets of an action situation).

This piece focuses on four elements most germane to this stage of the analysis: actors/participants, positions, actions, and control. Applied to non-state policy actors, these elements suggest something about (1) who and how many *actors* (informal, non-sovereigns) are *participating* in the policy process, (2) what *positions* non-state actors hold in the process, (3) what policy *actions* they are allowed to take (e.g. enforcement, formation, modification, etc.), and (4) what level of *control* non-states have over their initiatives (i.e. whether they must first seek permission, etc.).

3.3.3 *Levels of Analysis*

The preceding action situation analysis, in order to be representational, must be contextualized within a series of analytic levels—operational, collective choice, constitutional, and meta-constitutional (Ostrom *et al.* 1994; E. Ostrom 1999). In other words, the IAD framework contemplates the reality that the participants, positions, actions, outcomes, information, control, and costs/benefits are not homogenous across various situations. Levels of analysis are linked by the context elements of the IAD framework: physical/material conditions, community attributes, and, the focus of this analysis—rules (see Figure 3A.1). The primary level of analysis is the operational level, the domain of situations directly affecting the world, for example, construction of a school, delivery of health services, etc. Operational action situations are, in addition to physical/material conditions and community attributes, shaped by collective-choice rules-in-use. Operational situations include the activities of provision, production, distribution, appropriation, assignment, and consumption. Collective-choice situations (action situation determining how operational action situations are structured) are shaped by constitutional rules-in-use, and constitutional situations (action situation determining how collective-choice situations are structured) are shaped by meta-constitutional rules-in-use. Unlike operational situations, the activities circumscribed by collective choice, constitutional, and meta-constitutional situations are marked by the activities of prescribing, invoking, monitoring, applying, and enforcing.

In challenging the Westphalian paradigm, it is with these pre-operational levels that the global influence of NGOs is most appropriately associated. At the more operational action levels, policy influence would be diminished by the more pressing tasks of policy execution, and by the layers of collective and constitutional authority arranging the stage for the operational activities. I remind here, by way of illustration, that in a substantive policy field such as health services, and under the Westphalian paradigm, states with sole access, for example, to treaty making, would be considered the primary if not sole agenda setters for world health policy—articulating/authorizing the priorities and specifying operational channels for policy implementation.

Up to the current analysis, and in the traditional Westphalian paradigm, non-state actors have been viewed as a very prolific feature of operational action situations and occasionally of collective-choice situations. Indeed, in the present state of worldwide public management reforms, of which devolution has been an integral component (Thompson 1997), many non-state actors are at the forefront of such operational activities as provision, production, distribution, appropriation, assignment, and consumption. One might even argue that the government management reforms are evidence of the collective-choice and constitutional level actions that have structured the operational situations, of which non-state and often less formal actors are integral parts.

At the operational level, non-state actors would appear to take up the definitional function that Peter Dobkin Hall (1987) ascribes organizations in defining an aspect of the nonprofit sector: assuming and performing those public tasks delegated by states. Non-sovereigns, acting solely at these more operational levels, would affirm the Westphalian paradigm characterized by sovereigns monopolistically populating the 'upper' action levels (collective choice, constitutional, meta-constitutional), prescribing policy for and delegating policy tasks to operational actors.

3.4 Soft Law: Challenging the Sovereign Monopoly Under a Global Paradigm

The foundation of a Westphalian model confirming that non-sovereigns function solely in the realm of policy execution has been weakened by the increasingly expansive roles of non-sovereigns. While collectives such as

NGOs and other informal organizations have been predominantly viewed as operational actors with operational goals and missions (e.g. provision, production, distribution, appropriation, assignment, and consumption, in terms of the IAD framework), many authors have noted what appears to be non-sovereign potency at the collective-choice and constitutional action levels as well. Evidence suggests that a global paradigm should, in the least, supplement the Westphalian paradigm.

In preface to exploring these observations of non-sovereign potencies, it is important to note the dynamics that many ascribe to, giving rise to the growth in numbers, if not powers, of non-sovereigns. These dynamics attribute the increased population of non-sovereign organizations, such as international non-governmental organizations (INGOs), to the decline of the state (Lindenberg and Dobel 1999, e.g. eroding trust in sovereign governments, decline in public sector resources, privatization, failed states; Salamon 1999); emergence and successful specification of global problems, where for example, transnational environmental problems require transnational action (Nowrot 1999); denationalization of multinational corporations (Grossman and Bradlow 1993; Nowrot 1999); and developments in communications/information technologies (Grossman and Bradlow 1993; Salamon and Anheier 1999; Gamble and Ku 2000).

While these dynamics certainly offer legitimate and ample explanation justifying analysis of global non-sovereign actors, it is not immediately clear how these explanations illuminate the mechanisms empowering non-sovereigns beyond the operational action level. I take up here one important innovation of non-sovereign influence and relate it to the variables of the IAD to do just that. The innovation to which I refer is known as 'soft law'.

An understanding of soft law can be reached by first reviewing fundamental concepts of international law. Traditionally international policies, or international law, could be located in one of two places: treaties or customary law. Following the Westphalian paradigm, the former constituted those laws manifest as 'written agreements between states' while the latter constituted 'uncodified, but equally binding rules based on long-standing behaviour that states accept as compulsory' (Ratner 1998: 67). Ratner notes that much of this former category is eventually codified into hard law, but that recent years have seen the rise of a third category of international law: soft law. Ratner also notes that the growth of soft law has shared some correspondence with two other dynamics: the general aversion of sovereign nations to adopt binding international rules and the growth in number of global actors.

Grant (1999: 456) defines soft law as those 'statements intermediate between law and the merely hortatory... international norms still in the process of formation'. Although lacking the binding power of hard treaty law or international customary law, soft law's significance, like that of customary law, is in its potential to influence states and other global actors. As I cited previously, international norms are becoming increasingly important in shaping the direction of policy (see Sikkink 2002), often serving as intermediate/preparatory steps to hard law. As such, soft law has become a new gateway, whose entrance is not necessarily limited to sovereign actors, into creating internationally binding law and policy.

Scholars (Ratner 1998) observe that the normative expectations induced by soft law develop more gradually than hard treaty law, but more quickly than waiting for the evolution of customary law. Grant (1999: 456) confirms that soft law constitutes 'rules in *statu nascendi* [and] may be advanced by their commitment to paper... [I]f endorsed by further instruments and by practice, such statements can become binding *erga omnes*'. In essence, the evolution of soft law can legally subject sovereign nation-states to the expectations of those organizations creating and promoting soft law.

Relating this discussion back to the IAD framework, soft law is a legally significant innovation by which non-sovereign organizations can wield influence in more than just the operational action level, undiminished by the fact that they are not sovereign bodies under the Westphalian model. Not circumscribed by the cross-national thoroughfares traditionally accommodating the generation and modification of policy, soft law is an avenue through which non-sovereign organizations can assume activities such as prescribing, invoking, monitoring, applying, and enforcing policy. Again, because soft law allows non-sovereigns to participate in policy formation independent of 'sovereign' external authority and control, soft law becomes a vehicle conveying non-sovereign actors into action situations (collective choice, constitutional, and meta-constitutional) solely occupied by sovereigns under the Westphalian paradigm. Figure 3.1 depicts soft law's role in conveying non-sovereigns into policy activities beyond operational situations. Policy activities are listed by level of action situation in Figure 3A.1.

Observations of such influence are widely evident including authors highlighting

- non-sovereigns' expanding role in the global political world, including nongovernmental organizations' 'effects on agenda setting and the evolution of public attention to global goals' (Martin 1999: 59; Sen 1999),

Figure 3.1. Soft law's effect on institutional policy arrangements

- that international 'development cooperation increasingly requires that states interact productively with nonstate actors' (Martin 1999: 59), and
- that in considering international forums there is a need for a 'new form of tripatism... emphasizing the need to encourage more systematic consultation and cooperation among government, civil society, and business' (Kaul *et al.* 1999: 480).

Specific examples of non-sovereign influence range from the policy areas of world health (Chen *et al.* 1999; Zacher 1999), economic development (Krut 1997), and international justice (Sen 1999; Christensen 2001/2002; Drezner 2001); land mine policy (Price 1998; Kaul *et al.* 1999); race relations (Bouget and Prouteau 2002); international investment and securities (Walker 2001); and international security and peace (Hamburg and Holl 1999; Mendez 1999).

While the impact of non-sovereign organizations in relation to soft law certainly varies along a continuum, conceptualizing instances of soft law activities as actual evidence of collective-choice, constitutional, and meta-constitutional levels of activities is helpful.

Prescribing and invoking. Krut illustrates the ability of non-sovereign entities to prescribe and invoke policy in noting that non-governmental organizations 'accredited to ECOSOC [United Nations Economic and Social Council] have the right to formally state their views and participate in... a global conference or meeting. They can, for example, make their views known in position papers circulated via UN distribution channels along with the other official documents' (1997: 40). UN Deputy Secretary-General Frechette (1998) has indicated that such status for non-sovereigns is only likely to increase in breadth and depth.

Possibly the most prolific and current example of this influence has been the formation of the International Criminal Court (ICC), whose first justices were sworn into office during the writing of this manuscript (11 March 2003). With far-reaching implications over the globe's nation-states and citizens (e.g. Christensen 2001/2002), the creation of the ICC has been credited in significant part to the soft law, specifically the Rome Statute, energized by INGOs (Drezner 2001). The same has been said for the international treaty to ban land mines (Price 1998).

Monitoring. Although not necessarily a manifestation of soft law, Brinkerhoff and Coston (1999) evidence NGOs' role in monitoring policy pursuits. Internationally recognized organizations such as Amnesty International and Greenpeace symbolize a host of organizations monitoring states' progress on various issues, for example, environmental protection and human rights (Hobe 1997). As in the case of the ICC, evidence gathered from these monitoring pursuits, however, has been used to establish and give credibility to the norms created by soft law.

Applying and enforcing policy. Hobe (1997) and Abbott and Snidal (2000) offer evidence of NGOs' role in the enforcement of policy. From the field of environmental law, for example, the International Union for the Conservation of Nature and Natural Resources (IUCNNR) has been delegated power to directly implement environmental policy (Hobe 1997).

3.5 Implications and Conclusion

The preceding specification of non-governmental activities occupying space traditionally reserved for sovereign states emphasizes the mechanisms that would empower non-sovereigns beyond the traditional Westphalian, operational roles. Beginning with the context articulated in IAD, soft law introduces a change in the rules-in-use that have traditionally structured the policy process. Because rules-in-use are integral determinants of the action arena at every level of analysis (see Ostrom *et al.* 1994: 37 and Figure 3A.1), soft law's impact is far-reaching. The discussion that follows further elaborates how soft law impacts rules-in-use, thereby introducing non-sovereigns to action situations formerly off-limits in the Westphalian world (see Figure 3.1).

Soft law impacts *entry and exit (boundary) rules*, imbuing non-sovereigns with policy potency beyond the traditional operational-level notions of policy execution. Relatedly, evidence suggests that *position rules* have also been altered by the soft law process, allowing non-sovereigns to occupy positions traditionally reserved for sovereigns, positions from which policy is prescribed, invoked, monitored, applied, and enforced. Soft law significantly alters *scope rules* by delimiting the functional impact of non-sovereign policy actors. While Westphalian rules-in-use appeared to limit non-sovereign functionality to operational-level actions such as policy execution (see Figure 3.1) (e.g. production, distribution, appropriation, assignment, and consumption), soft law grants collective-action, constitutional, and meta-constitutional functionalities to non-sovereigns—giving them voice in the structuring of operational and other action arenas.

Soft law has implications for *authority* and *aggregation rules* as well, by altering the set of actions that actors 'must, may, or may not take' and the 'level of control that an actor in a position exercises in the selection of an action' (Ostrom *et al.* 2002: 292). Again, the Westphalian model would limit policy formulation and enforcement to sovereign actors. With the introduction and growing legitimacy of the third type of international law (soft law), actions previously beyond the authority of non-sovereigns are now within their authority. Concerning aggregation, although the normative expectations created by non-sovereigns must eventually be confirmed by the accepted practice by sovereign states to be credible and binding, examples such as the establishment of the ICC certainly illustrate the reality of non-sovereign control in the policy process.

As the various levels of action arenas are impacted by the rules-in-use just discussed, there is a growing body of observations evidencing an expansion in the participants, positions, actions, and control traditionally seen under the Westphalian paradigm. These rules-in-use comprise significant mechanisms by which soft law empowers non-sovereigns beyond the operational-level action arena (see Figure 3.1).

The implications for development and the informal sector include the following: access to development policy creation and change is not restricted to cross-national channels bricked with sovereignty. Soft law introduces new dynamics influencing the institutional arrangements of the policy process, whether viewed internationally or globally. Those fields of policy more heavily populated by active non-sovereign participants are more likely to be subject to the normative expectations formulated by these groups. Accordingly, inasmuch as these fields include development policy (e.g. Krut 1997), their agendas are influenced to varying degrees by the impact of non-sovereigns empowered by changing rules-in-use through soft law. Although we have traditionally conceived of society in terms of sovereignty and state (Hart, chapter 2, this volume), soft law's impact opens to non-sovereigns the process of enabling humans to solve problems. Where sovereigns have been limited to facilitate the betterment of humanity, or have even interfered with the process, the promise of empowering capacity of soft law is especially meaningful.

By detailing this empowerment, I have offered a starting point to a fuller comprehension of how the 'informal' sector can begin to act without the levels of external, sovereign authority formerly required under the Westphalian paradigm. I am not suggesting that with the innovation of soft law non-sovereigns can act unilaterally in all development policy; the concept and framework of state will still need to be addressed. Indeed, many scholars rightly caution that 'internationally generated imports succeed only where the local situation allows them to be nationalized—made part of indigenous structures and practices' (Garth and Dezalay 2002: 6). What I offer here is a framework to transcend the sovereign/non-sovereign dichotomy, a global paradigm to supplement the Westphalian paradigm, an avenue for development policy that should not be overlooked.

As only select IAD components are raised in this chapter, the institutional analysis framework still has much to offer in fully exploring the importance of the informal sector, including relevant incentives and patterns of interaction in the world policy process. For example, work suggesting that the communications environment is altering government/non-governmental relationships (Brainard and Siplon 2002) might be examined as physical/material conditions or community attributes that impact the structuring of an action arena (see Ostrom *et al.* 1994: 37). Work highlighting the ability of NGOs to influence policy at multiple levels (Bouget and Prouteau 2002) could benefit from the IAD framework's articulation and linking of multiple levels of analysis. Future analyses should utilize the richness of the framework to identify relevant variables and relationships.

The analysis here suggests a supplementation, if not a shift in world paradigms used to understand development policy and the sectors influencing that policy. While the Westphalian paradigm is still highly relevant, policy inquiries should recognize the mechanisms that would affirm a more global model less rooted in the concept of sovereignty. This shift is reflected by reiterating O'Toole and Hanf's (2002: 160) observation that '[t]o an increasing degree, a government's success in pursuing domestically defined national objectives depends on how effectively it can act within changing institutional contexts, including new transnational institutions'.

Appendix

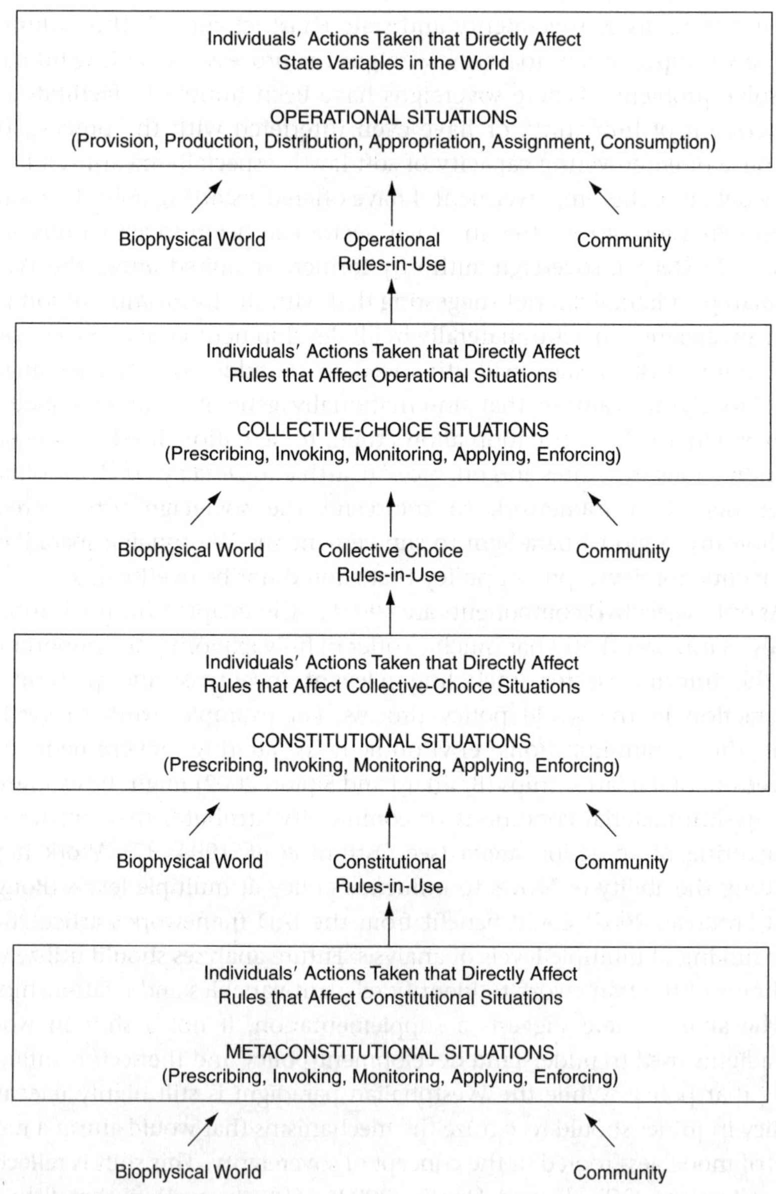

Figure 3A.1. Levels of action situations

Source: Ostrom (1999) 'Institutional Rational Choice: An Assessment of the IAD Framework', in P. Sabatier (ed.), *Theories of the Policy Process*. Boulder, CO: Westview Press, p. 60. Reproduced by permission of Westview Press, a member of Perseus Books, L.L.C.

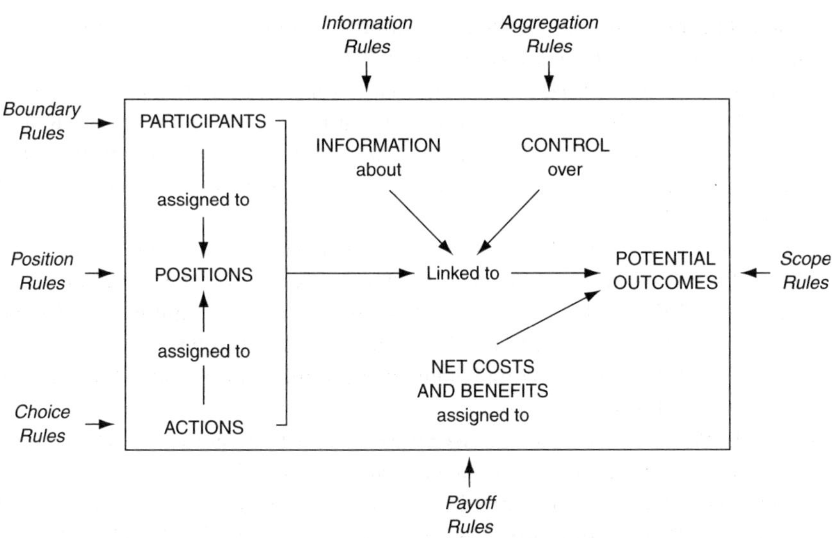

Figure 3A.2. Types of rules, relationships to action situation

Source: Ostrom (2005b) *Understanding Institutional Diversity*. Princeton, NJ: Princeton University Press, p. 189 (Figure 7.1). Reprinted by kind permission of Princeton University Press.

References

Abbott, K. W. and D. Snidal (2000). 'Hard and Soft Law in International Governance'. *International Organization*, 54(3): 421–56.

Allison, G. T. (1969). 'Conceptual Models and the Cuban Missile Crisis'. *American Political Science Review*, 63: 689–718.

Benvenisti, E. (1999). 'Exit and Voice in the Age of Globalization'. *Michigan Law Review*, 98(1): 167.

Bouget, D. and L. Prouteau (2002). 'National and Supranational Government-NGO Relations: Anti-discrimination Policy Formation in the European Union'. *Public Administration and Development*, 22: 31–7.

Brainard, L. A. and P. D. Siplon (2002). 'The Internet and NGO-Government Relations: Injecting Chaos into Order'. *Public Administration and Development*, 22: 63–72.

Brinkerhoff, D. W. and J. M. Coston (1999). 'International Development Management in a Globalized World'. *Public Administration Review*, 59(4): 346.

Chen, L. C., T. G. Evans, and R. A. Cash (1999). 'Health as a Global Public Good', in I. Kaul, I. Grunberg, and M. A. Stern (eds), *Global Public Goods: International Cooperation in the 21st Century*. Oxford: Oxford University Press, pp. 284–305.

Christensen, R. K. (2001/2002). 'Getting to Peace by Reconciling Notions of Justice: The Importance of Considering Discrepancies Between Civil and Common Legal

Systems in the Formation of the International Criminal Court'. *UCLA Journal of International Law and Foreign Affairs*, 6(2): 391–423.

Christensen, R. K. (2004). 'International Nongovernmental Organizations: Globalization, Policy Learning, and the Nation-State', in D. Levi-Faur and E. Vigoda-Gadot (eds), *International Public Policy and Management: Policy Learning Beyond Regional, Cultural, and Political Boundaries*. New York: Marcel Dekker, pp. 45–66.

de Soto, H. and Instituto Libertad y Democracia (Lima Peru). (1989). *The Other Path: The Invisible Revolution in the Third World*. New York: Harper and Row.

Delbruck, J. (1997). 'The Role of the United Nations in Dealing with Global Problems'. *Indiana Journal of Global Legal Studies*, 4(2): 277–96.

Diver, C. S. (1981). 'Policymaking Paradigms in Administrative Law'. *Harvard Law Review*, 95: 393–434.

Drezner, D. W. (2001). 'On the Balance Between International Law and Democratic Sovereignty'. *Chicago Journal of International Law*, 2(2): 321–36.

Frechette, D. S.-G. L. (1998). United Nations Press Release, DSG/SM/38. Accessed 7 March 2006, from http://www.un.org/News/Press/docs/1998/19981203.dsgsm38.html

Gamble, J. K. and C. Ku (2000). 'International Law—New Actors and New Technologies: Center Stage for NGOs'? *Law and Policy in International Business*, 31(2): 221.

Garth, B. G. and Y. Dezalay (2002). 'Introduction', in Y. Dezalay and B. G. Garth (eds), *Global Prescriptions: The Production, Exportation, and Importation of a New Legal Orthodoxy*. Ann Arbor, MI: University of Michigan Press, pp. 1–36.

Gibson, C., K. Andersson, E. Ostrom, and S. Shivakumar (2005). *The Samaritan's Dilemma: The Political Economy of Development Aid*. Oxford: Oxford University Press.

Grant, T. D. (1999). 'Defining Statehood: The Montevideo Convention and its Discontents'. *Columbia Journal of Transnational Law*, 37(2): 403–57.

Grossman, C. and D. D. Bradlow (1993). 'Are we Being Propelled Towards a People-Centered Transnational Legal Order?'. *American University Journal of International Law and Policy*, 9(Fall): 1–25.

Hall, P. D. (1987). 'A Historical Overview of the Private Nonprofit Sector', in W. W. Powell (ed.), *The Nonprofit Sector: A Research Handbook*. Princeton: Yale University, pp. 3–26.

Hamburg, D. A. and J. E. Holl (1999). 'Preventing Deadly Conflict: From Global Housekeeping to Neighbourhood Watch', in I. Kaul, I. Grunberg, and M. A. Stern (eds), *Global Public Goods: International Cooperation in the 21st Century*. Oxford: Oxford University Press, pp. 366–81.

Hobe, S. (1997). 'Global Challenges to Statehood: The Increasingly Important Role of Nongovernmental Organizations'. *Indiana Journal of Global Legal Studies*, 5(1): 191–209.

Kanbur, R. (2001). 'Economic Policy, Distribution and Poverty: The Nature of the Disagreements'. *World Development*, 29(6): 1083–94. Reprinted 2004 in

A. Shorrocks and R. van der Hoeven (eds), *Growth, Inequality and Poverty*. Oxford: Oxford University Press for UNU-WIDER.

Kaul, I., I. Grunberg, and M. A. Stern (1999). 'Conclusion: Global Public Goods: Concepts, Policies, and Strategies', in I. Kaul, I. Grunberg, and M. A. Stern (eds), *Global Public Goods: International Cooperation in the 21st Century*. Oxford: Oxford University Press, pp. 450–507.

Kettl, D. F. (2000). 'The Transformation of Governance: Globalization, Devolution, and the Role of Government'. *Public Administration Review*, 60(6): 488.

Kiser, L. L. and E. Ostrom (1982). 'The Three Worlds of Action: A Metatheoretical Synthesis of Institutional Approaches', in E. Ostrom (ed.), *Strategies of Political Inquiry*. Beverly Hills, CA: Sage, pp. 179–222.

Krut, R. (1997). 'Globalization and Civil Society: NGO Influence in International Decision-making', Discussion Paper No. 83. Accessed (March 2004) from http://www.unrisd.org/unrisd/website/document.nsf/(httpPublications)/87428A38D3E0403380256B650043B768.

Lindbloom, C. (1959). 'The Science of Muddling Through'. *Public Administration Review*, 19: 79–88.

Lindenberg, M. and J. P. Dobel (1999). 'The Challenges of Globalization for Northern International Relief and Development NGOs'. *Nonprofit and Voluntary Sector Quarterly*, 28(Suppl.): 4–24.

Lipton, M. (1991). 'The State-Market Dilemma, Civil Society, and Structural Adjustment'. *The Round Table*, 317(1): 21–31.

Martin, L. L. (1999). 'The Political Economy of International Cooperation', in I. Kaul, I. Grunberg, and M. A. Stern (eds), *Global Public Goods: International Cooperation in the 21st Century*. Oxford: Oxford University Press, pp. 51–64.

Mendez, R. P. (1999). 'Peace as a Global Public Good', in I. Kaul, I. Grunberg, and M. A. Stern (eds), *Global Public Goods: International Cooperation in the 21st Century*. Oxford: Oxford University Press, pp. 382–416.

Nowrot, K. (1999). 'Legal Consequences of Globalization: The Status of Non-governmental Organizations Under International Law'. *Indiana Journal of Global Legal Studies*, 6(2): 579–645.

O'Toole Jr., L. J. and K. I. Hanf (2002). 'American Public Administration and Impacts of International Governance'. *Public Administration Review*, 62(4): 158–69.

Oakerson, R. J. (1992). 'Analyzing the Commons: A Framework', in D. Bromley *et al.* (eds), *Making the Commons Work: Theory, Practice, and Policy*. San Francisco, CA: ICS Press, pp. 41–59.

Ostrom, E. (1999). 'Institutional Rational Choice: An Assessment of the IAD Framework', in P. Sabatier (ed.), *Theories of the Policy Process*. Boulder, CO: Westview Press, pp. 35–72.

Ostrom, E. (2005a). 'Unlocking Public Entrepreneurship and Public Economies'. Discussion Paper No. 2005/01. Helsinki: UNU-WIDER.

Ostrom, E. (2005b). *Understanding Institutional Diversity*. Princeton, NJ: Princeton University Press.

Ostrom, E., R. Gardner, and J. Walker (1994). *Rules, Games, and Common-pool Resources*. Ann Arbor, MI: University of Michigan Press.

Ostrom, E., C. Gibson, S. Shivakumar, and K. Andersson (2002). *Aid, Incentives, and Sustainability: An Institutional Analysis of Development Cooperation*. Stockholm: Sida.

Ostrom, E., R. B. Parks, and G. Whitaker (1978). *Patterns of Metropolitan Policing*. Cambridge, MA: Ballinger.

Ostrom, V. (1999). 'Polycentricity', in M. McGinnis (ed.), *Polycentricity and Local Public Economies: Readings from the Workshop in Political Theory and Policy Analysis*. Ann Arbor, MI: University of Michigan Press, pp. 52–74.

Price, R. (1998). 'Reversing the Gun Sights: Transnational Civil Society'. *International Organization*, 52(3): 613.

Ratner, S. R. (1998). 'International Law: The Trials of Global Norms'. *Foreign Policy*, 110: 65.

Salamon, L. M. (1999). 'Preface', in L. M. Salamon (ed.), *Global Civil Society: Dimensions of the Nonprofit Sector*. Baltimore, MD: Johns Hopkins Center for Civil Society Studies, pp. xvii–xix.

Salamon, L. M. and H. K. Anheier (1999). 'Civil Society in Comparative Perspective', in L. M. Salamon (ed.), *Global Civil Society: Dimensions of the Nonprofit Sector*. Baltimore, MD: Johns Hopkins Center for Civil Society Studies, pp. 3–39.

Scott, W. R. and J. W. Meyer (1991). 'The Organization of Societal Sectors: Proposition and Early Evidence', in W. W. Powell and P. J. DiMaggio (eds), *The New Institutionalism in Organizational Analysis*. Chicago: University of Chicago Press, pp. 108–40.

Seita, A. Y. (1997). 'Globalization and the Convergence of Values'. *Cornell International Law Journal*, 30(2): 429–91.

Sen, A. (1999). 'Global Justice: Beyond International Equity', in I. Kaul, I. Grunberg, and M. A. Stern (eds), *Global Public Goods: International Cooperation in the 21st Century*. Oxford: Oxford University Press, pp. 116–25.

Sikkink, K. (2002). 'Transnational Advocacy Networks and the Social Construction of Legal Rules', in Y. Dezalay and B. G. Garth (eds), *Global Prescriptions: The Production, Exportation, and Importation of a New Legal Orthodoxy*. Ann Arbor, MI: University of Michigan Press, pp. 37–64.

Slaughter, A. (1995). 'International Law in a World of Liberal States'. *European Journal of International Law*, 6(4): 503–38.

Teubner, G. (1997). 'Foreword: Legal Regimes of Global Non-state Actors', in G. Teubner (ed.), *Global Law without a State: Studies in Modern Law and Policy*. Aldershot: Dartmouth Publishing, pp. xiii–xvii.

Thomas, J. (2001). 'What Is the Informal Economy, Anyway'? *SAIS Review*, XXI(1): 1–11.

Thompson, F. (1997). 'Defining the New Public Management', in L. R. Jones, K. Schedler, and S. W. Wade (eds), *International Perspectives on the New Public*

Management, Advances in International Comparative Management, Supplement 3. Greenwich, CT: JAI Press, pp. 1–14.

Walker, A. (2001). 'NGOs, Business, and International Investment: The Multilateral Agreement on Investment, Seattle, and Beyond'. *Global Governance: A Review of Multilateralism and International Organizations*, 7(1): 51–73.

Wise, C. R. (1997). 'The Future of Public Law: Beyond Administrative Law and National Borders', in P. J. Cooper and C. A. Newland (eds), *Handbook of Public Law and Administration*. San Francisco, CA: Jossey-Bass, pp. 569–87.

Zacher, M. W. (1999). 'Global Epidemiological Surveillance: International Cooperation to Monitor Infectious Diseases', in I. Kaul, I. Grunberg, and M. A. Stern (eds), *Global Public Goods: International Cooperation in the 21st Century*. Oxford: Oxford University Press, pp. 266–83.

4

The relevance of the concepts of formality and informality: a theoretical appraisal

Alice Sindzingre[1]

4.1 Introduction

Since its first appearance in the 1970s, the concept of informality has referred to highly heterogeneous phenomena and measurement methods, and has been explored by development microeconomics and institutional economics via the notions of formal and informal institutions and contracts (Hart 1973). This plurality of meanings and instruments calls into question the concept's validity. This chapter synthesizes the critical issues within both a development economics and an institutional economics perspective. It highlights the continuity of 'formal' and 'informal' phenomena as well as the weaknesses of most criteria that discriminate between the two categories. It proposes a theoretical approach toward institutions according to which all institutions, be they formal or informal, include forms and contents. The latter's dynamics are explained in terms of core attributes of institutions and rules: relevance, credibility, and enforceability. This approach enables one to understand the impact, resilience, and transformation of institutions and the links between them.

The following section examines the conceptual problems inherent in the concept of informality, especially the plurality and heterogeneity of the phenomena and of measurement. It highlights definitional

[1] The author thanks the participants in the EGDI-WIDER conference for their comments, and particularly Ravi Kanbur for very stimulating suggestions, though the usual caveat applies.

weaknesses, the logical inconsistencies of the formal–informal dualism, and the continuity between the two categories. From an institutional perspective, the third section shows the difficulty in establishing criteria of formal and informal institutions and contracts. Criteria such as the credibility of rules and enforcement capacity have greater explanatory power. Together with the distinction between the forms and contents of institutions, these features more accurately explain the structure and transformation of activities and institutions, which are described through the formal–informal duality.

4.2 The Concept of Informality: Heterogeneity and Inconsistencies

The term 'informal' was coined by Keith Hart in his article on informal income opportunities in Ghana, while the 1972 International Labour Office report on employment and poverty in Kenya was the starting point of the subsequent notoriety of the 'informal sector'.[2]

4.2.1 *Heterogeneous Phenomena and Dualisms*

The literature highlights the vagueness and plurality of definitions of the informal economy[3] as well as the difficulty in measuring phenomena that are not well defined, as shown by the wide range of terms: non-observed, irregular, unofficial, second, hidden, shadow, parallel, subterranean, informal, cash economy, black market, unmeasured, unrecorded, untaxed, non-structured, petty production, and unorganized.

Over time, the informal sector has come to refer to increasingly heterogeneous phenomena. The informal sector may sometimes be distinguished from the informal economy. It refers to unregulated labour-intensive activities, self-employed entrepreneurs, micro and small enterprises, activities that take place outside state regulations or formal firms, unregistered activities, or which include various degrees of illegality, such as escaping taxation, non-compliance with labour regulations, financial transactions outside the monitoring of the state or banks (from capital flight to petty village moneylenders), and smuggling. Casual work and domestic labour also may or may not be considered as belonging to the

[2] International Labour Office (1972); a history of the concept is in Bangasser (2000).

[3] The fuzziness of the concept of informality is highlighted since the 1970s; see Bromley (1978), Peattie (1987).

informal sector. The multiplicity of definitions and lack of clear conceptual boundaries make it difficult to view these activities as forming a 'sector'.

The formal–informal dualism is sometimes confused with other dualisms, for example, state–non-state, public–private, large–small firms, rigid–flexible norms, market–non-market institutions, Western origin–'traditional', written–unwritten rules, impersonal–personal and efficient–inefficient enforcement, the latter relying on personal exchanges and mechanisms of trust and reputation.[4] The formal–informal dualism is also associated with the core model of economic dualism, that is, the dualistic nature of labour markets in developing countries. The informal sector is a residual of distortions pushing wages above equilibrium level and hence workers into the unprotected informal sector. This two-sector model (industrial vs. agricultural, capitalists vs. farmers) was elaborated by Arthur Lewis in his analysis of the labour surplus moving from agriculture to industry and urban jobs (the unlimited supply of rural labour as a condition of industrialization).[5] The informal sector refers to the non-agricultural and low-productivity sector where the unskilled are in excess supply vis-à-vis demand.[6]

4.2.2 *Plurality and Heterogeneity of Measurement Methods*

Definitional problems also stem from the plurality of methodologies aimed at quantifying informal activities.[7] There is no unique statistical aggregate that corresponds to the concept of informal economy. Statistical certainty is limited to the sub-sectors, such as the types of enterprises or employment that fulfil certain criteria of size, organization, payment of particular taxes, and so on.

The quantification of the phenomena assimilated into the concept of unobserved economy is deduced through various tools that produce large approximations: national accounts, macro-models—based on monetary flows or stocks, indicators,[8] discrepancies, or sets of explanatory variables (e.g. tax, regulation)—and household and enterprise surveys.[9] These

[4] Analysed by Fafchamps (1992), Platteau (1994), Greif (1989).

[5] Lewis (1954); the model is also presented in Bardhan and Udry (1999).

[6] Bourguignon and Morrisson (1998) show that it has been assimilated with other dualisms, such as rural–urban income differentials.

[7] Morrisson and Mead (1996) show that there is little relationship between different measurements based on size, registration, payment of taxes, and conformity to labour regulations.

[8] See Johnson *et al.* (1997) for an estimation via the electricity consumption.

[9] See the OECD Handbook (2002).

quantification exercises rely on several definitions (e.g. underground, informal) and methods that cannot be added up so as to provide a rigorous idea of the economic extent of the informal sector. The plurality of measurement methods leads to large variations in estimates as well as figures that are both high and highly aggregated. For example, the informal economy ('unreported income from the production of legal goods and services') in 2000 would have thus represented 41 per cent of the gross national income (GNI) in developing countries (Schneider and Enste 2000; Schneider 2002). Likewise, informal employment would have represented between one-half to three-quarters of non-agricultural employment in developing countries, but the figures are higher if informal employment in agriculture is included.[10]

4.2.3 *The Logical Inconsistencies of the Definitional Criteria*

The definitional criteria display logical inconsistencies in terms of hierarchy and exclusiveness. The informal economy is defined via the criterion of a form, that is, a negative form (not being 'formal'), which coexists, however, with a series of substantive criteria that refer to categories and characteristics of firms with variable and non exclusive attributes (e.g. being small firms, urban, unregistered, and so on). The 15th ICLS[11] Resolution (1993), which is the source of the system of national accounts (SNA93) definition, defines the informal sector as 'units engaged in production', 'generating employment and incomes', displaying a 'low level of organisation', and relying on 'casual employment', 'personal and social relations', 'rather than contractual arrangements with formal guarantees'.[12] Here a ('negative') form is at the same time defined as a set of features.

Another logical problem is that informal activities may be defined as a sector (manufacturing or services). They also refer to firm features (small-scale, family or self-employment-based, low productivity, low barriers to entry, and low skills) as well as to employment. The ILO recognizes that the enterprise-based definition of the 15th ICLS cannot apprehend informal employment (Hussmanns 2004a). The informal economy refers to a type of activity for the ILO, that is, employment in the informal sector

[10] For data, see International Labour Office (2002a; 2002b).

[11] 15th International Conference of Labour Statistics.

[12] Paragraph 5(1) of the ICLS Resolution of 1993, quoted in the OECD Handbook (2002: 162).

plus informal employment outside of the informal sector.[13] The levels of the sector and the firm differ, as firms may be heterogeneous (both formal and informal).

The formal–informal dualism may lead to trivial observations, as it represents a partition of the world in two categories. Both categories are defined by default and are residuals of each other. These logical problems are a dimension of measurement problems. For example, one of the large surveys of the informal sector in Niger (1987–88) found that 99 per cent of the enterprises were informal, as the informal sector was defined by default—all enterprises that did not pay taxes on profits (Augeraud 1991).

4.2.4 *Concepts that Stem from Measurement Objectives*

Concepts logically pre-exist vis-à-vis the methods that are devised for testing them. In the case of the informal sector, methods often construct the concept, which has contributed to the plurality of its meanings. There is a discrepancy between the informal sector as an artefact of national accounts with specific criteria (e.g. the 'non-observed' economy), which is coherent with other macroeconomic aggregates and allows for international comparisons,[14] and the plurality of its meanings at the microeconomic level. At the microeconomic level, the targets of household, employment and small enterprises surveys are not necessarily homogeneous with those of national accounts and macro-models (e.g. understanding the dynamics of micro-enterprises).

Consensual definitions have stemmed from national accountants' objectives of measurement, such as achieving exhaustive and comparable estimates of GDP and defining economic production according to the SNA93. Informal sector production is defined as the 'productive activities conducted by unincorporated enterprises in the household sector that are unregistered'. The 1993 ICLS on which the SNA93 is based has recognized the difficulties of merging a political and analytical concept with a statistical concept. It highlights the two possible definitions of the informal sector: Through the relationship with the legal and administrative system, where informality is equated with non-registration, or as a specific form of production, which contradicts the first definition, as this form of production may include registered firms.

[13] But not for the labour statisticians of the 17th ICLS (2003) who maintained the separation between the informal sector and informal employment; see Hussmanns (2004b).

[14] Within the 1993 System of National Accounts (SNA93); see OECD *et al.* (2002).

4.2.5 *Concepts Determined by Policy Objectives*

The concept of 'informal' has been significantly influenced by policy and operationalization objectives. National accounts are a matter of national interest and are politically sensitive.[15] Due to their importance in many developing countries—particularly in low-income and aid-dependent countries—international organizations have had a crucial role in the expansion and shaping of the concept. These have given rise to studies of the informal sector that were determined by political and policy goals. The meanings of the informal sector have been influenced by thinking as to how it reacts to economic reform and its possible roles in policy-making—for example, the training of small scale enterprises or the impact of government regulation and 'business climate'.[16]

In Keith Hart's study, informal activities were analysed as multiple opportunities for increasing the income of the poor. The focus on dualism was developed later, for example by the ILO. The Bretton Woods institutions had an interest in the informal sector because of accuracy of the calculations of GDPs and growth, and the strengthening of the capacities of the statistical services. Taxation has also been a key issue for the IMF in the context of stabilization programmes. The informal sector was viewed as a factor in the low level of revenue and has been the subject of various reform proposals—for example, presumptive taxation or taxation of production factors (Taube and Tadesse 1996).

4.2.6 *Non-discriminating Characteristics: Registration, Barriers to Entry, and Income*

The features of informality do not constitute necessary or sufficient characteristics that would unambiguously assign phenomena in either the formal or informal category. Even the labour statisticians of the 15th ICLS have recommended avoiding a dualist segmentation of the economy and employment: certain activities that are excluded from the informal sector are not necessarily formal, such as domestic unpaid services or small-scale agriculture. For the ILO, the informal economy contrasts with the formal economy, but also with the criminal economy and the 'reproductive or care' economy (International Labour Office 2002b).

The continuity between economic activities may be demonstrated in opposition to the hypothesis of segmentation. The apparent discontinuity

[15] And may be 'national tales'; see Tanzi (1999).

[16] As argued by de Soto (1989).

may be an endogenous response to heavy state regulation and should disappear if the latter were to be relaxed (de Soto 1989; Djankov *et al.* 2003). There are numerous linkages between formal (public and private) and informal markets: for example, formal firms hiring workers via informal sub-contracting, informal firms using inputs produced in the formal economy and informal lenders applying for bank credit (Aryeetey *et al.* 1996). Furthermore, individual multiactivity is a dimension of poverty and uncertain environments.[17] In Russia, labour markets display the three statuses of formality, informality, and multiactivity, the most precarious situation being to possess only one formal job (Kalugina and Najman 2002). Individuals may implement rational risk-mitigating strategies and shift from the formal to the informal and vice-versa or manage parallel activities.[18] Households are heterogeneous and may include members who work in both the formal and the informal sector.

A supposed characteristic of the informal sector is the unrecorded character of its activities. The latter is, however, more a matter of a continuum than a binary dichotomy. Informal firms are often registered by state services (at least a segment of their activity) and pay certain taxes (licenses or taxes on equipment).[19] Low barriers to entry are supposed to characterize the informal sector, as well as competitiveness and being unregulated. Barriers to entry may indeed be features of the informal sector, created, for example, by a lack of skills, of credit,[20] or of informal networks and similar trust-building devices, which may be highly structured in accordance with complex social rules.[21] The informal sector may therefore be a fragmented market and split between insiders and outsiders (Bardhan and Udry 1999). Differences are more complex than a simple dichotomy. Informal firms may be less capital-intensive, have little access to credit, with heads being less educated but they may be efficient.[22]

Finally, the informal sector is often characterized by lower levels of income relative to the formal sector—informality being a 'survival mechanism'. The informal sector, however, displays large variations in earnings. Informal enterprise heads may have higher earnings than the average wage in the formal sector, but employees may earn less than the

[17] Highlighted by Hart (1973: 78).

[18] Including civil service jobs; see Sindzingre (1998).

[19] In Morrisson (1995), two-thirds of micro-enterprises were paying taxes in Thailand and three-quarters in Tunisia.

[20] Kingdon and Knight (2004) on South Africa; Younger (1996) on Ghana; Mills and Sahn (1996) on Guinea; Sindzingre (1998) on Benin.

[21] On the informal sector as an 'entrepreneurial sector'; see Maloney (2004).

[22] For example, in formal African firms, as in Kenya; see Bigsten *et al.* (2000).

official minimum wage. In terms of wages and working conditions, workers in the informal sector may be in a worse situation than informal entrepreneurs and workers in the formal sector.[23] The return on skills is more of a determining factor in explaining wage differentials and unemployment, and the dichotomies skilled–unskilled and employed–unemployed may be more pertinent than formal–informal (Teal 2000).

4.3 Deepening the Institutional Perspective

The continuity between formal and informal phenomena also operates at the level of institutions. The analysis of institutions suggests a more accurate dichotomy that distinguishes the forms and contents of institutions and their respective dynamics. The focus on institutions shows that instead of the formal versus informal dichotomy, the phenomena gathered under the concept of informality may be explained by other characteristics, in particular, the credibility and enforceability of institutions and contracts, be they formal or informal.

4.3.1 *Informal Institutions, Contracts, and Norms: Confusing Characteristics*

The concept of informality has been explored by Douglass North in his analyses of institutional change (North 1990; 1991). As is well-known, North defines institutions as constraints that structure political, economic, and social interactions and consist of informal—that is, self-enforcing—constraints (sanctions, taboos, customs, traditions, codes of conduct, conventions, and norms of behaviour) and formal regulations (constitutions, laws, and property rights). Formal constraints are 'created', written, and intentional, whereas informal constraints evolve over time and are unwritten. The role of institutions is to reduce uncertainty, introduce regularity, and stability by establishing a stable (but not necessarily efficient) structure to human interaction.

The concept of informality has also been used in development microeconomics with notions such as informal exchanges, transactions, norms, contracts, interlinked arrangements determined by informational constraints, and operating in fragmented markets (credit, insurance, labour, and land). They underlie, for example, tied labour, sharecropping,

[23] Ozorio de Almeida *et al.* (1995), Mazumdar with Mazaheri (2000).

insurance, and risk-pooling mechanisms. Informal exchanges and contracts are contrasted with formal ones, that is, written and guaranteed by a state, and are therefore implicitly equated with unwritten and 'traditional' ones.[24] Informal arrangements, transactions, and contracts are supported by mechanisms such as personal and repeated exchanges, trust, and reputation, in environments that are characterized by uncertainty, problems of collective action, and free-riding.

Formal contracts are therefore equated with written ones and contrasted with informal contracts, unwritten, and outside the state's sphere, though these equivalences are rarely theoretically justified. Whether formal or informal, features such as asymmetric information or problems of incentives are more pertinent in explaining the functioning of institutions and contracts. To argue that because a rule is written, its nature changes accordingly, requires a theory of the cognitive effects of writing on human thought and behaviour.[25] Trust may also be viewed as an indispensable element in the efficiency of formal (written) contracts, as it reduces transaction costs and improves credibility. Moreover, informal transactions may not only stem from contracts but also from social norms that are by definition not voluntary, for example redistribution within social networks: these transactions constitute 'informal insurance', but this is only one of their functions—and a function is not the cause of a norm. These norms may also entail no reciprocity. Economic networks may depend on 'fundamental social relationships' between individuals (Udry and Conley 2004). Pre-existing social statuses (through kinship, ethnicity) may ease trust rather than trust easing informal transactions. Informal transactions may be the actualization of pre-existing statuses, which *ex ante* include exchange obligations (in labour, goods, and individuals) (Platteau 1994). Likewise, informal contracts may efficiently organize market transactions as well as non-market ones.

Finally, the equation of formal institutions with written, intentional creations often results in equating them with complex institutions. This property of complexity is not discriminating and informal institutions also include highly complex rules.[26] These problems of conceptual boundaries also explain the frequently inconclusive character of models

[24] Such as the 'bazaar economy', defined by Geertz (1978) as repeated exchanges in a 'noisy' and uncertain environment.

[25] This has been investigated by cognitive science and anthropology, see Goody (1986), but rarely by development economics.

[26] Examples of complex traditional kinship, political, and ritual systems being innumerable.

that include informal phenomena as one of their variables (often based on very simple indicators) (Sindzingre 2004).

4.3.2 *Cognitive Foundations of Institutions: The Issue of Credibility*

Douglass North has recognized that informal rules were 'extensions, elaborations and modifications' of formal rules and formed a continuum. Individuals make permanent cognitive tradeoffs between multiple norms from various origins (state, kinship, and so on) and assign relevance and credibility to given institutions according to their assessment of situations. Individuals are rational in the sense that they minimize the cognitive costs of mental processes given their limited information (North 1990: 40). For individuals, the fact whether rules are 'formal', written, or coming from the state, does not determine their credibility in a particular situation and is no more relevant than the many other attributes that orient individuals' tradeoffs regarding compliance with it: especially rule's credibility and the benefits or costs of complying with it. State rules and institutions may be less credible in certain developing countries than local institutions (e.g. social insurance networks). When individuals are exposed to competing norms ('modern' and 'traditional'), tradeoffs are determined more by the relevance and credibility of the norms, and hence by historical and cognitive path dependence. Credibility is also a key property of contracts, as the notion of contract entails a capacity to commit, whether the contract is formal or informal.

Douglass North rightly insisted on the cognitive dimension of institutions ('cognitive institutionalism') and on mental models in the shaping of institutions.[27] Learning processes, however, are more determining for North than relevance and credibility. He maintains the distinction between formal (result of human design) and informal institutions (result of spontaneous interaction) (Mantzavinos *et al.* 2003: 7). These formal–informal and cognitive distinctions cannot be assimilated, however. Informal institutions, even in North's sense of traditions, also result from human design. Furthermore, these distinctions do not explain the core question of institutional transformation, that is, why some institutions and rules are more resilient, credible, and complied with than others.

The state is supposed to constitute a discriminating element. Norms and contracts are said to be formal not only because they are written, but also because they are guaranteed by a governmental legal system, in contrast

[27] North (1996) on cognitive science, Denzau and North (1994) on mental models and institutions.

with norms that are maintained 'privately' by social groups (e.g. traditions) through personal transactions and reputational mechanisms. This distinction, however, is not convincing. In developed countries, contracts are also supported by trust and cooperative and reputational self-reinforcing mechanisms in parallel with government-enforced laws (Seabright 2004). 'Informal' cannot be equated with 'trust' and 'formal' with 'written and guaranteed by the state'. In many developing countries, states are undermined by problems of political legitimacy and institutional credibility.[28] Formal contracts may be guaranteed by a state legal system but may be less credible than 'informal' contracts guaranteed by other sources of authority built over time.[29]

In the perspective of methodological individualism—that is, if the acceptance of rules is considered to be primarily a psychological phenomenon—there is a cognitive continuity between the formal and the informal. In regard to the respect of commitments and the choice of non-opportunistic behaviour (e.g. paying off a sum due), individual trade-offs depend on the credibility of the enforcement, the benefits, and rewards.[30]

4.3.3 *The Criterion of Enforcement*

Rules and institutions are cognitive representations that individuals find relevant—more credible, less cognitively, and costly in a given environment. These cognitive representations have the property of being normative, that is, of providing instructions for other representations and behaviour.[31] Effective enforcement is an essential dimension of institutions as rules of the game, for individuals' rules must constitute binding cognitive states (Aoki 2001). A key dimension of all institutions, formal and informal, is that they are individually shared beliefs, which bind behaviour at a collective level. Both informal and formal institutions get their binding dimension from their links to other institutions (e.g. an informal credit transaction from the common kinship of the contractors) and are subjected to historical change.

Power relationships also shape the particular actualizations and transformations of institutions, both formal and informal, for example the

[28] On credibility as a key issue in sub-Saharan Africa, Collier and Patillo (2000).

[29] On time as an intrinsic dimension of institutions, Arrow (1998).

[30] On 'rational' trade-offs favouring local relevance against the national public good, Wantchekon (2003).

[31] This cognitive theory of relevance is developed in Sperber and Wilson (1986); see also Sindzingre (2003).

capacity for an individual to exercise her rights (such as land rights). Informal and unwritten rules are as coercive, enforceable, and subjected to sanctions as are formal laws and judgements. Conversely, North's formal regulations (constitutions, laws, and property rights) may be ignored, especially in developing countries with weakly institutionalized states. Group norms are coercive because they represent low-cost trust in uncertain environments and high costs (exclusion) in the event of a breach; they also represent information transmission and coordination of punishment supporting a reputation mechanism and in a self-fulfilling way (economic losses in case of non-compliance) (Akerlof 1976; Greif 1993).

Informal contract enforcement mechanisms may be even more credible on account of motives such as preserving personal relationships and trust, and formal enforcement (courts) may be viewed as less relevant.[32] Informal contract enforcement may similarly be more efficient: informal lenders may enjoy higher loan repayment rates than formal lenders without litigation in courts (Aryeetey 1998). The presence of states is not pertinent for these mechanisms of enforceability to function.[33] The various mechanisms underlying the credibility and compliance with rules have more explanatory power as to the effectiveness of rules than the dichotomy of formality versus informality.

4.3.4 *Form and Contents of Institutions*

Formal institutions and norms are often analysed as antagonistic vis-à-vis informal ones: formal norms may erase informal norms or be 'captured' by them, which is viewed as a factor in the failure of reform in transition and developing countries (Hoff and Stiglitz 2004). There are, however, no theoretical grounds for such an intrinsic difference of nature between both categories. Similarly, the form of an institution is often simply viewed as being the totality of the institution in question, for example the legal protection of property rights offering effective protection. Yet all institutions include both an organization (form) and implicit, traditional, path-dependent contents and meanings. All institutions are characterized by their forms—their definitions, names, and modes of organization—and 'contents'—their meanings, functions, relevance, and elements. These two levels are subject to distinct and continuous transformation due to historical processes and their environments. Institutional forms and

[32] Fafchamps (1996) on the example of commercial contracts in Ghana.

[33] As shown by Greif (1997).

contents are resilient or disappear depending on their relevance and credibility in the minds of individuals, which in turn depends on their perception of the events, history, and the environment to which they are exposed.

Institutional forms have particular contents, relevance, and functions on account of (1) their combination (e.g. hierarchical or complementary)[34] with other institutional forms and contents, and their exposure to the broader environment and (2) the absence of certain institutions. For example, in the context of weak state institutions, rural institutional forms may be endowed with the functions of the state, such as managing taxation, redistribution, and equity issues, while the forms of public institutions may be perceived as individual predatory activities. The effective content of economic institutions may depend on the ways in which they are articulated with other institutions, especially political institutions. This link determines, for example, the efficiency of a revenue service, which may otherwise be an institutional form that is 'filled' by various rationales (personal interest, creating employment, fulfilling solidarity obligations,[35] among other things). Similarly, the functions and credibility of a political institutional form such as courts may depend on an executive and a legal system which are also credible and accountable. On the other hand, a particular function may correspond to various forms of institutions.[36] 'Informal' institutions are no different, as they also have evolving forms and contents. For example, individuals may assign a market content to kinship reciprocity norms—they may use these norms, for example, as assets in labour markets (as in the case of the exploitation of kin members in a farm or enterprise).

Institutions are not defined *ex ante* by specific, necessary, and sufficient sets of forms and functions: in the course of time and institutional transformation, certain combinations are perceived by individuals as being more credible than others and therefore may be enforced. Functions and meanings may become irrelevant, whereas the institutional form remains intact (e.g. traditional systems of reciprocity). The specific interpretation of institutions by individuals, the ways they shape individual behaviour, and their modes of transformation are *ex ante* underdetermined for formal as well as informal institutions.

[34] On complementarity and hierarchy as explaining the transformation of institutions, Aoki (2001).

[35] Market institutions may also be 'filled' by kinship norms, as shown by Hoff and Sen (2005).

[36] As highlighted by Rodrik (2002).

4.4 Conclusion

Some dichotomies give rise to as many problems as the solutions they are aimed to provide. This chapter has shown that the concept of informality may not improve the understanding of the phenomena to which they have been applied. This dichotomy gathers empirical facts that are heterogeneous and has different meanings, depending on the theoretical approach and method. Furthermore, characteristics of informality that could be specific to it are difficult to find. A distinction between institutional forms and contents has been suggested, as has been a focus on criteria such as credibility and enforceability. They may more accurately explain the dynamics of informal activities and institutional transformation than does the formal–informal dualism.

References

Akerlof, G. (1976). 'The Economics of Caste and of the Rat Race and other Woeful Tales'. *Quarterly Journal of Economics*, 90(4): 599–617.

Aoki, M. (2001). *Toward a Comparative Institutional Analysis*. Cambridge, MA: MIT Press.

Arrow, K. J. (1998). 'The Place of Institutions in the Economy: A Theoretical Perspective', in Y. Hayami and M. Aoki (eds), *The Institutional Foundations of East Asian Economic Development*. London: Macmillan, pp. 39–48.

Aryeetey, E. (1998). *Informal Finance for Private Sector Development in Africa*. Background paper for the African Development Report. Tunis: African Development Bank.

Aryeetey, E., H. Hettige, M. Nissanke, and W. Steel (1996). 'Financial Market Fragmentation and Reforms in Sub-Saharan Africa'. Discussion Paper 356. Washington, DC: World Bank.

Augeraud, P. (1991). 'Exploitation de l'enquête secteur informel Niger 1987–88 pour la comptabilité nationale'. *Stateco*, 65: 33–62.

Bangasser, P. E. (2000). *The ILO and the Informal Sector: An Institutional History*. Geneva: International Labour Office.

Bardhan, P. and C. Udry (1999). *Development Microeconomics*. Oxford: Oxford University Press.

Bigsten, A., P. Kimuyu, and K. Lundvall (2000). *Are Formal and Informal Small Firms Really Different? Evidence from Kenyan Manufacturing*. Conference on 'Opportunities in Africa'. Oxford: Centre for the Study of African Economies.

Bourguignon, F. and C. Morrisson (1998). 'Inequality and Development: the Role of Dualism'. *Journal of Development Economics*, 57: 233–57.

Bromley, R. (1978). 'Introduction: The Urban Informal Sector: Why Is it Worth Discussing?'. *World Development*, 6(9–10): 1033–9.

Collier, P. and C. Patillo (eds) (2000). *Investment and Risk in Africa*. London: Macmillan.

Denzau, A. T. and D. C. North (1994). 'Shared Mental Models: Ideologies and Institutions'. *Kyklos*, 47(1): 3–31.

de Soto, H. (1989). *The Other Path*. London: I. B. Taurus.

Djankov, S., R. La Porta, F. Lopez de Silanes, A. Shleifer, and J. C. Botero (2003). 'The Regulation of Labor'. Working Paper 9756. Cambridge, MA: NBER.

Fafchamps, M. (1992). 'Solidarity Networks in Preindustrial Societies: Rational Peasants with a Moral Economy'. *Economic Development and Cultural Change*, 41(1): 147–74.

Fafchamps, M. (1996). 'The Enforcement of Commercial Contracts in Ghana'. *World Development*, 24(3): 427–48.

Geertz, C. (1978). 'The Bazaar Economy: Information and Search in Peasant Marketing'. *American Economic Review*, 68(2): 28–32.

Goody, J. (1986). *The Logic of Writing and the Organisation of Society*. Cambridge: Cambridge University Press.

Greif, A. (1989). 'Reputation and Coalitions in Medieval Trade: Evidence on the Maghribi Traders'. *Journal of Economic History*, XLIX(4): 857–82.

Greif, A. (1993). 'Contract Enforceability and Economic Institutions in Early Trade: The Maghribi Traders' Coalition'. *American Economic Review*, 83(3) (June): 525–48.

Greif, A. (1997). *On the Social Foundations and Historical Development of Institutions that Facilitate Impersonal Exchange: From the Community Responsibility System to Individual Legal Responsibility in Pre-modern Europe*. Department of Economics Working Paper 97–016. Stanford: Stanford University.

Hart, K. (1973). 'Informal Income Opportunities and Urban Employment in Ghana'. *Journal of Modern African Studies*, 11(1): 61–89.

Hoff, K. and A. Sen (2005). 'The Kin System as A Poverty Trap'?, in S. Bowles, S. N. Durlauf, and K. Hoff (eds), *Poverty Traps*. Princeton, NJ: Princeton University Press and Russell Sage Foundation, pp. 95–115.

Hoff, K. and J. E. Stiglitz (2004). 'After the Big Bang: Obstacles to the Emergence of the Rule of Law in Post-Communist Societies'. *American Economic Review*, 94(3): 753–63.

Hussmanns, R. (2004a). *Defining and Measuring Informal Employment*. Geneva: International Labour Office, Bureau of Statistics.

Hussmanns, R. (2004b). *Statistical Definition of Informal Employment: Guidelines Endorsed by the Seventeenth International Conference of Labour Statisticians (2003)*. Geneva: International Labour Office, Bureau of Statistics.

International Labour Office (1972). *Employment, Incomes and Inequality: A Strategy for Increasing Productive Employment in Kenya*. Geneva: International Labour Office.

International Labour Office (2002a). *Decent Work and the Informal Economy*. Geneva: International Labour Office.

International Labour Office (2002b). *Women and Men in the Informal Economy: A Statistical Picture*. Geneva: International Labour Office.

Johnson, S., D. Kaufmann, and A. Shleifer (1997). 'The Unofficial Economy in Transition'. *Brookings Papers on Economic Activity*, 2: 159–239.

Kalugina, E. and B. Najman (2002). *Labour and Poverty in Russia Self-rated Perceptions and Monetary Evaluations*. Conference on 'Unofficial Activities in Transition Countries'. Zagreb: Institute of Public Finance.

Kingdon, G. G. and J. Knight (2004). 'Unemployment in South Africa: The Nature of the Beast'. *World Development*, 32(3): 391–408.

Lewis, W. A. (1954). 'Economic Development with Unlimited Supplies of Labour'. *Manchester School*, 22: 139–91.

Maloney, W. F. (2004). 'Informality Revisited', *World Development*, 32(7): 1159–78.

Mantzavinos, C., D. C. North, and S. Shariq (2003). *Learning, Institutions and Economic Performance*. Preprint 2003/13. Bonn: Max Planck Institute for Research on Collective Goods.

Mazumdar, D. with A. Mazaheri (2000). *Wages and Employment in Africa*. RPED Paper 109. Washington, DC: World Bank.

Mills, B. and D. E. Sahn (1996). 'Life after Public Sector Job Loss in Guinea', in D. E. Sahn (ed.), *Economic Reform and the Poor in Africa*. Oxford: Clarendon Press, pp. 203–30.

Morrisson, C. (1995). *What Institutional Framework for the Informal Sector*? Policy Brief 10. Paris: OECD.

Morrisson, C. and D. Mead (1996). 'Pour une nouvelle définition du secteur informel'. *Revue d'Economie du Développement*, 3: 3–26.

North, D. C. (1990). *Institutions, Institutional Change and Economic Performance*. New York: Cambridge University Press.

North, D. C. (1991). 'Institutions'. *Journal of Economic Perspectives*, 5(1): 97–112.

North, D. C. (1996). *Economics and Cognitive Science*. St Louis: Washington University.

OECD-ILO-IMF-CIS Stat (2002). *Measuring the Non-Observed Economy: A Handbook*. Paris: OECD.

Ozorio de Almeida, A. L., L. F. Alves, and S. E. M. Graham (1995). *Poverty, Deregulation and Employment in the Informal Sector of Mexico*. Washington, DC: World Bank.

Peattie, L. (1987). 'An Idea in Good Currency and How It Grew: The Informal Sector'. *World Development*, 15(7): 851–60.

Platteau, J. P. (1994). 'Behind the Market Stage Where Real Societies Exist: I: The Role of Public and Private Order Institutions'. *Journal of Development Studies*, 30(3): 533–77; II: 'The Role of Moral Norms', 30(4): 753–817.

Rodrik, D. (2002). *Getting Institutions Right*. DICE Report 2/2004. Munich: CESifo.

Schneider, F. (2002). *Size and Measurement of the Informal Economy in 110 Countries around the World*. Canberra: Australian National University, Australian National Tax Centre.

Schneider, F. and D. Enste (2000). 'Shadow Economies: Size, Causes and Consequences'. *Journal of Economic Literature*, 38(1): 77–114.

Seabright, P. (2004). *The Company of Strangers: A Natural History of Economic Life*. Princeton, NJ: Princeton University Press.

Sindzingre, A. (1998). 'Réseaux, organisations et marchés: exemples du Bénin'. *Autrepart (IRD)*, 6: 73–90.

Sindzingre, A. (2003). *'Institutions and Development: A Theoretical Contribution'*. Conference on 'Economics for the Future', 17–19 September. Cambridge: Cambridge Journal of Economics.

Sindzingre, A. (2004).' "Truth", "Efficiency", and Multilateral Institutions: A Political Economy of Development Economics'. *New Political Economy*, 9(2): 233–49.

Sperber, D. and D. Wilson (1986). *Relevance: Communication and Cognition*. Cambridge, MA: Harvard University Press.

Tanzi, V. (1999). 'Uses and Abuses of Estimates of the Underground Economy'. *Economic Journal*, 109(456): 338–47.

Taube, G. and H. Tadesse (1996). *Presumptive Taxation in Sub-Saharan Africa: Experiences and Prospects*. Working Paper WP/96/5. Washington, DC: IMF.

Teal, F. (2000). *Employment and Unemployment in Sub-Saharan Africa: An Overview*. Conference on 'Opportunities in Africa'. Oxford: Centre for the Study of African Economies.

Udry, C. R. and T. G. Conley (2004). *Social Networks in Ghana*. Discussion Paper 888. New Haven: Yale University Economic Growth Center.

Wantchekon, L. (2003). 'Clientelism and Voting Behavior: Evidence from a Field Experiment in Benin'. *World Politics*, 55: 399–422.

Younger, S. (1996). 'Labor Market Consequences of Retrenchment for Civil Servants in Ghana', in D. E. Sahn (ed.), *Economic Reform and the Poor in Africa*. Oxford: Clarendon Press, pp. 185–202 .

5

Rethinking the informal economy: linkages with the formal economy and the formal regulatory environment

Martha Alter Chen

Since it was 'discovered' in Africa in the early 1970s, the informal economy has been subject to interpretation and debate and has gone in and out of fashion in international development circles. Despite the debates and critiques, the informal economy has continued to prove a useful concept to many policymakers, activists, and researchers because of the reality it captures—the large share of economic units and workers that remain outside the world of regulated economic activities and protected employment relationships—is so large and significant. Today there is renewed interest in the informal economy worldwide. This re-convergence of interest stems from two basic facts. First, despite predictions of its eventual demise, the informal economy has not only grown in many countries but also emerged in new guises and unexpected places. Second, despite continuing debates about its defining features, supporting informal enterprises and improving informal jobs are increasingly recognized as key pathways to promoting growth and reducing poverty.

This chapter explores the relationship of the informal economy to the formal economy and the formal regulatory environment. It begins with a comparison, in Section 5.1, of the earlier concept of the 'informal sector' with a new expanded concept of the 'informal economy' and a discussion of the size, composition, and segmentation of the informal economy broadly defined. Section 5.2 discusses the linkages between the informal economy and the formal economy, on one hand, and the formal regulatory environment, on the other. The concluding section suggests why and how more equitable linkages between the informal economy and the formal economy should be promoted through an appropriate policy and regulatory environment.

5.1 The Informal Economy

The recent re-convergence of interest in the informal economy has been accompanied by significant rethinking of the concept, at least in some circles. The rethinking about the informal economy, summarized below, includes a new term and expanded definition, recognition of its segmented structure, and a revised set of assumptions about its defining features. This section concludes with a broad summary of available statistics on women and men in the informal economy.

5.1.1 *New Term and Expanded Definition*

In recent years, a group of informed activists and researchers, including members of the global research policy network Women in Informal Employment: Globalizing and Organizing (WIEGO), have worked with the International Labour Organization (ILO) to broaden the earlier concept and definition of the informal sector to incorporate certain types of informal employment that were not included in the earlier concept and definition (including the official international statistical definition). They seek to include the whole of informality, as it is manifested in industrialized, transitional and developing economies and the real world dynamics in labour markets today, particularly the employment arrangements of the working poor. These observers want to extend the focus to include not only *enterprises* that are not legally regulated but also *employment relationships* that are not legally regulated or protected. In brief, the new definition of the informal economy focuses on the nature of employment in addition to the characteristics of enterprises. It also includes informal employment both within and outside agriculture.

Under this new definition, the informal economy is comprised of all forms of 'informal employment'—that is, employment without labour or social protection—both inside and outside informal enterprises, including both self-employment in small unregistered enterprises and wage employment in unprotected jobs.

5.1.2 *Key Features of the Informal Economy*

What follows is a discussion of key features of the informal economy broadly defined, including: its significance and permanence, the continuum of employment relations within it, and its segmented structure. The discussion ends on the issue of its legality or illegality as there is a widespread misconception that the informal economy is somehow illegal or is the equivalent of the underground, or even criminal, economy.

Significance and permanence. The recent re-convergence of interest in the informal economy stems from the recognition that the informal economy is growing; is a permanent, not a short-term, phenomenon; and is a feature of modern capitalist development, not just traditional economies, associated with both growth and global integration. For these reasons, the informal economy should be viewed not as a marginal or peripheral sector but as a basic component—the base, if you will—of the total economy.

Continuum of economic relations. Economic relations—of production, distribution, and employment—tend to fall at some point on a continuum between pure 'formal' relations (i.e. regulated and protected) at one pole and pure 'informal' relations (i.e. unregulated and unprotected) at the other, with many categories in between. Depending on their circumstances, workers and units are known to move with varying ease and speed along the continuum and/or to operate simultaneously at different points on the continuum. Consider, for example, the self-employed garment maker who supplements her earnings by stitching clothes under a sub-contract, or shifts to working on a sub-contract for a firm when her customers decide they prefer ready-made garments rather than tailor-made ones. Or consider the public sector employee who has an informal job on the side.

Moreover, the formal and the informal ends of the economic continuum are often dynamically linked. For instance, many informal enterprises have production or distribution relations with formal enterprises, supplying inputs, finished goods or services either through direct transactions or sub-contracting arrangements. Also, many formal enterprises hire wage workers under informal employment relations. For example, many part-time workers, temporary workers, and homeworkers work for formal enterprises through contracting or sub-contracting arrangements.

Segmentation. The informal economy consists of a range of informal enterprises and informal jobs. Yet there are meaningful ways to classify its various segments as follows:

- *Self-employment in informal enterprises*: workers in small unregistered or unincorporated enterprises, including:
  - employers
  - own account operators: both, heads of family enterprises and single person operators
  - unpaid family workers
- *Wage employment in informal jobs*: workers without worker benefits or social protection who work for formal or informal firms, for households or with no fixed employer, including:
  - employees of informal enterprises
  - other informal wage workers such as:
    - casual or day labourers
    - domestic workers
    - unregistered or undeclared workers
    - some temporary or part-time workers[1]
  - industrial outworkers (also called homeworkers).

From recent research findings and official data, two stylized global facts emerge about the segmented informal economy. The first fact is that there are significant gaps in earnings within the informal economy: on average, employers have the highest earnings; followed by their employees and other more 'regular' informal wage workers; own account operators; 'casual' informal wage workers; and industrial outworkers. The second is that, around the world, men tend to be over-represented in the top segment; women tend to be over-represented in the bottom segments; and the shares of men and women in the intermediate segments tend to vary across sectors and countries. These twin facts are depicted graphically in Figure 5.1.

The net result is a significant gender gap in earnings within the informal economy, with women earning less on average than men.[2] An additional fact, not captured in Figure 5.1, is that there is further segmentation and earning gaps within these broad status categories. Women tend to work in different types of activities, associated with different levels of earning, than men—with the result that they typically earn less even within specific segments of the informal economy. Some of this difference can be explained by the fact that men tend to embody more human capital due to educational

[1] Those temporary and part-time workers who are covered by labour legislation and statutory social protection benefits are *not* included in the informal economy.

[2] For a detailed analysis of available statistics on the gender segmentation of the informal economy and the linkages between working in the informal economy, and being a woman or man, and being poor, see Chen *et al.* (2004).

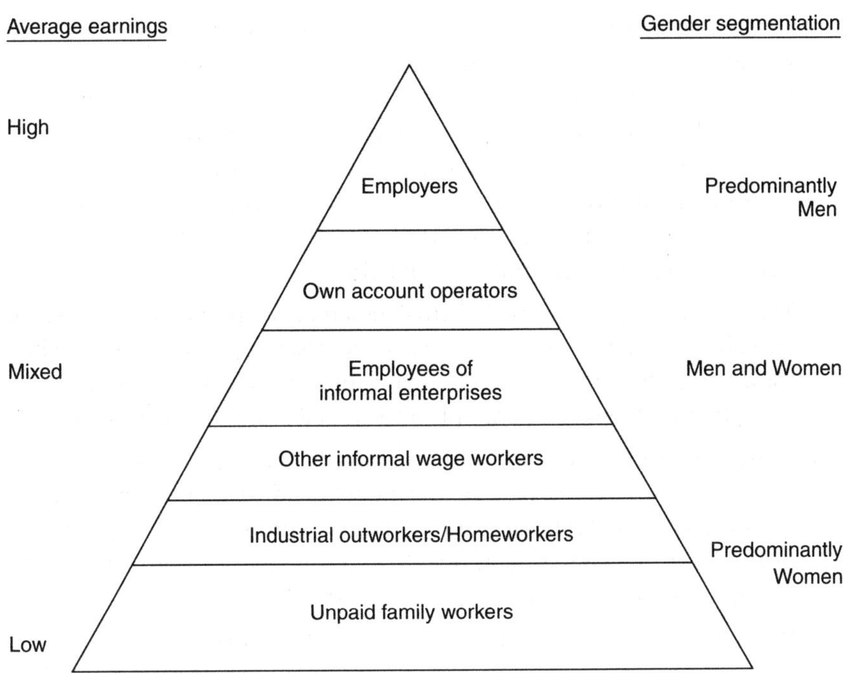

Figure 5.1. Segmentation of the informal economy

discrimination against girls, especially in certain societies (e.g. in North India and Pakistan). This difference can also be explained by the fact that men tend to have *better tools* of the trade, operate from *better work sites/spaces* and have *greater access to productive assets and financial capital.* In addition, or as a result, men often produce or sell a *higher volume* or a *different range* of goods and services. For instance, among street vendors in some countries, men are more likely to sell non-perishables while women are more likely to sell perishable goods (such as fruits and vegetables). In addition, men are more likely to sell from push-carts or bicycles while women are more likely to sell from baskets, or simply from a cloth spread on the ground.

LEGALITY OR SEMI-LEGALITY

Previously, there was a widespread assumption that the informal sector was comprised of unregistered and unregulated enterprises whose owner operators choose to avoid registration and, thereby, taxation. While it is important to understand informal employment in relation to the legal framework in any given country, this is far from being the whole story.

- There is a distinction between illegal *processes or arrangements* and illegal *goods and services*. While production or employment arrangements in the informal economy are often semi-legal or illegal, most informal workers and enterprises produce and/or distribute legal goods and services. Admittedly, one part of the informal economy—the criminal economy—operates illegally and deals in illegal goods and services. But it is only a small part of a larger whole that is, for the most part, not illegal or criminal (Thomas 1992).
- Many owner operators of informal enterprises operate semi-legally or illegally because the regulatory environment is too punitive, too cumbersome or simply non-existent. Also, many informal activities do not generate enough output, employment or income to fall into existing tax brackets.
- Most owner operators would be willing to pay registration fees and taxes if they were to receive the benefits of formality (enjoyed by registered businesses). For instance, street vendors who now pay a mix of legal and illegal fees would welcome the security that comes with being legally recognized (Chen *et al.* 2004; 2005).
- It is important to note that, in the case of informal wage work, it is usually not the workers but their employers, whether in formal or informal firms, who are avoiding registration and taxation.

More fundamentally, most informal workers associate operating outside the legal regulatory framework with costs rather than benefits. Most self-employed and wage workers in the informal economy are deprived of secure work, worker's benefits, social protection, and representation or voice. The self-employed must take care of themselves and their enterprises, as well as their employees (if they hire others), or unpaid contributing family members (if they run a family business). Moreover, they often face competitive disadvantages vis-à-vis larger formal firms in capital and product markets. Informal wage workers also have to take care of themselves as they receive few (if any) employer-sponsored benefits. In addition, both groups receive little (if any) legal protection through their work or from their governments. As a result of these and other factors, a higher proportion of the informal workforce than of the formal workforce is poor. Table 5.1 summarizes the key differences between the old and new views of the informal economy.

5.1.3 *Women and Men in the Informal Economy*

Compiling statistics on the size, composition, and contribution of the informal economy is hampered by the lack of sufficient data. While many

Table 5.1. Old and new views of the informal economy

The old view	The new view
The informal sector is the traditional economy that will wither away and die with modern, industrial growth.	The informal economy is 'here to stay' and expanding with modern, industrial growth.
It is only marginally productive.	It is a major provider of employment, goods and services for lower-income groups. It contributes a significant share of GDP.
It exists separately from the formal economy.	It is linked to the formal economy—it produces for, trades with, distributes for and provides services to the formal economy.
It represents a reserve pool of surplus labour.	Much of the recent rise in informal employment is due to the decline in formal employment or to the informalization of previously formal employment relationships.
It is comprised mostly of street traders and very small-scale producers.	It is made up of a wide range of informal occupations—both 'resilient old forms' such as casual day labour in construction and agriculture as well as 'emerging new ones' such as temporary and part-time jobs plus homework for high tech industries.
Most of those in the sector are entrepreneurs who run illegal and unregistered enterprises in order to avoid regulation and taxation.	It is made up of non-standard wage workers as well as entrepreneurs and self-employed persons producing legal goods and services, albeit through irregular or unregulated means. Most entrepreneurs and the self-employed are amenable to, and would welcome, efforts to reduce barriers to registration and related transaction costs and to increase benefits from regulation; and most informal wage workers would welcome more stable jobs and workers' rights.
Work in the informal economy is comprised mostly of survival activities and thus is not a subject for economic policy.	Informal enterprises include not only survival activities but also stable enterprises and dynamic growing businesses, and informal employment includes not only self-employment but also wage employment. All forms of informal employment are affected by most (if not all) economic policies.

countries have now undertaken a survey on employment in the informal sector, very few countries undertake these on a regular basis. Furthermore, only a handful of countries have collected data to measure informal employment outside informal enterprises. In addition, the available data are not comprehensive. Many countries exclude agriculture from their measurement of the informal sector while others measure only the urban informal sector. In most developing countries, however, a majority of the informal workforce may well be in agriculture. There are also a number of problems that limit the international comparability of data. However, in the absence of reliable data collected directly, various indirect methods to estimate the size and composition of the informal economy can be used. What follows is a summary of main findings from the most recent and most comprehensive set of estimates of the informal economy in developing countries, including its gender dimensions, using indirect methods where necessary.[3]

SIZE OF THE INFORMAL ECONOMY

Informal employment broadly defined comprises one-half to three-quarters of non-agricultural employment in developing countries: specifically, 48 per cent in North Africa; 51 per cent in Latin America; 65 per cent in Asia; and 72 per cent in sub-Saharan Africa. If South Africa is excluded, the share of informal employment in non-agricultural employment rises to 78 per cent in sub-Saharan Africa; and if comparable data were available for other countries in South Asia in addition to India, the regional average for Asia would likely be much higher.

Some countries include informal employment in agriculture in their estimates. This significantly increases the proportion of informal employment: from 83 per cent of *non-agricultural* employment to 93 per cent of *total* employment in India; from 55 to 62 per cent in Mexico; and from 28 to 34 per cent in South Africa respectively.

Informal employment is generally a larger source of employment for women than for men in the developing world. Other than in North Africa, where 43 per cent of women workers are in informal employment, 60 per cent or more of women non-agricultural workers in the developing world are informally employed. In sub-Saharan Africa, 84 per cent of women non-agricultural workers are informally employed compared to 63 per cent of men; and in Latin America the figures are 58 per cent of women in comparison to 48 per cent of men. In Asia, the proportion is 65 per cent for both women and men.

COMPOSITION OF THE INFORMAL ECONOMY

As noted earlier, the informal economy is comprised of both self-employment in informal enterprises (i.e. small and/or unregistered) and

[3] This section draws from an ILO statistical booklet prepared by Martha Chen and Joann Vanek that includes data compiled by Jacques Charmes for anywhere from 25–70 countries, depending on the specific estimate, as well as case studies for India, Mexico, South Africa, and OECD countries (International Labour Office 2002). Data available since 2002 were supplied by Jacques Charmes.

wage employment in informal jobs (i.e. without secure contracts, worker benefits, or social protection). In developing regions, *self-employment* comprises a greater share of informal employment outside of agriculture (and even more inside of agriculture) than wage employment: specifically, self-employment represents 70 per cent of informal employment in sub-Saharan Africa, 62 per cent in North Africa, 60 per cent in Latin America, and 59 per cent in Asia. If South Africa is excluded, since black-owned businesses prohibited during the apartheid era have only recently been recognized and reported, the share of self-employment in informal employment increases to 81 per cent in sub-Saharan Africa.

Informal *wage* employment is also significant in developing countries, comprising 30–40 per cent of total informal employment (outside of agriculture). Informal wage employment is comprised of employees of informal enterprises as well as various types of informal wage workers who work for formal enterprises, households, or no fixed employer (see definition above).

5.2 Links with the Formal Economy and Formal Regulatory Environment

A key issue in the debates on the informal economy is whether and how the informal economy and formal economy are linked. However, these debates have tended to blur the distinction between the formal economy and the formal regulatory environment and the relationship of the informal enterprises and informal workers to each other. But it is important to distinguish between the:

- *formal economy*: comprising regulated economic units and protected workers
- *formal regulatory environment*: comprising government policies, laws, and regulations

This section discusses the linkages between informal enterprises and workers and, the formal economy and the formal regulatory environment. In real life, of course, it is often hard to know what is driving what: as large formal registered enterprises are often involved in 'setting' formal policies and regulations; and formal policies and regulations are often biased towards formal registered firms to the disadvantage of both informal enterprises and informal wage workers.

5.2.1 *The Formal Economy*

Over the years, the debates on the informal economy crystallized into three dominant schools of thought: dualism, structuralism, and legalism. Each of these has a different perspective on how the informal and formal economies are linked. The dualists argue that informal units and activities have few (if any) linkages to the formal economy but, rather, operate as a distinct sector of the economy; and that informal workers comprise the less-advantaged sector of a dualistic labour market (Sethuraman 1976; Tokman 1978). Unlike the dualists, structuralists see the informal and formal economies as intrinsically linked. To increase competitiveness, capitalist firms in the formal economy are seen to reduce their input costs, including labour costs, by promoting informal production and employment relationships with subordinated economic units and workers. According to structuralists, both informal enterprises and informal wage workers are subordinated to the interests of capitalist development, providing cheap goods and services (Moser 1978; Portes *et al.* 1989). The legalists focus on the relationship between informal entrepreneurs/enterprises and the formal regulatory environment, not formal firms. But they acknowledge that capitalist interests—what Hernando de Soto (1989) calls 'mercantilist' interests—collude with government to set the bureaucratic 'rules of the game'.

Given the heterogeneity of the informal economy, there is some truth to each of these perspectives. But the reality of informal employment is more complex than these perspectives would suggest. What follows is a summary of various ways in which informal enterprises and workers are linked to formal firms.

INFORMAL ENTERPRISES AND FORMAL FIRMS

Few informal enterprises, except perhaps some survival activities, operate in total isolation from formal firms. Most source raw materials from and/or supply finished goods to formal firms either directly or through intermediate (often informal) firms. Sourcing and supplying of goods or services can take place through *individual transactions* but are more likely to take place through a *sub-sector network* of commercial relationships or a *value chain* of sub-contracted relationships.

To understand the linkages between informal enterprises and formal firms it is important to consider the nature of the production system through which they are linked. This is because the nature of the linkage—specifically, the allocation of authority (over the work situation and the outcome of work done) and economic risk between the informal and formal firm—varies according to the nature of the production system. For instance, a garment maker might produce for the open market (with some authority and all of the risk) or for a supply firm linked to a multinational company (with little authority but much of the risk in the form of non-wage costs, rejected goods, and delayed payments). Types of production systems include:

- *Individual transactions*: some informal enterprises or own account operators exchange goods and services with formal firms in what might be characterized as open or pure market exchange (in the sense of independent units transacting with each other). In such cases, the more competitive firm in terms of market knowledge and power—as well as the ability to adjust if the transaction does not proceed—controls the exchange or transaction.
- *Sub-sectors*: many informal enterprises or own account operators produce and exchange goods and services with formal firms in what are called sub-sectors, networks of independent units involved in the production and distribution of a product or commodity. In such networks, individual units are involved in transactions with suppliers and customers. The terms and conditions of these transactions are largely governed by the more competitive firm in specific transactions (as above) but also by the 'rules of the game' for the sub-sector as a whole, which typically are determined by dominant firms in the sub-sector.
- *Value chains*: some informal enterprises and own account operators and, by definition, all industrial outworkers produce goods within a value chain. The terms and conditions of production in value chains are determined largely by the lead firm: a large national firm in most domestic chains and a large trans-national corporation in most global value chains. However, the major suppliers to whom the lead firm sub-contracts work—also often formal firms—also help determine the terms and conditions of work that they sub-contract to informal firms and workers down the chain.

In sum, in the manufacturing sector in particular, informal enterprises are quite likely to have linkages with formal firms. But these commercial relationships are not likely to be regulated, although this differs from one context to another. In the provision of services, such as catering, transport, and construction, there is greater possibility of de-linking from formal firms.

INFORMAL WORKERS AND FORMAL FIRMS

Historically, the 'employment relationship' has represented the cornerstone—the central legal concept—around which labour law and collective bargaining agreements have sought to recognize and protect the rights of workers. Whatever its precise definition in different national contexts, it has represented 'a universal notion that links a person, called the employee (frequently referred to as 'the worker') with another person, called the employer to whom she or he provides labour or services under certain conditions in return for remuneration' (International Labour Office 2003).

The concept of employment relationship has always excluded those workers who are self-employed. Increasingly, some wage workers have found themselves to be, in effect, without legal recognition or protection because their employment relationship is either:

- *Disguised*: the employment relationship is deliberately disguised by giving it the appearance of a relationship of a different legal nature. For example, the lead firm in a sub-contracting chain may claim that it has a 'sales–purchase'—or commercial—relationship with those who produce goods for it, rather than a sub-contracted employment relationship. In Ahmedabad City, India, many *bidi* (hand-rolled cigarettes) traders now claim that they sell tobacco and other raw materials to those who produce bidis and buy the finished bidis from them. This is because the bidi-traders are trying to avoid employer contributions to a retirement fund being demanded by the bidi-rollers (Chen forthcoming).
- *Ambiguous*: the employment relationship is objectively ambiguous as there is a doubt whether an employment relationship really exists. This is the case, for instance, with street vendors who depend on a single supplier for goods or sell goods on commission for a distributor.
- *Not clearly defined*: the employment relationship clearly exists but it is not clear who the employer is, what rights the worker has, and who is responsible for securing these rights. For example, in value chain production, it is not clear who the real employer is: the lead firm, the supply firm, or the sub-contractor? Similarly, in the case of temporary work, it is not clear who the real employer is: the agency that supplies temporary workers or the firms that hire them on a temporary basis? Or in the case of day labourers or seasonal labourers in agriculture and construction, whether the labour contractor or gang master is the employer?

Under each of these employment relationships, workers tend not to be protected under labour law or collective bargaining agreements: in brief, they are informally employed. It is important to note that, in many such cases, the employer seeks to disguise the employment relationship or avoid definition of who is responsible; and that the employer in question may well represent a formal firm, not an informal enterprise (International Labour Office 2003).

Beginning in the 1980s, formal firms in some developed countries began to favour flexible labour relationships. This form of labour market segmentation took place in the interest of flexible specialized production, not in response to rising wage rates or labour costs (Piore and Sabel 1984). Also increasingly since the 1980s, many formal firms in developed countries have decided to sub-contract production to workers in developing countries: some of whom are relatively protected (e.g. those who work in call centres) while others are not protected (e.g. many of those who work in assembly factories). Production under this form of labour market segmentation takes place in developing countries where labour costs are low and there is no real threat of rising wages due to legislation or unionization. In producing countries, there is often further segmentation between the core semi-permanent workforce and a peripheral temporary workforce that is mobilized during peak seasons and demobilized during slack seasons (what has been called a 'permanent temporary workforce'). Depending on the context, the effect is to shift uncertainty from permanent employees to 'permanent temporary' employees or from 'permanent temporary' employees to industrial outworkers.

In sum, many formal firms prefer informal employment relationships, in the interest of flexible specialized production, global competition, or (simply) reduced labour costs. The related point is that formal firms choose these types of informal employment relationships as a means to avoiding their formal obligations as employers. In such cases, it is the formal firm not the informal worker that decides to operate informally and enjoys the benefits of informality. This reality points to the need to re-examine the notion that informal employment is 'voluntary' from the perspective of informal wage workers, not just of the self-employed.

5.2.2 *The Formal Regulatory Environment*

The three dominant schools of thought also view the relationship between the informal economy and the formal regulatory environment in different ways. With regard to informal enterprises, dualists pay relatively little attention to government regulations *per se* but focus instead on government provision of necessary support services: notably, credit and business development services. In regard to informal wage workers, some dualists subscribe to the neo-classical economics notion that government intervention in labour markets leads to wage rigidities which, in turn, lead to more informal employment. The legalists believe that government deregulation would lead to increased economic freedom and entrepreneurship among working people, especially in developing countries (de Soto 1989). However, the founder of the legalist school—Hernando de Soto—recently advocated one form of regulation: namely, the *formalization* of property rights for the informal workforce to help them convert their informally-held assets into real assets (de Soto 2000). In marked contrast, the structuralists see a role for government in regulating the unequal relationships between 'big businesses' and subordinated informal producers and workers: they advocate the regulation of commercial relations in the case of informal producers and the regulation of employment relations in the case of informal wage workers.

OVER-REGULATION

As noted earlier, the legalists have focused on excessive regulations that create barriers to working formally. However, over-regulation may raise barriers and costs not only to operating formally but also to operating informally. Consider the case of gum collectors in India. Following the nationalization of the forests in India, gum and other forest products came under the control of the National and State Forest Departments with the result that trading these products requires a government licence. Although there is a thriving open market for gum that includes textile and pharmaceutical companies, those who collect gum must sell gum to the Forest Development Corporation; to sell in the open market requires a special licence. Most gum collectors—except those who can afford to obtain a licence—must sell to the Forest Development Corporation for below market prices (Crowell 2003).

Consider also the case of salt makers in India. The cheapest way to transport salt within India is via railway. Historically, small salt producers have not been able to transport their salt by train because of a long-standing government regulation that stipulates that salt farmers need to own a minimum of 90 acres of land to be eligible to book a train wagon. Given that most small salt farmers lease land from the government or local landlords, they are not eligible to use rail transport, and have to use private transport; thus small salt farmers face high transportation costs and remain less competitive than larger salt farmers (Crowell 2003).

DEREGULATION

As part of economic restructuring and liberalization, there has been a fair amount of *deregulation*, particularly of financial and labour markets. Deregulation of labour markets is associated with the rise of informalization or flexible labour markets. It should be noted that workers are caught between two contradictory trends: *rapid flexibilization* of the employment relationship (making it easy for employers to contract and expand their workforce as needed) and *slow liberalization* of labour mobility (making it difficult for labour to move easily and quickly across borders or even to cities within the same country) (Chen *et al.* 2004).[4] Labour advocates have argued for *re-regulation* of labour markets to protect informal wage workers from the economic risks and uncertainty associated with flexibility and informalization.

LACK OF REGULATION

The regulatory environment often overlooks whole categories of the informal economy. A *missing* regulatory environment can be as costly to informal operators as an *excessive* regulatory environment. For example, city governments tend to adopt either of two stances towards street trade: trying to eliminate it or turning a blind eye to it. Either stance has a punitive effect: eviction, harassment, and the demand for bribes by police, municipal officials, and other vested interests. Few cities have adopted a coherent policy—or set of regulations—towards street trade. Rather, most cities assign the handling of street traders to those departments—such as the police—that deal with law and order (Bhowmik 2004; Mitullah 2004).

The different perspectives on regulation outlined above are appropriate for the specific components of the informal economy to which they refer: the legalists focus on informal *enterprises* (and informal *commercial* relationships); labour advocates focus on informal *jobs* (and informal *employment* relationships); and those concerned about street vendors focus on the regulation of *urban space* and *informal trade*. Arguably, for each component of the informal economy, what is needed is *appropriate regulation*, not complete deregulation or the lack of regulation.

[4] Liberalization of labour markets implies (1) wage flexibility, (2) flexibility in contractual arrangements, and (3) limited regulation in terms of the conditions under which labour is exchanged. It should be noted that international labour mobility is often excluded from discussions of labour market flexibility.

5.3 Promoting More Equitable Linkages

Given that the informal economy is here to stay and that the informal and formal economies are intrinsically linked, what is needed is an appropriate policy response that promotes more equitable linkages between the two, and that balances the relative costs and benefits of working formally and/ or informally. While the focus here is on the role of government, there is a role for all stakeholders, including formal firms in promoting socially responsible corporate practices, and for organizations of informal workers in policymaking.

Reflecting the schools of thought outlined above, policymakers have taken differing stances on the informal economy: some view informal workers as a nuisance to be eliminated or regulated; others see them as a vulnerable group to be assisted through social policies; still others see them as entrepreneurs to be freed from government regulations. Another perspective sees the informal workforce as comprising unprotected producers and workers who need to be covered by labour legislation. Subscribing to one or another of these, policymakers tend to over react to the informal economy, trying to discourage it altogether, to treat it as a social problem, or to promote it as a solution to economic stagnation.

But at the core of the debate on the informal economy is the oft-repeated and greatly misunderstood question of whether to formalize the informal economy. However, it is not clear what is meant by 'formalization'. To many policymakers, formalization means that informal enterprises should obtain a licence, register their accounts, and pay taxes. But to the self-employed these represent the costs of entry into the formal economy. What they would like is to receive the benefits of operating formally in return for paying these costs, including: enforceable commercial contracts; legal ownership of their place of business and means of production; tax breaks and incentive packages to increase their competitiveness; membership in trade associations; and statutory social protection. But what about informal wage workers? To them, formalization means obtaining a formal wage job—or converting their current job into a formal job—with secure contract, worker benefits, and social protection.

Taking into account the different meanings of formalization, the feasibility of formalizing the informal economy is unclear. First, most bureaucracies would not be able to handle the volume of licence applications and tax forms if all informal businesses were to be formalized. Second, most bureaucracies would claim that they cannot afford to offer informal businesses the incentives and benefits that formal businesses receive. Third, recent trends suggest that employment growth is not keeping pace with the demand for jobs—there simply are not enough jobs to go around, especially given the very sharp rise in the proportion of people who are of working age in many countries. Finally, available evidence suggests that employers are more inclined to convert formal jobs into informal jobs—rather than the other way around.

The formalization debate should be turned on its head by recognizing, first, that formalization has different meanings for different segments of the informal economy and, second, that it is unlikely that most informal producers and workers can be formalized—although efforts should be made to do so. Further, the formalization debate needs to take into account the benefits due to informal enterprises if they operate formally and to wage workers if they get a formal job; and the costs of working informally for both the self-employed and the wage employed. The policy challenge is to decrease the costs of working informally and to increase the benefits of working formally.

References

Bhowmik, S. (2004). *Survey of Research on Street Vendors in Asia*. Unpublished manuscript. Cambridge, MA: WIEGO.

Chen, M. A. (forthcoming). *Self-Employed Women: The Membership of SEWA*. Ahmedabad, India: Self-Employed Women's Association.

Chen, M. A., J. Vanek, and M. Carr (2004). *Mainstreaming Informal Employment and Gender in Poverty Reduction: A Handbook for Policy-Makers and Other Stakeholders*. London: Commonwealth Secretariat.

Chen, M. A., J. Vanek, F. Lund, J. Heintz with R. Jhabvala and C. Bonner (2005). *Progress of the World's Women 2005: Women, Work, and Poverty*. New York: UNIFEM.

Crowell, D. W. (2003). *The SEWA Movement and Rural Development: The Banaskantha and Kutch Experience*. New Delhi: Sage Publications.

de Soto, H. (1989). *The Other Path: The Economic Answer to Terrorism*. New York: Harper Collins.

de Soto, H. (2000). *The Mystery of Capital: Why Capitalism Triumphs in the West and Fails Everywhere Else*. New York: Basic Books.

International Labour Office (2002). *Women and Men in the Informal Economy: A Statistical Picture*. Geneva: International Labour Office. Available online at: http://www.ilo.org/public/English/employment/gems/download/women.pdf, accessed 22 March 2006.

International Labour Office (2003). *Scope of the Employment Relationship: Report IV, International Labour Conference, 91st Session*. Geneva: International Labour Office.

Mitullah, W. (2004). *A Review of Street Trade in Africa*. Unpublished manuscript. Cambridge, MA: WIEGO.

Moser, C. N. (1978). 'Informal Sector or Petty Commodity Production: Dualism or Independence in Urban Development'. *World Development*, 6: 1041–64.

Piore, M. and C. Sabel (1984). *The Second Industrial Divide*. New York: Basic Books.

Portes, A., M. Castells, and L. A. Benton (eds) (1989). *The Informal Economy: Studies in Advanced and Less Developed Countries*. Baltimore: Johns Hopkins University Press.

Sethuraman, S. V. (1976). 'The Urban Informal Sector: Concept, Measurement and Policy'. *International Labour Review*, 114(1): 69–81.

Thomas, J. J. (1992). *Informal Economic Activity*. London: Harvester Wheatsheaf.

Tokman, V. (1978). 'An Exploration into the Nature of the Informal-Formal Sector Relationship'. *World Development*, 6(9/10): 1065–75.

6

Formal and informal enterprises: concept, definition, and measurement issues in India

M. R. Narayana

6.1 Introduction

Formal and informal enterprises have long co-existed in all sectors of the Indian economy. Only with comparable concepts, definitions, and measurements can their *relative* economic contributions and performance be analysed: without them, formal and informal enterprises should be analysed separately.

This chapter assesses the comparability of concepts, definitions, and measurements of formal and informal enterprises in India, using the latest available official databases. Hence, it provides a basis for (1) continuity and poolability of data on formal and informal enterprises and (2) comparison of Indian experience with the rest of the world. On conceptualizing, defining, and measuring the formal and informal enterprises at the global level (e.g. by the International Labour Organization) see Chen (chapter 5) and Sindzingre (chapter 4, both in this volume).[1]

The main conclusion of this chapter is that: differences in concepts and definitions exceed similarities; hence the databases cannot be used to compare economic contributions and performance between the formal and informal enterprises; standardization of concepts, definitions, and measurements between the formal and informal enterprises, and among

[1] In addition, papers presented for the meetings of the Expert Group on Informal Sector Statistics (Delhi Group) highlight the measurement issues in select Asian, Latin American, and African countries. These papers are available at: http://mospi.nic.in/mospi_informal_sector.htm

informal enterprises is needed to design and evaluate (1) promotional measures (e.g. labour laws including social security) for informal enterprises, (2) appropriate linkages between formal and informal enterprises.

The rest of the chapter is organized as follows. Section 6.2 examines the comparability of official concepts and definitions of the formal and informal enterprises in India. In Section 6.3, economic contributions and performance of formal and informal enterprises are analysed by the latest available databases. Conclusions and policy implications are presented in section 6.4.

6.2 Concepts and Definitions

Different concepts and definitions are used for distinguishing between formal and informal enterprises and sectors. Box 6.1 summarizes these distinctions by formal/organized/registered/regulated/enterprises, and informal/unorganized/unregistered/unregulated enterprises.

In essence, (1) the unorganized sector is wider in scope than the informal sector to include unregistered,[2] unregulated, and informal enterprises;[3] and (2) employment size is the basic criterion for distinguishing enterprises in both the formal and informal sectors. Thus, the concepts and definitions of formal and informal enterprises follow the enterprise approach in India.[4]

The above concepts and definitions are not specific to Small Scale Enterprises (SSEs), as they are defined on different (e.g. non-employment

[2] Legislation relating to various labour laws and social security does not apply for enterprises with less than 10 workers with power and 20 without power. Consequently, unregulated sector is characterized by labour relations not based on contractual arrangements with formal guarantees (e.g. wages and social security benefits).

[3] Outside India, informal sector is included as a part of 'irregular economy'. For instance, according to McIntyre, 'the term irregular economy indicates all economic activities that are totally or partially outside formal institutions. As such, the irregular economy includes "underground", "informal", "shadow", and criminal economy, and the like. The shadow sector consists of any type of economic activity which citizens deliberately or consciously conceal from observation in order to minimize costs, for example by tax evasion. The criminal sector includes any economic activity government enforcement institutions might act against forcibly, to stop them functioning' (McIntyre 2003: 17).

[4] The other approach to conceptualizing and defining of the formal and informal sector is in terms of characteristics of persons involved and/or characteristics of their employment. This approach is called labour approach. It makes an essential distinction between employment in informal sector and informal employment, because 'the enterprise definition of the informal sector is unable to capture all aspects of the increasing so-called "informalization" of employment, which has led to a rise in various forms of informal (or non-standard, atypical, alternative, irregular, precarious, etc.) employment, in parallel to the growth of the informal sector that can be observed in many countries' (Hussmans 2004: 1).

Box 6.1 CONCEPTS AND DEFINITIONS OF FORMAL AND INFORMAL SECTORS AND ENTERPRISES IN INDIA

Formal and Informal Sectors and Enterprises

Informal sector is defined in terms of all unincorporated proprietary enterprises and partnership enterprises. In this definition,

- an enterprise is an undertaking, which is engaged in the production and/or distribution of some goods and/or services meant for the purpose of sale, whether fully or partly;
- proprietary enterprises are those where an individual is the sole owner of the enterprise. Partnership enterprises are those where partners (from the same household or different households) agree to share the profits of a business carried on by all or any one of them acting for all; and
- an enterprise is distinguished between an *Own Account Enterprise* (OAE) and an *Establishment*. An OAE is run by household labour, usually without any hired worker employed on a fairly regular basis. An Establishment has less than ten workers with at least one hired labourer on a fairly regular basis. An Establishment is further distinguished between a Directory Establishment (DE) and a Non-directory Establishment (NDE). A DE (or NDE) employs more than five workers (or less than six workers) with at least one hired labourer.

Consequently, all non-informal sectors and enterprises define the formal sectors and enterprises.

Organized and Unorganized Sectors and Enterprises

Organized and unorganized sectors are defined in different contexts.

- First, organized sector comprises of enterprises, and information (e.g. statistical data) on their activities are available or collected regularly (e.g. registered manufacturing units). In contrast, information on activities of unorganized enterprises is neither regulated under any legal provision, nor regular account on their activities maintained by the enterprises themselves.
- Second, manufacturing units (i.e. all manufacturing, processing, and repair and maintenance services units), registered (or not registered) under the Factory Act 1948, belong to the organized (or unorganized) sector. That is, factories employing 10 or more (or less than 10) workers and using power, or employing 20 or more (or less than 20) workers without using power, in the reference year, belong to the registered (or unregistered) manufacturing sector. This implies that the unregistered sector includes OAE.
- Third, enterprises covered (or not covered) by the Annual Survey of Industries (ASI) fall under the purview of the organized (or unorganized) sector.

Unorganized and Informal Sectors and Enterprises

The unorganized sector includes unincorporated proprietary or partnership enterprises, enterprises run by co-operative societies, trusts, and private and public limited companies (non ASI). Thus, informal sector is a part of unorganized sector in India.

Source: Compiled from National Sample Survey Organisation (2001), section 1.

Box 6.2 CONCEPTS AND DEFINITIONS OF INDIA'S SMALL SCALE ENTERPRISES, 2001–02

Small scale enterprises	Investment limit (on historical cost of plant and machinery), and other conditions
1. Small scale industry	In general: Rs. 10 million (US$0.21 million) Special case: Rs. 50 million (US$1.05 million) in Hosiery and Hand tool industry
2. Ancillary undertaking	Rs. 10 million (US$0.21 million), provided that 50 per cent of total output should be for other undertakings
3. Export oriented enterprise	Rs. 10 million (or US$0.21 million), provided 30 per cent of output is exported
4. Tiny industry	Rs. 2.5 million (or US$0.05 million)
5. Small Scale Service and Business (Industry related) enterprises	Rs. 1 million (US$0.02 million)
6. Women enterprises	Rs. 10 million (or US$0.21 million) and 51 per cent equity are held by women
	Turnover limit for excise duty exemptions and concessions
Small scale enterprises in registered and unregistered sector	Rs. 30 million (or US$0.63 million).

Note: Exchange rate (annual average in 2001–02) is equal to Rs. 47.69 per US$1 (Reserve Bank of India 2003).
Source: Compiled from Government of India (2001).

size) criteria, such as, investment and turnover limits.[5] This is evident in Box 6.2.

In short, the concepts and definitions of formal, informal, and small scale enterprises are not comparable in India.[6] Further, these enterprises cannot be categorized on a mutually exclusive basis due to data issues. For instance, under the multiple registrations system, an SSE can register under the Factories Act as well as with the Directorate of Industries and Commerce. This implies that a part of organized enterprises includes registered SSEs. In the same way, unorganized sector includes informal and unregistered SSEs.[7]

[5] Investment limit entitles the SSEs for various policy support and incentives. This is evident, for instance, in government of India's Comprehensive Policy Package for SSIs and Tiny Sector 2000 in terms of fiscal support, credit support, infrastructure support, support for technological upgradation and quality improvement, marketing support, entrepreneurship development, facilitating prompt payment, and rehabilitation of sick enterprises. The details are available in Annexure-4 in Government of India (2001).

[6] Nevertheless, studies in India have compared between registered SSEs and unorganized manufacturing units by select indicators, such as, value added and ownership pattern, on the ground that the unorganized sector is composed of unregistered SSE. This is evident in the government of India's reports on SSEs (Government of India 1997; 2001).

[7] This implies that categorization of enterprises, such as, SSEs and informal enterprises, non-SSEs and formal enterprises, SSEs and formal enterprises, and non-SSEs and informal enterprises is not plausible.

Thus, in terms of measurement, different databases on the enterprises show different coverage of enterprises. From the published databases, it is not possible to separate out enterprises according to a particular definition. This data problem is the main reason for non-comparability of enterprises across the databases. This implies that the Indian databases, which measure the economic contributions and performance of the enterprises by different concepts and definitions, should be separately analysed in terms of their rich diversities.

6.3 Measurement of Economic Contributions and Performance

Economic contributions and performance of formal and informal enterprises are analysed by specific categories and from the latest databases. To start with, organized and unorganized enterprises are analysed, as they include the informal enterprises, registered and unregistered manufacturing enterprises, and registered and unregistered SSEs. Each database is useful to construct select indicators to measure for relative economic contributions, and performance of enterprises by different sub-categories (e.g. by manufacturing and non-manufacturing sectors, and by rural and urban distinctions). Throughout, all analysis is done at the national level of aggregation.[8]

6.3.1 *Unorganized and Organized Enterprises*

Economic Census-1998 (conducted from March–June 1998) measures the contribution of unorganized sector by number of enterprises and workers.[9] Enterprises include Own Account Enterprises (OAEs), Directory Establishments (DEs) and Non-Directory Establishments (NDEs). Both agricultural enterprises (AEs) and non-agricultural enterprises (NAEs) are covered in the Census.[10] The contributions are indicated by spatial

[8] India is a federal economy, and industry and labour are in the concurrent list of the Indian constitution. Both the federal and state level governments have regulatory and promotional functions in industry and labour sectors. Nevertheless, to restrict the scope of this chapter, no disaggregate analysis at the state level is attempted.

[9] Previous Economic Census was conducted in 1977, 1981 and 1991. A comparison of results of these previous censuses with the Census 1998 is presented in Chapter V in Central Statistical Organisation (2001).

[10] In addition, the Census provides the following non-employment related information. First, self-financing accounts for 82.94 per cent of total finances. Second, share of total establishments with 'private others' (i.e. other than private non-profit institutions,

distribution and employment size by OAEs, DEs, and NDEs in rural and urban regions (Table 6.1).[11] The indicators reveal the following insights.

First, NAEs dominate the total number of units in the unorganized sector. For instance, 85 per cent of OAEs, 96 per cent of NDEs, and 97 per cent of DEs belong to NAEs.[12] Within the total number of NAEs, rural OAEs are more than the urban OAEs. Within the rural and urban NAEs, OAEs constitute the highest share and is followed by NDEs and DEs.

Second, NAEs dominate the total number of workers in the unorganized sector. That is, 83 per cent of workers in OAEs, 95 per cent of workers in NDEs, and 98 per cent of DEs workers belong to NAEs. Within the total number of workers in NAEs, urban workers have a higher share (56 per cent) than the share of rural workers (41 per cent). While rural workers dominate in OAEs (47 per cent), workers in NDEs (59 per cent) and DEs (67 per cent) dominate in urban areas.

Third, manufacturing sector does not have a higher share as compared to service sector in total number of NAEs. For instance, 21 per cent of OAEs, 16 per cent of NDEs, and 34 per cent of DEs belong to manufacturing sector in the NAEs. However, within the total number of manufacturing units, OAEs dominate in both rural and urban areas, but rural OAEs are more than the urban OAEs. Within the rural and urban manufacturing units, OAEs constitute the highest share and is followed by NDEs and DEs.

Fourth, manufacturing workers do not constitute a higher share than service sector workers in total number of workers in NAEs. For instance, 26 per cent of workers in OAEs, 19 per cent of workers in NDEs, and 38 per cent of workers in DEs belong to manufacturing sector in NAEs. Within the total number of workers in manufacturing units, rural workers have a higher share (52 per cent) than the share of urban workers (48 per cent).

co-operatives, and government) is equal to 97.90 per cent (96.72 per cent rural and 98.84 per cent urban). Third, share of enterprises owned by socially vulnerable groups (e.g. Scheduled Castes and Tribes, and Other Backward Castes) is equal to 64.96 per cent (69.03 per cent rural and 54.41 per cent urban). Fourth, share of non-perennial (or non-seasonal) enterprises is equal to 10.34 per cent (12.7 per cent rural and 4.22 per cent urban). Fifth, share of enterprises without premises is equal to 12.42 per cent (13.88 per cent rural and 8.66 per cent urban). Sixth, share of enterprises without using power or fuel is equal to 65.96 per cent (66.55 per cent rural and 64.42 per cent urban). Seventh, share of female workers in enterprises is equal to 30.77 per cent (33.34 per cent rural and 24.46 per cent urban) and in total Establishments is equal to 17.10 per cent (4.36 per cent rural and 1.60 per cent urban). Eighth, the share of child workers in total Establishments is equal to 2.78 per cent (4.36 per cent rural and 1.60 per cent urban).

[11] The Economic Census did not collect any information on production and investment of unorganized enterprises. Thus, more realistic performance indicators, such as, employment per unit of capital or per unit of output is not computable for unorganized enterprises.

[12] Throughout, all numbers are rounded off to the nearest per cent.

Table 6.1. Economic contribution and performance of unorganized enterprises in India, 1998

Indicators of economic contribution and performance	Rural				Urban				Combined			
	OAEs	NDEs	DEs	Total	OAEs	NDEs	DEs	Total	OAEs	NDEs	DEs	Total
1. Total no. of NAEs (in millions)	10.71	3.19	0.60	14.51	7.56	3.80	1.00	12.37	18.27	6.99	1.61	26.87
% to rural or urban or nation's total	73.86	21.97	4.17	100.00	61.12	30.77	8.12	100.00	67.99	26.02	5.99	100.00
% to nation's total	58.64	45.59	37.59	53.98	41.36	54.41	62.41	46.02	100.00	100.00	100.00	100.00
% to combined total of AEs and NAEs	78.78	92.13	9.36	61.68	97.15	98.83	99.41	97.84	85.47	95.66	96.91	88.55
2. Total no. of workers in NAEs (in millions)	15.81	7.27	10.69	33.77	11.07	10.43	21.28	42.78	26.89	17.70	31.96	76.55
% to rural or urban or nation's total	46.83	21.53	31.65	100.00	25.88	24.39	49.73	100.00	35.12	23.12	41.75	100.00
% to nation's total	58.81	41.06	33.43	44.11	41.19	58.94	66.57	55.89	100.00	100.00	100.00	100.00
% to combined total of AEs and NAEs	76.24	90.98	96.10	84.74	96.63	98.70	99.61	98.60	83.39	95.38	98.35	91.90
3. Total no. of manufacturing enterprises (in millions)	2.76	0.53	0.22	3.52	1.06	0.64	0.32	2.02	3.83	1.17	0.54	5.54
% to rural or urban or nation's total	78.53	15.11	6.37	100.00	52.66	31.45	15.88	100.00	69.09	21.07	9.84	100.00
% to nation's total	72.19	45.54	41.10	63.52	27.81	54.46	58.90	36.48	100.00	100.00	100.00	100.00
% to total NAEs	25.77	16.67	37.02	24.24	14.07	16.70	31.95	16.33	20.93	16.68	33.86	20.60
4. Total no. of workers in manufacturing enterprises (in millions)	5.01	1.43	5.21	11.65	2.04	1.93	6.91	10.88	7.05	3.36	12.12	22.53
% to rural or urban or nation's total	42.99	12.28	44.73	100.00	18.75	17.75	63.50	100.00	31.28	14.93	53.79	100.00
% to nation's total	71.05	42.54	42.98	51.70	28.95	57.46	57.02	48.30	100.00	100.00	100.00	100.00
% to total NAEs	31.67	19.68	48.75	34.49	18.42	18.52	32.48	25.43	26.21	19.00	37.92	29.43
5. Average employment												
Combined total of AEs and NAEs	1.53	2.31	1.72	1.69	1.47	2.75	21.15	3.43	1.51	2.54	19.58	2.74
AEs	1.71	2.65	0.07	0.67	1.74	3.04	14.03	2.23	1.72	2.70	10.47	1.94
NAEs	1.48	2.28	17.67	2.33	1.47	2.74	21.19	3.46	1.47	2.53	19.87	2.85
Manufacturing enterprises	1.81	2.69	23.27	3.31	1.92	3.04	21.54	5.39	1.84	2.88	22.25	4.07

Notes:

AEs = agricultural enterprises; NAEs = non-agricultural enterprises.
OAEs = Own Account Enterprises; DEs = Directory Establishments; and NDEs = Non-Directory Establishments.
Average employment is equal to number of workers per enterprise.

Source: Computed by using the basic data in Central Statistical Organisation (2001).

Within the rural and urban manufacturing workers, workers in DEs dominate over workers in OAEs and NDEs.

Fifth, average employment in manufacturing enterprises is higher than in informal enterprises or in agricultural enterprises or in NAEs. In particular, manufacturing DEs have the highest average employment and is followed by average employment in NDE and OAE in both rural and urban areas.

The performance of employment generation in the unorganized sector discussed here, may be compared with the organized sector in 1998–99. The government of India publishes the organized employment data on an annual basis by public and private sectors as well as by industry.[13]

Total organized employment in 1999 is equal to 28 million persons and the share of non-agriculture employment is equal to 95 per cent (27 million persons). The share of manufacturing employment in the total organized employment is equal to 24 per cent (7 million persons). In the same way, the share of manufacturing employment in the total non-agriculture employment is equal to 25 per cent (Government of India 2004a: Table 3.1 and 3.2).

A comparison between the organized and unorganized employment levels provides us with the following evidence. First, the size of total employment in unorganized agriculture (7 million) is five times higher than employment size in organized agricultural sector. Second, the size of total employment in NAEs in unorganized sector (77 million) is three times higher than the total non-agricultural employment in organized sector. Third, the size of unorganized manufacturing employment (23 million) is three times higher than the organized manufacturing employment. Thus, unorganized sector is more contributory than organized sector in generating employment in both AEs and NAEs.[14]

[13] The organized sector covers all Establishments in the public sector and all non-agricultural Establishments employing ten or more persons. Industry wise data helps in separating the agricultural and non-agricultural and manufacturing and non-manufacturing employment within the organized sector. In essence, organized employment data includes, but is not restricted to, factory employment. Thus, employment data from the ASI is not used for comparison purposes.

[14] Agricultural enterprises and Establishments are those engaged (excluding in agricultural production and plantation) in raising of livestocks, agricultural services, hunting, trapping, forestry, logging, and fishing. Non-agricultural enterprises are those engaged in mining and quarrying; manufacturing (as per NIC-1987); electricity, gas, and water; construction; wholesale and retail trade; restaurants and hotels; transport; storage and warehousing; communications; financial, insurance, real estate, and business services; community, social, and personal services; and other (unspecified) activities. This implies that non-manufacturing NAEs belong to service enterprises.

6.3.2 *Informal Enterprises*

A national sample survey on India's informal sector was conducted in 1999–2000 (National Sample Survey Organisation 2001). This survey was the first of its kind in India and covered the non-agricultural enterprises.[15] The survey data measures the contribution and performance of rural and urban enterprises by number of enterprises and workers, value added and sources of net surplus, utilization of assets and sources of debt financing.[16] These indicators (Table 6.2) reveal the following insights into the measurement issues.

NATURE, COMPOSITION, AND LOCATION OF ENTERPRISES

Informal enterprises include OAEs and Establishments. Of the total informal enterprises, OAEs (87 per cent) constitute the largest share. Of the total OAEs, rural OAEs are higher than urban OAEs; and of the total Establishments, urban Establishments are higher than rural Establishments.

Manufacturing sector does not have a higher share as compared to service sector in total number of informal enterprises. For instance, 32 per cent of OAEs, 34 per cent of Establishments and 32 per cent of total informal enterprises belong to manufacturing sector.

DISTRIBUTION OF WORKERS

Number of workers in informal enterprises is relatively higher in OAEs (71 per cent).[17] Within the rural and urban areas, the share of workers in OAEs is higher than in Establishments. Of the total workers in OAEs, share of workers in rural OAEs is higher than in urban OAEs. On the other hand, of the total workers in Establishments, share of workers in urban Establishments is higher than in rural Establishments. Thus, rural OAEs and urban Establishments are major sources of employment in the informal enterprises.

Informal manufacturing workers do not constitute a higher share than service sector workers in total number of workers. For instance, 36 per cent

[15] The non-agricultural enterprises include manufacturing (as per NIC 1998 at 2-digit level from 15–37); construction; wholesale and retail trade; repair of motor vehicles, motor cycles, and personal and household goods; hotels and restaurants; transport, storage and communications; financial intermediations; real estate, renting, and business activities; education; health and social works; and other community, social, and personal services. Thus, non-manufacturing enterprises belong to service enterprises.

[16] The sample design and technique of estimation are outlined in chapter 2 in National Sample Survey Organisation (2001).

[17] A supplementary information on workers is the share of female workers: 9.84 per cent in all units (11.94 per cent in rural areas and 6.74 per cent in urban areas).

Table 6.2. Economic contribution and performance of informal enterprises in India, 1999–2000

Indicators of economic contribution and performance		Rural			Urban			Combined		
		OAEs	ESTMs	Total	OAEs	ESTMs	Total	OAEs	ESTMs	Total
1. No. of enterprises (in millions)		23.66	1.41	25.07	15.14	4.20	19.34	38.80	5.61	44.41
% to total (rural + urban)		60.97	25.14	56.44	39.03	74.86	43.56	100.00	100.00	100.00
% to rural or urban or nation's total		94.37	5.63	100.00	78.28	21.72	100.00	87.36	12.64	100.00
2. No. of manufacturing enterprises (in millions)		9.01	0.61	9.61	3.35	1.31	4.66	12.35	1.92	14.27
% to total (rural + urban)		72.91	31.71	67.37	27.09	68.29	32.63	100.00	100.00	100.00
% to rural or urban or nation's total		93.67	6.33	100.00	71.87	28.13	100.00	86.56	13.44	100.00
% to total enterprises		38.07	43.10	38.35	22.10	31.17	24.07	31.83	34.17	32.13
3. Total no. of workers in all enterprises (in millions)		34.14	5.67	39.81	22.11	17.86	39.97	56.25	23.53	79.78
% to total (rural + urban)		60.69	24.10	49.90	39.31	75.90	50.10	100.00	100.00	100.00
% to rural or urban or nation's total		85.76	14.24	100.00	55.32	44.68	100.00	70.51	29.49	100.00
4. Total no. of workers in manufacturing units (in millions)		14.87	2.83	17.69	5.57	6.40	11.97	20.44	9.23	29.66
% to total (rural + urban)		72.75	30.66	59.64	27.25	69.34	40.36	100.00	100.00	100.00
% to rural or urban or nation's total		84.06	16.00	100.00	46.53	53.47	100.00	68.89	31.11	100.00
% to all informal enterprises		43.56	49.91	44.44	25.19	35.83	29.95	36.34	39.23	37.18
5. Average employment										
All informal enterprises		1.44	4.02	1.59	1.46	4.25	2.07	1.45	4.19	1.80
Non-manufacturing enterprises		1.32	3.54	1.43	1.40	3.96	1.91	1.35	3.87	1.66
Manufacturing enterprises		1.65	4.65	1.84	1.66	4.89	2.57	1.65	4.81	2.08
6. Value added										
Value added per worker in manufacturing enterprises:	Rs.	8961.41	22660.89	11158.09	15580.54	35228.26	26085.59	10765.16	31375.00	17182.43
	US$	206.82	522.98	257.51	359.58	813.02	602.02	248.45	724.09	396.55
Ratio of value added per worker in all informal enterprises to manufacturing enterprises		1.50	1.08	1.35	1.61	1.24	1.28	1.67	1.25	1.41
Ratio of value added per worker in non-manufacturing to manufacturing enterprises		1.89	1.16	1.62	1.81	1.38	1.40	2.06	1.41	1.65
Net surplus as % of total value added in all informal enterprises		96.01	56.89	86.81	91.74	59.37	72.70	93.67	59.00	77.04

Net surplus as % of total value added per manufactuirng enterprise		96.35	55.27	82.88	93.29	50.43	62.59	95.14	51.54	70.56
Net surplus as % of total value added per non-manufacturing enterprise		95.87	58.29	88.77	91.45	62.80	75.68	93.26	62.27	79.31
Emoluments as % of value added per informal enterprise		1.27	36.61	9.58	1.95	31.90	19.56	1.64	32.61	16.49
Emoluments as % of value added per manufacturing enterprise		2.12	39.22	14.29	2.46	42.91	31.43	2.26	42.07	24.70
Emoluments as % of value added per non-manufacturing enterprise		0.92	34.35	7.24	1.86	27.67	16.06	1.47	28.45	13.61
Ratio of total receipts to total expenditure in informal enterprises		1.38	1.33	1.37	1.28	1.17	1.20	1.32	1.19	1.24
Ratio of total receipts to total expenditure in manufacturing enterprises		2.00	1.48	1.74	1.89	1.45	1.53	1.96	1.46	1.59
Ratio of total receipts to total expenditure in non-manufacturing enterprises		1.30	1.26	1.29	1.25	1.14	1.17	1.27	1.15	1.19
7. Use of assets										
Total market value of assets per manufacturing enterprise:	Rs.	15042.05	131023.22	22380.70	47174.38	352236.84	133003.61	23746.38	282084.50	58473.84
	US$	347.15	3023.85	516.52	1088.72	8129.17	3069.55	548.04	6510.14	1349.50
Ratio of market value of assets per informal enterprise to manufacturing enterprise		1.32	1.17	1.22	1.51	1.28	1.15	1.68	1.33	1.41
Ratio of market value of assets per non-manufacturing enterprise to manufacturing enterprise		1.52	1.29	1.36	1.65	1.41	1.20	1.99	1.50	1.60
Hired assets as % of total assets of all informal enterprises		20.37	18.55	19.80	47.60	42.51	44.35	39.32	40.07	39.75
Hired assets as % of total assets in manufacturing enterprises		11.56	16.57	13.41	37.29	35.05	35.62	25.41	32.32	29.89
Hired assets as % of total assets of non-manufacturing enterprises		23.94	19.71	22.72	49.37	44.92	46.66	42.58	42.74	42.67
Rents on hired assets as % of total value added in all informal enterprises		1.71	2.13	1.81	5.76	4.97	5.29	3.92	4.54	4.22
Rents on hired assets as % of total value added in manufacturing enterprises		0.80	1.51	1.03	3.51	4.22	4.02	1.87	3.62	2.86
Rents on hired assets as % of total value added in non-manufacturing enterprises		2.08	2.67	2.19	6.17	5.27	5.68	4.49	4.96	4.70

Table 6.2. (*Continued*)

Indicators of economic contribution and performance		Rural			Urban			Combined		
		OAEs	ESTMs	Total	OAEs	ESTMs	Total	OAEs	ESTMs	Total
8. Debt financing										
Total amount of borrowings by	Rs. in million	26922.00	34245.08	61167.07	42529.50	194732.65	237262.15	69451.50	228977.72	298429.23
informal enterprises	US$ in million	621.32	790.33	1411.66	981.53	4494.18	5475.70	1602.85	5284.51	6887.36
% of borrowings by manufacturing enterprises		16.71	43.13	31.50	6.12	18.78	16.51	10.23	22.42	19.59
% of borrowings from institutional sources by enterprises										
All informal enterprises		70.83	85.50	79.05	56.12	51.80	52.57	61.82	56.84	58.00
Manufacturing enterprises		70.77	84.58	81.36	70.71	58.80	59.59	70.75	66.22	66.77
Non-manufacturing enterprises		70.84	86.20	77.98	55.17	50.18	51.19	60.81	54.13	55.86
% of borrowings from private money lenders										
All informal enterprises		12.52	6.93	9.39	11.01	14.78	14.10	11.59	13.60	13.14
Manufacturing enterprises		15.20	6.24	8.33	10.55	8.00	8.17	13.50	7.49	8.22
Non-manufacturing enterprises		11.98	7.46	9.88	11.04	16.34	15.27	11.38	15.37	14.33
% of interest payments to institutional sources										
All informal enterprises		64.93	82.10	73.81	50.13	53.84	52.98	55.78	8.51	57.72
Manufacturing enterprises		69.91	83.20	79.48	63.99	77.57	76.17	67.54	79.30	77.35
Non-manufacturing enterprises		63.88	81.31	71.37	49.06	48.37	48.55	54.31	52.45	53.04
% of interest payments to private money lenders										
All informal enterprises		20.40	11.13	15.61	14.93	12.25	12.86	17.02	12.06	13.49
Manufacturing enterprises		21.15	10.14	13.22	22.04	12.33	13.33	21.50	11.66	13.29
Non-manufacturing enterprises		20.24	11.84	16.63	14.38	12.23	12.77	16.46	12.18	13.53
Interest payments as % of total value added										
All informal enterprises		1.27	4.50	2.02	1.70	4.03	3.06	1.51	4.10	2.74
Manufacturing enterprises		0.76	4.08	1.84	0.78	2.62	2.10	0.77	2.94	2.00
Non-manufacturing enterprises		1.05	2.61	1.41	1.58	3.27	2.57	1.34	3.17	2.21

Notes:

OAEs = Own Account Enterprises; ESTMs = Establishments.

Average employment is equal to number of workers per enterprise.

Source: Computed by using the basic data in National Sample Survey Organisation (2001).

of workers in OAEs, 39 per cent of workers in Establishments, and 37 per cent of total workers belong to manufacturing sector. Within the rural and urban manufacturing workers, share of workers in OAEs (or Establishments) is higher in rural (or urban) areas.

At the national level, average employment in informal manufacturing enterprises is equal to two (or two for OAEs and five for Establishments). This indicator is higher for Establishments than OAEs in both rural and urban areas. Further, in both rural and urban areas, average employment in manufacturing enterprises is higher than in all informal enterprises and service enterprises. Thus, average employment generation is highest in manufacturing enterprises than in all informal enterprises in general, and in service enterprises in particular.

VALUE ADDED

Measurement of value added per worker (as an indicator of labour productivity), and extent and sources of net surplus per enterprise (as indicators of profitability), is compared between all informal enterprises, manufacturing enterprises, and non-manufacturing enterprises below. The comparison offers the following evidence.[18]

- Labour productivity is higher in urban enterprises than in rural enterprises, and higher in Establishments than in OAEs in both rural and urban areas.
- Labour productivity in manufacturing enterprises is lower than in all informal enterprises or non-manufacturing enterprises. Thus, the ratio of value added per worker in all informal or non-manufacturing enterprises to manufacturing enterprises exceeds unity for OAEs and Establishments in both rural and urban areas. In both cases, of course, labour productivity is lower because physical and human capital per unit of labour are higher; correspondingly, the productivity of physical and human capital is lower.
- Ratio of net surplus to total factor income is higher in all OAEs than in Establishments in both rural and urban areas. For instance, the ratio is equal to 96 (or 55) per cent in manufacturing OAEs (or Establishments) in rural areas and 939 (50) per cent in urban areas. This is mainly

[18] Gross value added is computed by the factor income and product methods. In the factor income approach, value added is equal to sum of factor incomes: interest to investors, rent to owners of land and buildings, emolument to workers, and the residual (net surplus) to the entrepreneur. In the product approach, value added is equal to the difference between total receipts and total expenditure. Value added by the product approach is used below for computation of value added per worker.

attributable to the higher factor payments in Establishments than in OAEs. For instance, of the factor payments, a higher share is evident for emoluments (due to the presence of hired labour) in value added per Establishment than in value added per OAE. Thus, emoluments as a percentage of value added per manufacturing OAE (or Establishment) is equal to 2 (or 39) per cent in rural areas and 2 (or 44) per cent in urban areas, or 2 (or 42) per cent at the national level. In fact, this percentage is highest for manufacturing enterprises than for all informal or non-manufacturing enterprises. Thus, the share of labour cost in value added per manufacturing enterprise is highest in the informal sector.

- Ratio of total receipts to total expenditure is higher in manufacturing enterprises than in all informal or non-manufacturing enterprises in both rural and urban areas. Thus, profitability (or net surplus) per manufacturing enterprise is highest among the informal enterprises in India, notwithstanding a lower labour productivity and higher labour cost.

UTILIZATION OF ASSETS

Total assets used by informal enterprises are equal to owned and/or hired assets. They are in the form of land and building, plant and machinery, and transport equipment. These assets are contributory to long-term production and employment generation. Analysis of current market value of assets by all informal enterprises, manufacturing enterprises, and non-manufacturing enterprises in rural and urban areas leads to the following insights.

- In both rural and urban areas, market value of total assets per manufacturing enterprise is smaller than per informal or non-manufacturing enterprise. Thus, the ratio of market value of assets per informal (or non-manufacturing) enterprise to manufacturing enterprise exceeds unity for OAEs and Establishments in both rural and urban areas. In fact, manufacturing enterprises are not the larger users of total assets per enterprise as compared to all informal enterprises or non-manufacturing enterprises.[19]
- Share of hired assets in manufacturing enterprises is smaller than in all informal enterprises or non-manufacturing enterprises. Further, share of hired assets in Establishments exceeds that in OAEs in both rural and urban areas. Thus, the share of rent on hired assets in the total value

[19] This result is mainly attributable to aggregation of all assets in all non-manufacturing or informal enterprises. For instance, transport activities, storage, and communication activities are the largest creators of transport equipment; wholesale and retail trade are the largest creators of land and building assets; and manufacturing activities are the largest creators of plant and machinery.

added is smaller in manufacturing enterprises than in all informal enterprises or in non-manufacturing enterprises. Other things being equal, this implies a comparative cost advantage for manufacturing enterprises within the informal sector.

PATTERN OF DEBT FINANCING

Pattern of borrowings and payment of interest by all informal enterprises, manufacturing and non-manufacturing enterprises are measured by ten different sources. The formal or institutional sources include term lending institutions, commercial banks, and cooperative banks and societies. Informal or non-institutional sources include private moneylenders, business partners, suppliers and contractors, friends and relatives. These data are useful to measure the extent of debt financing and interest payment by sources of borrowing, and interest cost in the value added.

Of the total borrowings of the informal enterprises, the share of manufacturing enterprises is equal to 20 per cent (32 per cent in rural areas and 17 per cent in urban areas). Of the enterprises, the share of manufacturing OAEs (or Establishments) is equal to 10 (or 22) per cent. However, manufacturing enterprises have a small share in total borrowings of informal enterprises.

Both the rural and urban enterprises are largely financed by institutional sources. However, rural enterprises have a larger share in formal sources than the urban enterprises. For instance, the sum of borrowings from the formal sources by rural (or urban) enterprises is equal to 79 (or 53) per cent; 79 (or 56) per cent by OAEs; and 86 (or 52) per cent by Establishments. Of the non-institutional sources, role of private moneylenders is noteworthy, as they supply about 13 per cent of total borrowings of the informal enterprises. In particular, urban enterprises borrow more from the private moneylenders than the rural enterprises.

In general, share of interest payments by sources correspond with the size of borrowings by the sources. Thus, the largest share of interest payments goes to institutional sources and is paid by the non-manufacturing enterprises. For instance, the sum of interest payments to institutional sources (or private moneylenders) by all informal enterprises is equal to 53 (or 1) per cent. The sum of interest payments to institutional sources (or private moneylenders) by all manufacturing enterprises is equal to 77 (or 13) per cent. In general, interest rates in the non-institutional sources are unregulated and are higher than in the institutional sources. Thus, other things being the same, higher borrowings from the non-institutional sources imply higher interest cost for informal enterprises.

Interest cost as a percentage of total value added shows three remarkable differences. First, the percentage is higher for urban enterprises than for rural enterprises. Second, the percentage is higher for Establishments than for OAEs in both rural and urban areas. Third, of the Establishments, rural manufacturing enterprises and urban non-manufacturing enterprises have the highest percentage.

Thus, the database on India's informal sector measures the multidimensional contributions and performance of rural and urban OAEs and Establishments to the national economy.

6.3.3 *Registered and Unregistered Manufacturing Enterprises*

Contribution of the registered and unregistered manufacturing sectors to national income by major product groups is measured in India's National Accounts Statistics (NAS).[20] This contribution is presented for select years (1993–94, 1998–99, and 2002–03) in Table 6.3.

India's GDP, at 1993–94 factor cost increased from Rs. 7813.45 billion in 1993–94 to Rs. 10827 billion in 1998–98 and to Rs. 13183 billion in 2002–03, but annual growth fell from 7 per cent in 1994–95 to 6 per cent in 1998–99 and to 4 per cent in 2002–03. Contribution of manufacturing sector to national income has remained around 17 per cent and that of registered (or unregistered) manufacturing sector at around 11 (or 6) per cent. Within the manufacturing GDP, the share of registered sector has been around 65 per cent. In terms of average growth over 1994–95 to 2002–03, the growth of GDP, manufacturing GDP, registered manufacturing GDP, and unregistered manufacturing GDP is similar at 6 per cent.

GDP by 20 major product groups shows that the average contribution of registered (or unregistered) manufacturing groups has increased by 1.56 (or 1.48) times from 1993–94 to 1998–99, and by 1.22 (or 1.19) times from 1998–99 to 2002–03.[21] However, average contribution per product group of the registered sector has remained double that of the unregistered sector. At the same time, relative variability (in terms of coefficient of variation) in the product-wise contribution has remained higher in the registered sector.

[20] Methodology and databases for these estimations are available at: http://mospi.nic.in/nas_snm.htm

[21] These 20 product groups (as per NIC-1998 at 2-digit level) include food products (20–21), beverages, tobacco, etc. (22), cotton textiles (23), wool, silk, etc. (24), jute textiles (25), textile products (26), wood, furniture, etc. (27), paper and printing, etc. (28), leather and fur products (29), chemicals, etc. (30), rubber and petroleum, etc. (31), non-metallic products (32), basic metal industries (33), metal products (34), non-electric machinery, tools and parts (35), electric machinery (36), and transport equipment (37).

Table 6.3. Economic contribution and performance of registered and unregistered enterprises in India, 1993–94 to 2002–03

Indicators of economic contribution and performance			1993–94	1998–99	2002–03
1. Total GDP at factor cost and constant (or 1993–94) prices: Rs. in millions			7813450	10827480	13183210
2. Annual growth of GDP (%)			7.3*	6.5	4.00
3. Share of manufacturing to total GDP (%)			16.06	17.05	17.22
4. Share of registered manufacturing sector to total GDP (%)			10.48	11.09	11.36
5. Share of unregistered manufacturing sector to total GDP (%)			5.58	5.95	5.86
6. Share of registered sector in total manufacturing in GDP (%)			65.24	65.08	65.99
7. Average growth (%) during 1994–95 to 2002–03					
GDP	5.84				
Manufacturing sector	5.88				
Registered manufacturing	6.09				
Unregistered manufacturing	5.51				
8. Descriptive statistics of manufacturing GDP by 20 product groups					
Registered manufacturing		Mean GDP	453740.00	664350.00	811190.00
		Coefficient of variation (%)	8.37	9.64	9.40
Unregistered manufacturing		Mean GDP	225810.00	333390.00	396010.00
		Coefficient of variation (%)	6.15	5.58	5.25

Note:
*refers to 1994–95.
All descriptive statistics are computed for unadjusted GDP for financial intermediation services indirectly measured due to lack of product-specific adjustment values.

Source: Computed by using the basic data in Central Statistical Organisation (2004).

In addition, the contribution of product groups differs between the registered and unregistered sectors. For instance, within the registered sector, important product groups include chemicals, basic metals, food products, and rubber and petroleum products. The combined share of these four product groups in registered manufacturing GDP is equal to 46 per cent in 1993–94, 48 per cent in 1998–99, and 48 per cent in 2002–03. On the other hand, the important products in unregistered manufacturing GDP comprise food products including beverages and tobacco, cotton textiles, wood and furniture, metal products, and other manufacturing products. The combined share of these six products in unregistered manufacturing GDP is equal to 54 per cent in 1993–94, 51 per cent in 1998–99, and 47 per cent in 2002–03. This is due to declining (or emerging) share of cotton textiles and wood and furniture products (or non-metallic products and repair services).

6.3.4 *Registered and Unregistered Small Scale Enterprises*

The Third All India Census of Small Scale Industries was conducted in 2002–03 for the reference year 2001–02.[22] The Census definition and composition of SSEs are the same as given in Box 6.2. The Census covered both the registered and unregistered enterprises.[23] In particular, the coverage is 100 per cent of the 2.26 million registered enterprises. Of the registered enterprises, 61 per cent are working (hence, the remaining 39 per cent are closed) enterprises. The estimated number of unregistered enterprises is equal to 9.15 million.[24] In total, 5983 (or 2680) products are produced by registered (or unregistered) SSEs. Using these data, indicators for economic contribution and performance of SSEs are constructed (Table 6.4). All analyses for registered (or unregistered) enterprises below refer to working (or total estimated) enterprises.

[22] The First (or Second) All India Census of SSIs is conducted in 1970 (or 1987–88).

[23] An enterprise is called a registered (or an unregistered) enterprise, if it is (or is not) permanently registered with the Directorate of Industries in a State or Union Territory as on 31 March 2001. Reasons for non-registration (by per cent of unregistered SSEs) include (1) not interested (39.86 per cent); (2) no knowledge of such provisions (53.13 per cent); and (3) complicated procedures (3.87 per cent). Thus, reasons for not registering are not explicitly motivated by the familiar devil's deal: 'a kind of unspoken deal between politicians and their constituents—a myriad of small-firm owners, many in the informal sector, that is "if you vote for me, according to this exchange, I won't collect taxes from you; I won't make you comply with other tax, environmental, or labour regulations; and I will keep the police and inspectors from harassing you". This will be known here as tacit understanding of "the devil's deal" because it causes informality to become more attractive, and formalisation less attractive, than they otherwise might be' (Tendler 2002).

[24] The sample design, size, coverage, and estimation procedures are outlined in chapter IV in Government of India (2004b).

Table 6.4. Economic contribution and performance of small scale enterprises in India, 2001–02

Indicators of economic contribution and performance	Registered	Unregistered
1. No. of SSEs (in millions)	2.26	9.15
% of small scale industries (SSIs)	65.55	38.75
% of tiny enterprises among SSIs	97.90	99.99
% of ancillary enterprises among SSIs	5.08	2.44
% of women enterprises	10.00	10.13
2. Size and capitalization indicators		
Average output (Rs. in million at current prices)	1.48	0.09
Average fixed investment (Rs. in million at current prices)	0.67	0.07
Average investment on plant and machinery (Rs. in million at current prices)	0.22	0.03
Average employment (persons)	4.48	2.05
% of export enterprises	0.53	25.80
% of exports in total output	6.06	2.39
3. Performance indicators		
Employment per million rupees of gross output	3.03	23.75
Employment per million rupees of original value of plant and machinery	20.32	76.41
Employment per million rupees of total investment	6.71	30.00
4. Smallness of SSEs		
4.1 % of enterprises with gross value of output (at current prices)		
Upto Rs. 0.1 million	70.83	95.39
More than Rs. 0.1 million but less than or equal to Rs. 0.2 million	5.27	2.11
More than Rs. 0.2 million but less than or equal to Rs. 0.5 million	7.23	1.52
More than Rs. 0.5 million but less than or equal to Rs. 1 million	5.42	0.54
4.2 Of the enterprises with gross value of output of Rs. 1 million or less (or above Rs. 5 million)		
% of employment	61.65 (6.37)	97.63 (0.05)
% of fixed capital	30.77 (19.42)	93.7 (0.82)
% of original plant and machinery	33.89 (14.95)	93.51 (0.26)
% of total exports from	0.36 (78.33)	6.92 (89.52)
4.3 % of enterprises with:		
Upto one employee	23.61	42.59
More than 2 employees but less than or equal to 7 employees	64.83	56.13
More than 7 employees but less than or equal to 10 employees	5.71	0.79
4.4 Of the enterprises with less than or equal to 10 employees		
% of gross output	35.09	88.43
% of fixed capital	49.15	96.36
% of original plant and machinery	51.61	95.13
% of total exports from	10.08	9.57
5. Sickness of SSEs		
% of total sick enterprises	13.98	6.89
Reasons for sickness		
Lack of demand	58.00	69.00
Shortage of working capital	57.00	43.00
Non-availability of raw material	12.00	12.00
Power shortage	17.00	12.00
Labour problems	6.00	4.00
Marketing problems	37.00	36.00
Equipment problems	9.00	12.00
Management problems	5.00	3.00

Note:
Average value is computed by dividing the total value of a variable by total number of enterprises.

Source: Computed by using the basic data in Government of India (2004b).

SSIs account for a larger share in registered SSEs (66 per cent) and SSSBEs (or small scale service and business [industry related] enterprises) in unregistered SSEs (61 per cent). Tiny enterprises constitute about 98 per cent within the registered and unregistered SSIs. Share of ancillary (or women) enterprises is equal to 5 (or 10) per cent in registered enterprises and 2 (or 10) per cent in unregistered enterprises. Thus, heterogeneity in composition is evident in both registered and unregistered SSEs.[25]

Wide disparity exists between the registered and unregistered SSEs in size and capitalization indicators of SSEs. In essence, average output, average fixed investment, average investment on original value of plant and machinery, average employment, and per cent of exports in total output are higher for registered enterprises; and per cent of export enterprises is higher for unregistered enterprises.[26]

Difference in employment performance by registered and unregistered SSEs is remarkable. The unregistered SSEs show higher performance than the registered SSEs in all the three employment performance indicators: about eight times higher by employment per million rupees of gross output; about four times higher by employment per million rupees of original value of plant and machinery; and about four times higher by employment per million rupees of total investment.

Smallness of SSEs is evident in the output indicators. Per cent of registered (or unregistered) enterprises with value of gross output of less than or equal to Rs. 0.1 million is equal to 71 (or 95) per cent, or less than or equal to Rs. 1 million is equal to 89 (or 99 per cent). Unregistered enterprises with gross value of output with less than or equal to Rs. 1 million have the largest share in employment (98 per cent), fixed capital (94 per cent), and original plant and machinery (94 per cent). Enterprises with gross value of output of more than Rs. 5 million have the largest share in exports in both registered enterprises (78 per cent) and unregistered enterprises (90 per cent).

[25] Heterogeneity is further evident in the following features. Of the total registered (or unregistered) enterprises, the share of enterprises (1) under proprietary organization is 88.85 (or 96.9) per cent; (2) owned by Scheduled Castes, Scheduled Tribes, and Other Backward Classes is 48.88 (or 57.18) per cent; (3) managed by women is 8.32 (or 8.37) per cent; and (4) using electricity is 65.43 (or 44.01) per cent. In addition, about 26.23 (or 42.15) per cent of registered (or unregistered) enterprises do not need electric or non-electric power for their operations.

[26] The Development Commissioner for Small Scale Industries (DC-SSI) provides with annual estimated data on four performance indicators for SSIs: (1) cumulative total number of registered and unregistered units; (2) total value of annual production at current and constant prices; (3) cumulative total employment; and (4) total value of annual exports at current prices. Except for number of enterprises, no other data is distinguished between registered and unregistered SSIs. Hence, these performance indicators are not comparable with the performance indicators based on the Third Census data for SSEs.

Further, smallness of SSEs is evident in employment indicators. Per centage of registered (or unregistered) enterprises with less than or equal to ten employees is equal to 94 (or 99) per cent. These unregistered enterprises have the largest share in output (88 per cent), fixed capital (96 per cent), and original plant and machinery (95 per cent). However, enterprises with this employment size have a lesser share of exports in both registered enterprises (11 per cent) and unregistered enterprises (10 per cent).

Total sick enterprises constitute 14 (or 7) per cent of total registered (or unregistered) SSEs.[27] Lack of demand is the most important reason for sickness among the registered SSEs (58 per cent) and unregistered SSEs (69 per cent). The other important reasons for sickness for registered (or unregistered) enterprises include: working capital problems: 57 (or 43) per cent, marketing problems: 37 (or 36) per cent, power shortage: 17 (or 12) per cent, non-availability of raw materials: 12 (or 12) per cent, and equipment problems: 9 (or 12) per cent.

6.3.5 *Cluster of Registered and Unregistered Small Scale Enterprises*

Database on industrial clusters (Government of India 2003a, b; 2004b) provide valuable information on measuring the economic contribution and performance of SSIs and small and medium enterprises (SMEs) in clusters. In essence, these databases are not comparable due to (1) differences in definition for clusters, (2) composition of units (SSIs and SMEs), and (3) nature and number of indicators for spatial distribution and economic performance of clusters. Thus, select indicators are separately constructed and presented by the databases in Table 6.5.

Indicators based on the Small Industries Development Organisation (SIDO) database show remarkable differences in product and sector compositions, size of turnover, employment size, and number of units in the clusters. For instance, clusters marked by product homogeneity as single product clusters is equal to 89; product composition is heavily concentrated in three sectors (i.e. sector 7, sector 6 and sector 1 with their combined share equal to 65 per cent of total clusters); clusters with medium (or high) potential in technology upgradation is equal to 68 (or 29) per cent and in export promotion is equal to 42 (or 39) per cent; clusters with annual turnover of more than Rs. 1 billion is equal to 85 per cent; clusters with

[27] An enterprise is included in total sick SSEs if it has continuous decline in gross output over three consecutive financial years, and/or delay in repayment of institutional loans by more than 12 months, and/or erosion in the net worth due to accumulated losses to the extent of 50 per cent of its net worth during the preceding accounting year.

Table 6.5. Economic contributions and performance of industrial clusters of small-scale and medium enterprises in India

Indicators of economic contribution and performance
1. SIDO database—total number of clusters = 388
1.1 Single product clusters
1.2 Potential for technology upgradation
High
Medium
Low
1.3 Product composition
Sector 1
Sector 2
Sector 3
Sector 4
Sector 5
Sector 6
Sector 7
Sector 8
Sector 9
1.4 Potential for export promotion
High
Medium
Low
1.5 Annual value of turnover
More than Rs. 10 billion
Rs. 1 billion to Rs. 10 billion
Rs. 100 million to Rs. 1 billion
Less than Rs. 100 million
1.6 No. of enterprises
More than 10,000 enterprises
1000 enterprises to 10,000 enterprises
500 enterprises to 1000 enterprises
100 enterprises to 500 enterprises
Less than 100 enterprises
1.7 Size of employment
More than 100,000 persons
10,000 persons to 100,000 persons
1000 persons to 10,000 persons
Less than 1000 persons
2. Ministry of SSIs database—total number of clusters = 358
2.1 No. of natural clusters
2.2 No. of clusters manufacturing reserved products
2.3 Linkages
Large unit centred
Vertical
Horizontal
Both horizontal and vertical
2.4 Basis of cluster
Market based
Resource based
Infrastructure based

Table 6.5. *(Continued)*

3. Third All India Census of SSIs—total number of clusters in registered (or unregistered) SSEs = 1223 (or 819)

3.1. Size and capitalization indicators
No. of registered (or unregistered) SSIs per cluster
Gross output per rupee of fixed investment in registered (or unregistered) SSIs: Rs.
Gross output per employee in registered (or unregistered) SSIs: Rs. in million
Fixed assets per employee in registered (or unregistered) SSIs: Rs. in million

3.2. Performance indicators
Employment per million rupees of gross output in registered (or unregistered) SSIs
Employment per million rupees of total investment in registered (or unregistered) SSIs

Notes:
The sectoral composition of products are as follows.

Sector 1: Animal, vegetable, horticulture, forestry products, beverages, tobacco, and pan masala and non-drinkable water/spirit and alcohol (industrial use).

Sector 2: Ores, minerals, mineral fuels, lubricants, gas, and electricity.

Sector 3: Chemical and allied products.

Sector 4: Rubber, plastic, leather, and products thereof.

Sector 5: Wood, cork, thermocol and paper, and articles thereof.

Sector 6: Textile and textile articles.

Sector 7: Base metals, products thereof and machinery equipment, and parts thereof, excluding transport equipment.

Sector 8: Railways, airways, ships, road surface transport, and related equipment and parts.

Sector 9: Other manufactured articles and services, not elsewhere classified.

Source: Compiled and computed from the basic data in Government of India (2003a; 2003b; 2004b).

more than 1000 enterprises is equal to 47 per cent; and clusters with employment size of more than 1000 persons is equal to 98 per cent.

Ministry of SSIs database provides additional information on clusters in terms of (1) natural or policy induced clusters;[28] (2) reserved/unreserved nature of products; (3) the cluster being market based, resource based, or infrastructure based;[29] and (4) the nature of linkages by large unit based, vertical, horizontal, and vertical and horizontal.[30] The evidence shows that the highest number of clusters is natural (93 per cent) rather than induced; manufacture of unreserved items (56 per cent) rather than reserved items; horizontally linked (74 per cent) and horizontally and vertically linked (16 per cent) rather than large unit centred or vertically linked; and market based (58) and resource based (40 per cent) rather than infrastructure based.

[28] Clusters developed without (or with) deliberate policy intervention by the government are called natural (or induced or infrastructure-based) clusters.

[29] Resource includes raw materials and skilled labour. Infrastructure is largely in the form of public provisioning of economic infrastructure (e.g. industrial estates and technology parks).

[30] Horizontal clusters comprise enterprises, which process the raw materials, and produce and market the finished products by themselves with no scope for division of enterprises. Clusters of enterprises around a large enterprise or few large enterprises are called large enterprise based clusters. Vertical clusters are linked with large enterprises as suppliers or processors of raw materials or as subcontractors of large enterprises.

The Third All India Census of SSIs presents the cluster data by the registered and unregistered SSEs. A district having 100 (or 500) or more registered (or unregistered) SSI units, and engaged in manufacturing the same product as per Annual Survey of Industry Commodity Classification 2000 (at 5 digit), is considered a cluster for that product in that district. Number of SSI units per cluster, gross output per rupee of fixed assets at current prices (or a proxy indicator for output/capital ratio), gross output per employment at current prices (or a proxy indicator for output/labour ratio) and value of fixed assets per employment at current prices (or a proxy indicator for capital/labour ratio) are constructed as size and capitalization indicators. Except for number of SSIs per cluster, registered SSIs have higher value of these indicators than cluster of unregistered SSIs.[31]

Further, unregistered SSEs have higher performance in employment generation than the registered SSEs. For instance, employment per million rupees of gross output in registered (or unregistered) SSEs is equal to about 4 (or 32) persons. In the same way, employment per million rupees of total investment in registered (or unregistered) SSEs is equal to about 9 (or 52) persons. Most importantly, these performance indicators are higher as compared to employment performance of dispersed SSEs in Table 6.4. Thus, clustered SSEs are better performing in employment generation than the dispersed SSEs.

6.4 Conclusions and Policy Implications

Indian experiences are highly diversified in conceptualizing and defining of formal and informal sectors and enterprises, as well as in measuring the economic contributions and performance of these sectors and enterprises. The formal (or informal) sector comprises regulated (or unregulated), organized (or unorganized), and registered (or unregistered) enterprises. Informal enterprises are composed of OAEs, Establishments (DEs and NDEs), and unregistered SSEs. Definitions, measurements, and coverage of these enterprises vary by their databases. This implies that each database should be analysed in terms of its own strength and limitations, and both continuity and poolability of these data are not plausible. Thus, in order to establish comparability between the databases, concepts, definitions and measurements (including the method of data collection by census or survey techniques), of formal and informal enterprises need to be standardized by official data collection agencies. For instance, comparability requires

[31] Artisan clusters include stone carving, handloom, handicrafts, and handmade pottery.

that the enterprises in unorganized sector are classifiable by investment and turnover limits or SSEs are classifiable by nature of employment (e.g. hired or not) and size of employment (i.e. number of persons employed). As comparable database is essential to design and evaluate promotional policies (e.g. labour laws including social security) for informal sector, the need for standardization is a policy imperative for India.

Latest databases are useful to quantitative measurement of the economic contributions and performance of the formal and informal sectors in regard to national income, employment generation, production of goods, and use of assets in both rural and urban areas, linkages with the formal credit institutions and to cluster development. In particular, this measurement identifies their strength and potential to contribute for national economic growth and for broader income distribution through employment generation in both rural and urban India. As the ownership of informal enterprises is widely distributed, including among the socially vulnerable groups and women, development of informal sector has important non-economic implications in India.

Industrial clusters include the formal and informal manufacturing units in all sizes. In terms of size of production and employment generation, and possibilities for exports promotion and technology upgradation, clusters eliminate the disadvantages of smallness of dispersed SSEs. Most importantly, clusters facilitate for their linkages, both horizontal and vertical. Thus, they need to be promoted and strengthened, both at present and in future, as a strategy of linking formal and informal sectors and enterprises.

The analysis, conclusions and implications of this chapter serve as bases for comparison of relevant Indian experiences with other countries and offer lessons for other developing countries in building databases on informal sectors and enterprises.

References

Central Statistical Organisation (2001). *Economic Census 1998. All India Report.* New Delhi: Ministry of Statistics and Programme Implementation, Government of India.

Central Statistical Organisation (2004). *National Accounts Statistics 2004.* New Delhi: Ministry of Statistics and Programme Implementation, Government of India.

Government of India (1997). *Report of the Expert Committee on Small Enterprises.* New Delhi: Ministry of Industry.

Government of India (2001). *Report of the Study Group on Development of Small Scale Enterprises*. New Delhi: Planning Commission.

Government of India (2003a). *'Indian Clusters'*. New Delhi: http://www.laghu-udyog.com/clusters/clus/ovrclus.htm, Small Industry Development Organisation, Ministry of Small Scale Industry.

Government of India (2003b). *Cluster Development and Sector Programme: Achievements and New Initiatives by Ministry of SSI*. New Delhi: Development Commissioner (Small Scale Industries), Ministry of Small Scale Industries.

Government of India (2004a). *Economic Survey 2003–04*. New Delhi: Economic Division, Ministry of Finance.

Government of India (2004b). *Final Results: Third All India Census of Small Scale Industries 2001–02*. New Delhi: Development Commissioner (Small Scale Industries), Ministry of Small Scale Industries, Government of India.

Hussmans, R. (2004). 'Statistical Definition of Informal Employment: Guidelines Endorsed by the Seventeenth International Conference of Labour Statisticians (2003)', paper presented for the 7th Meeting of the Expert Group on Informal Sector Statistics (Delhi Group). New Delhi: 2–4 February.

McIntyre, R. J. (2003). 'Small Enterprises in Transition Economies: Causal Puzzles and Policy-Relevant Research', in R. J. McIntyre and B. Dallago (eds), *Small and Medium Enterprises in Transitional Economies*. New York: Palgrave Macmillan for UNU-WIDER, pp. 1–17.

National Sample Survey Organisation (2001). *Informal Sector in India 1999–2000*. New Delhi: Ministry of Statistics and Programme Implementation, Government of India.

Reserve Bank of India (2003). *Report on Currency and Finance 2001–02*. Mumbai: Reserve Bank of India.

Tendler, J. (2002). 'Small Firms, the Informal Sector and the Devil's Deal'. *IDS Bulletin*, 33(3): 98–104.

Part II

Empirical Studies of Policies and Interlinking

7

The impact of regulation on growth and informality: cross-country evidence*

Norman V. Loayza, Ana María Oviedo, and Luis Servén

7.1 Introduction

The enactment of regulation follows a process where valid social goals are mixed with the objectives of particular interest groups (see Djankov *et al.* 2002). Whatever their justifications and objectives, regulations are bound to have an impact beyond their area of control and exert an effect on the overall economy. This effect has two basic channels: the dynamics of firm restructuring and the formation and evolution of the informal sector. Concentrating on the latter channel, this chapter uses a large sample of industrial and developing countries to examine empirically the overall effect of business regulation on, respectively, economic growth and the relative size of the informal sector.[1]

The key to a healthy economy is the flexibility to manage negative shocks and take advantage of growth opportunities. Intentionally or not, regulation can impose rigidities and distort the incentives for factor reallocation, capital accumulation, competition, and innovation. For those firms that abide by the regulatory environment, this distorts the normal process of firm creation, growth, and disappearance—the Schumpeterian process of 'creative destruction'. Through this firm-dynamics channel, regulation

* This research has been supported by the World Bank's Latin America Regional Studies Programme. We are very grateful to Basudeb Guha-Khasnobis, Patricia Macchi, Janis Vehmaan-Kreula, participants in the EGDI-WIDER Conference on the Informal Sector (held in Helsinki in 2004), and an anonymous referee for useful comments.

[1] We explore the firm-dynamics channel in a related paper (Loayza *et al.* 2005b).

can have a macroeconomic impact by both worsening recessionary periods and reducing trend growth.

In the absence of perfect monitoring and compliance, some firms will find it optimal—or simply necessary—to evade regulations and work outside the strict legal regime. That regulations are evaded, however, does not imply that they cease to have an effect. The informal sector—the result of the loose aggregation of firms and activities outside the regulatory framework—is the second-best response of an economy facing shocks and trying to grow.[2] The response is second-best because it entails losing, at least partially, the advantages of legality, such as police and judicial protection, access to formal credit institutions, and participation in international markets. Trying to escape the control of the state forces many informal firms to remain sub-optimally small, use irregular procurement and distribution channels, and constantly divert resources to mask their activities or bribe officials. Therefore, when compared with a first-best response, the expansion of the informal sector often represents distorted and insufficient economic growth.[3] In addition, the informal sector can generate a negative externality that compounds its adverse effect on growth: informal activities use and congest public infrastructure without contributing the tax revenue to replenish it. Since public infrastructure complements private capital in the process of economic growth, a larger informal sector implies smaller growth through this mechanism.[4]

In assessing the impact of regulation, it is essential to consider that this impact is likely to depend not only on the quantity of regulation, but also on its quality. There are good reasons for this. On analytical grounds, certain types of regulation—such as those designed to enhance competition in goods or financial markets—should be expected to exert beneficial effects on economic performance, rather than adverse ones. More generally, countries with better institutions tend to create regulatory environments genuinely aimed to improve business conditions rather than

[2] For an excellent review of the causes and consequences of the informal sector, see Schneider and Enste (2000). Drawing from a public-choice approach, Gerxhani (2004) provides an interesting discussion of the differences of the informal sector in developed and developing countries. The classic study of informality is, of course, de Soto (1989).

[3] This does not necessarily mean that informal sector firms are not dynamic or lagging behind their formal counterparts (see Maloney 2004 for evidence on the dynamism of Latin American informal firms). In fact, in equilibrium the risk-adjusted returns in both sectors should be similar. The stagnation arguments presented in the text are relative to the first-best response and not with respect to a sclerotic economy unable to circumvent its regulation-induced rigidities.

[4] See Loayza (1996) for an endogenous-growth model highlighting the negative effect of informality through the congestion of public services.

privilege a few interest groups.[5] They are also more likely to enforce regulation in a transparent and even-handed manner, limiting the regulator's margin for arbitrariness and corruption that can place many firms at a disadvantage. All these arguments suggest that the quality of regulation is likely to be closely related to overall governance quality, and thus in our experiments we use governance indicators to capture and examine the importance of regulatory quality.

Before proceeding, we should mention two limitations of this study. First, this is only an exploration of the link between regulatory burden, informality, and economic growth. A complete study would include a full analysis of causal relationships and exact transmission mechanisms from regulation to informality and then growth. However, in a companion paper, we try to ascertain the causal impact of regulation on economic growth through an instrumental variable procedure (see Loayza *et al.* 2005b). There we find that the regulatory effect estimated through ordinary least squares is likely to also represent a causal impact, which leads us to believe that the relationships described in this chapter are more than mere correlations. Second, this study is only a partial evaluation of regulation since it focuses on its macroeconomic impact and does not consider whether the regulation's specific goals were accomplished or not.

The rest of the chapter is organized as follows. Section 7.2 describes the synthetic regulation indicators and presents some stylized facts concerning the patterns of regulation across countries. Section 7.3 reports estimates of the impact of regulation on, respectively, economic growth and the size of the informal sector. Section 7.4 offers some concluding remarks.

7.2 Measuring Business Regulation

In this section, we briefly describe our measures of regulation and their sources. We also discuss differences in regulation intensity across countries for different levels of economic development.

We construct indices to measure business regulation in the following seven areas: firm entry, labour markets, fiscal regulation, trade barriers, financial markets, contract enforcement, and bankruptcy regulation. The firm entry regulation index captures the legal difficulty that an entrepreneur faces to register and start a formal business. The labour market

[5] This is the argument in Claessens and Klapper (2002).

regulation index measures how difficult it is for a firm to adjust its labour force because of mandated hiring and firing costs, regulated wages, and the power of organized labour. The index of fiscal regulation aims to measure the burden to firms imposed by taxation and fiscal spending. The trade regulation index indicates the tariff and non-tariff barriers that prevent international trade competition. The financial markets regulation index captures the difficulty a firm faces in accessing capital markets because of credit rationing, interest rate controls, and excessive procedural and collateral requirements. The contract enforcement regulation index is a measure of how difficult it is for firms to turn to the justice system to resolve legal disputes in view of procedural complexity and burdensome red tape. Finally, the index of bankruptcy regulation reflects the inefficiency of the bankruptcy process caused by the justice system's inability to establish creditor priorities and enforce compensation.

Each index is obtained as an average of related components, normalized to vary within a unit interval with higher values representing heavier regulatory burden.[6] The components used to construct the seven synthetic indices are obtained from the following data sources: Doing Business (The World Bank Group), Index of Economic Freedom (The Heritage Foundation), Economic Freedom of the World (The Fraser Institute), Labour Market Indicators Database (Rama and Artecona 2002), The Corporate Tax Rate Survey (KPMG), and International Country Risk Guide (The PRS Group). Except for the Labour Market Indicators Database, all sources are public. Our sample covers 75 countries.

In most cases, data are based on surveys conducted in a single year (in the late 1990s) in a large group of countries; for components with observations for more than one year, we use average values over the period. Therefore, our indices should be interpreted as average regulation levels in the late 1990s. We should note, however, that regulation tends to stay constant over long periods of time.

Table 7.1 shows simple correlations between the seven regulation indices. The strong correlations among all but the fiscal burden and labour indices suggest that regulation policy comes in 'packages'. Judging from these correlations, we can distinguish three regulation categories: fiscal, labour, and product-market regulations, where the latter is a composite of the entry, trade, financial markets, bankruptcy, and contract enforcement indices. We obtain the product-market index by averaging the scores of

[6] We refer the interested reader to Loayza *et al.* (2005a) for details on the construction and components of the business regulation indices.

Table 7.1. Correlation coefficients between regulation indices

	Entry	Financial markets	Contract enforcement	Trade	Bankruptcy	Labour	Fiscal	Governance
Entry	1							
Financial markets	0.66***	1						
Contract enforcement	0.66***	0.58***	1					
Trade	0.63***	0.73***	0.62***	1				
Bankruptcy	0.52***	0.44***	0.53***	0.51***	1			
Labour	0.39***	0.1	0.44***	0.05	0.14	1		
Fiscal	−0.50***	−0.27**	−0.57***	−0.33***	−0.38***	−0.16	1	
Governance	−0.70***	−0.64***	−0.79***	−0.79***	−0.57***	−0.14	0.51***	1

	Product market	Labour	Fiscal	Overall	Governance
Product market	1				
Labour	0.26***	1			
Fiscal	−0.49**	−0.16	1		
Overall	0.97***	0.42***	−0.31***	1	
Governance	−0.86***	−0.18	0.52**	−0.80***	1

Notes: ** and *** denote significance at the 5% and 1% level, respectively.
Source: Authors' estimation.

the five components.[7] We also compute an overall regulation index by averaging the scores of all seven components. We choose to give equal weights to all components despite the strong correlation among the first five because we do not have any priors about the importance of labour market or fiscal regulation relative to the others.

Figure 7.1 depicts scatter plots of the overall, product-market, labour, and fiscal regulation indices against the (the log of) GDP per capita of all countries in the sample. The product-market regulation index is strongly negatively related to average income, and so is the overall regulation index, reflecting the fact that it loads heavily on product-market regulations. Labour regulation also has a negative correlation with average income, but it is smaller and not statistically significant. The relationship between fiscal regulation and income is strong but of the opposite sign as those of the other types of regulation: richer countries tend to have heavier fiscal regulation.

Finally, we use a governance index in order to assess the quality of regulation itself and the general context that determines how regulation

[7] The term 'product-market regulations' is taken from Nicoletti *et al.* (2000).

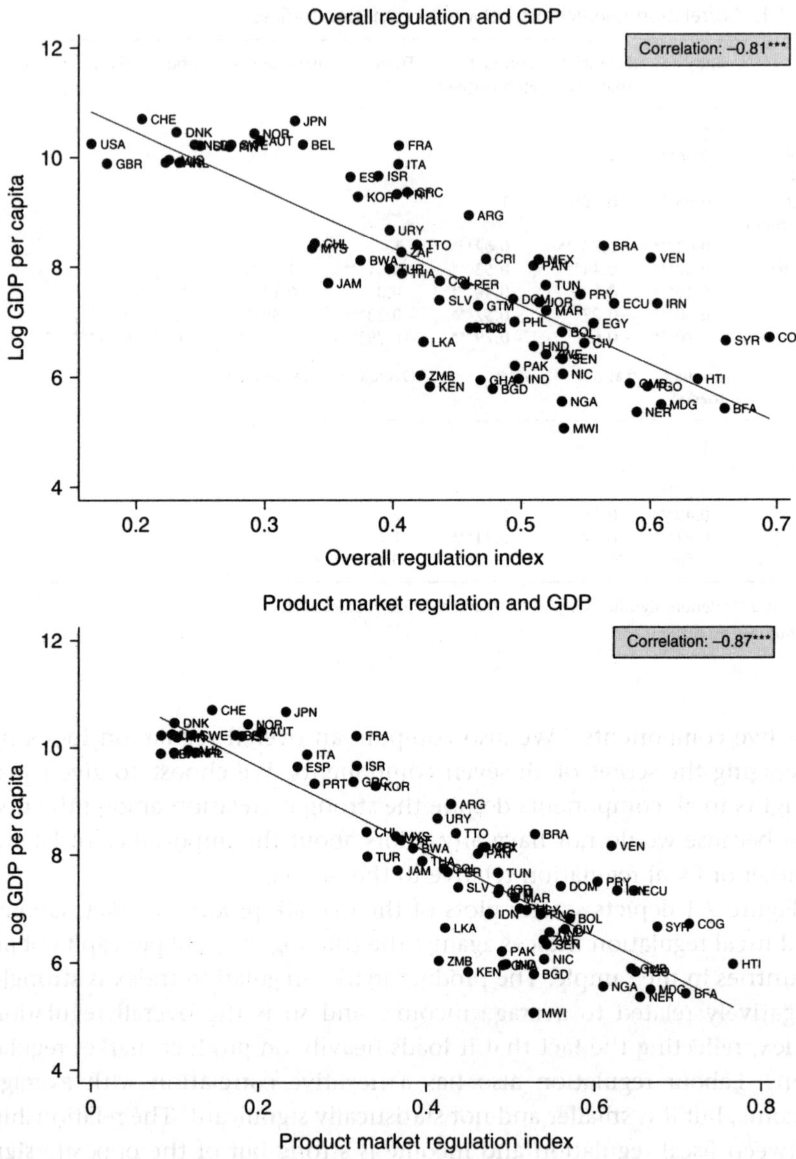

Figure 7.1. GDP per capita versus regulation indices

Notes: *** denotes significance at the 1% level.

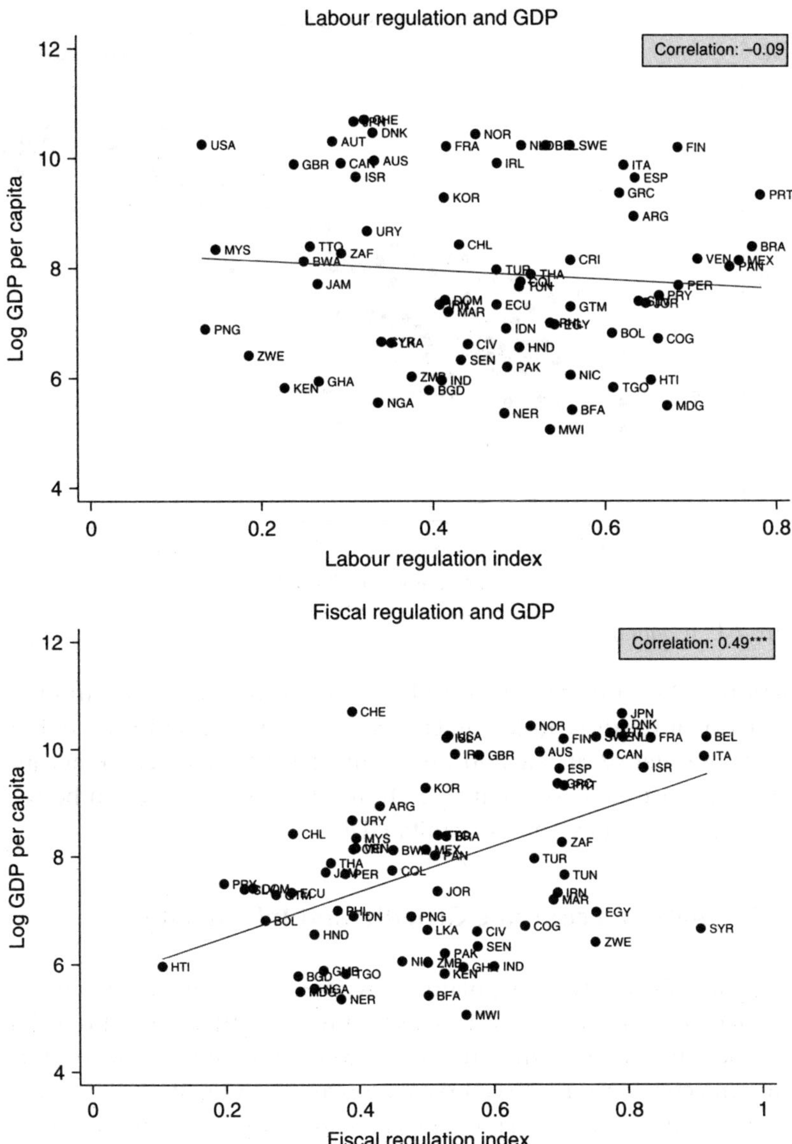

Figure 7.1. *(Continued)*

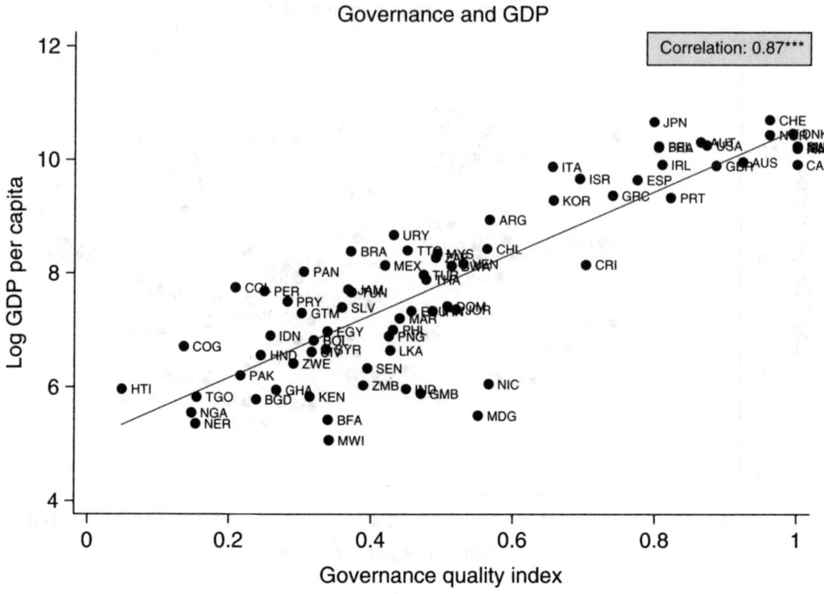

Figure 7.1. (*Continued*)

functions. We construct this index using three measures from the International Country Risk Guide: absence of corruption in the political system, prevalence of law and order, and level of democratic accountability. The last panel of Figure 7.1 shows the close connection between our governance index and per capita GDP.

7.3 Regulation, Economic Growth, and Informality

Having described how the regulatory environment varies across countries, our objective for this section is examining whether regulations have an impact on economic growth and the size of the informal sector. Establishing the connection between regulation and informality is the first step in understanding how regulation affects economic growth. In assessing the effect of the regulatory environment, it is important to consider that the quality of regulation is profoundly affected by the institutional context in which it is imposed. Thus, regulation's ultimate impact is likely to be affected by the country's level of institutional development. In order to explore the interaction between institutional progress and regulatory environment, we extend the basic empirical analysis by allowing the effects of regulation to vary with the measure of governance described above.

7.3.1 *Sample and Specification*

Our empirical methodology is based on cross-country regression analysis. We conduct separate regressions for each dependent variable of interest, namely, economic growth and the size of the informal sector. In each case, we use as explanatory variables a measure of regulation and a set of basic control variables. Table 7.2 presents descriptive statistics of all variables used in the chapter.

The sample consists of 72–75 countries, depending on the regression exercise. In the largest sample, we have 22 developed and 53 developing countries, of which 21 belong to Latin America, 22 to Africa and the Middle East, and 10 to Asia. Country observations for each variable correspond to averages for the 1990s. We are constrained to this decade because internationally comparable regulation measures are available only for this period.

The dependent variables are defined as follows. Regarding economic growth, its measure is standard in the literature and is given by the average annual growth rate of real GDP per capita. For our second dependent variable—the size of the informal sector—there is no standard measure. To the contrary, there is much dispute as to what exactly the informal sector is, and this controversy naturally extends to all attempts to measure it (see Schneider and Enste 2000). The definition we use in this chapter identifies informality with the evasion of regulation. This definition is not only the most relevant, given the focus of the chapter, but it has also become the most popular since the seminal work by de Soto (1989). The informal sector thus defined is a shadow economy whose size is best represented as a latent variable. This is the approach taken by Schneider (2004) to provide estimates of the size of the informal sector—as production in percentage of GDP—for 145 countries for the period 2000–03.[8]

Schneider's study combines the DYMIMIC (dynamic multiple-indicators multiple-causes) method, the physical input (electricity) method, and the excess currency-demand approach for the estimation of the informal sector as a latent variable. More precisely, the informal sector comprises (non-criminal) economic activities that go undeclared specifically in order to avoid compliance with costly regulation (in particular employment protection laws), tax payments, and social security contributions. It therefore excludes criminal activities and home-based production. We use Schneider's estimates because, first, they are the most

[8] Loayza (1996) uses a similar approach for his estimates of the informal sector in Latin American countries.

Table 7.2. Descriptive statistics

Years: 1990–2003, 72–75 countries

Variable	Mean	Median	Standard deviation	Minimum	Maximum
(a) Univariate statistics					
Growth rate of GDP per capita (%)	1.53	1.78	1.67	−2.71	6.22
Informal sector output (% of GDP)	33.64	34.55	14.69	8.60	67.83
Log of GDP per capita in logs in 1990	7.83	7.60	1.61	4.98	10.74
Log of secondary enrollment rate in 1990	3.86	3.97	0.69	1.89	4.78
Log of private domestic credit/GDP in 1990	3.42	3.35	0.93	0.68	5.29
Overall regulation index	0.44	0.46	0.12	0.16	0.69
Product market regulation index	0.42	0.45	0.18	0.08	0.77
Fiscal regulation index	0.53	0.52	0.19	0.10	0.92
Labour regulation index	0.47	0.48	0.16	0.13	0.78
Governance index	0.52	0.46	0.26	0.05	1.00

	Growth rate of GDP per capita	Informal sector output (% of GDP)	Log of GDP per capita in logs in 1990	Log of secondary enrollment rate in 1990	Log of private domestic credit/GDP in 1990	Overall regulation index	Product market regulation index	Fiscal regulation index	Labour regulation index	Governance index
(b) Correlation coefficients between dependent variables, control variables, and regulation indices										
Growth rate of GDP per capita	1									
Informal sector output (% of GDP)	−0.32***	1								
Log of GDP per capita in logs in 1990	0.33***	−0.69***	1							
Log of secondary enrollment rate in 1990	0.40***	−0.55***	0.83***	1						
Log of private domestic credit/GDP in 1990	0.31***	−0.63***	0.73***	0.55***	1					
Overall regulation index	−0.41***	0.62***	−0.80***	−0.67***	−0.66***	1				
Product market regulation index	−0.42***	0.67***	−0.87***	−0.73***	−0.69***	0.97***	1			
Fiscal regulation index	0.17	−0.51***	0.49***	0.49***	0.41***	−0.31***	−0.49***	1		
Labour regulation index	−0.14	0.24**	−0.08	−0.11	−0.23**	0.42***	0.26**	−0.16	1	
Governance index	0.35***	−0.78***	0.86***	0.68***	0.65***	−0.80***	−0.86***	0.51***	−0.14	1

Notes: ** and *** denote significance at the 5% and 1% level, respectively.

Source: Authors' estimation.

comprehensive in terms of country coverage; second, they have been checked to ensure their robustness to different methodologies; and third, they are used by a number of other studies, which helps the comparability of our results. However, as with the measurement of any other latent variable, these estimates of the size of the informal sector should be considered with caution. They are likely to pick up a large amount of measurement error; and in the particular case of the DYMIMIC procedure, the estimates depend largely on the theoretical relation between the variable of interest and the indicators, which may be subject to debate. Although highly important and interesting, a detailed discussion of the estimation of the informal sector is beyond the scope of this chapter.

As described in the previous section, our explanatory variables of interest in the growth and informality regressions are indices that quantify a country's regulatory burden. We consider, in turn, the overall regulation index and its three main components—the product-market, labour, and fiscal regulation indices. In extensions to the basic specification, we interact the regulation index with a governance proxy, which as already noted is constructed from information on experts' perceptions on public accountability, absence of corruption, and rule of law, as reported by the International Country Risk Guide.

The set of control variables for the growth regressions is taken from the standard cross-country empirical growth literature. It consists of the initial level of per capita real GDP (to account for convergence effects), the initial rate of secondary enrollment (as proxy for human capital investment), the initial ratio of private domestic credit to GDP (to account for financial depth), and a sub-Saharan dummy variable (to control for the particular conditions of civil conflict, mismanagement, and disease affecting this region).[9] For the regressions of the size of the informal sector, the control set is quite parsimonious consisting only of initial real GDP per capita. Despite its parsimony, this variable summarizes most elements of economic development and is crucially important as a control, given its strong relationship with both informality and regulation (see, as illustration, the corresponding bivariate correlations in Table 7.2).

7.3.2 *Results and Discussion*

We start with a visual exercise. Figures 7.2 and 7.3 show scatter plots that represent the simple relationship between the regulation indices and,

[9] The 'Africa dummy' has a long tradition in empirical growth studies; see for example Easterly and Levine (1997).

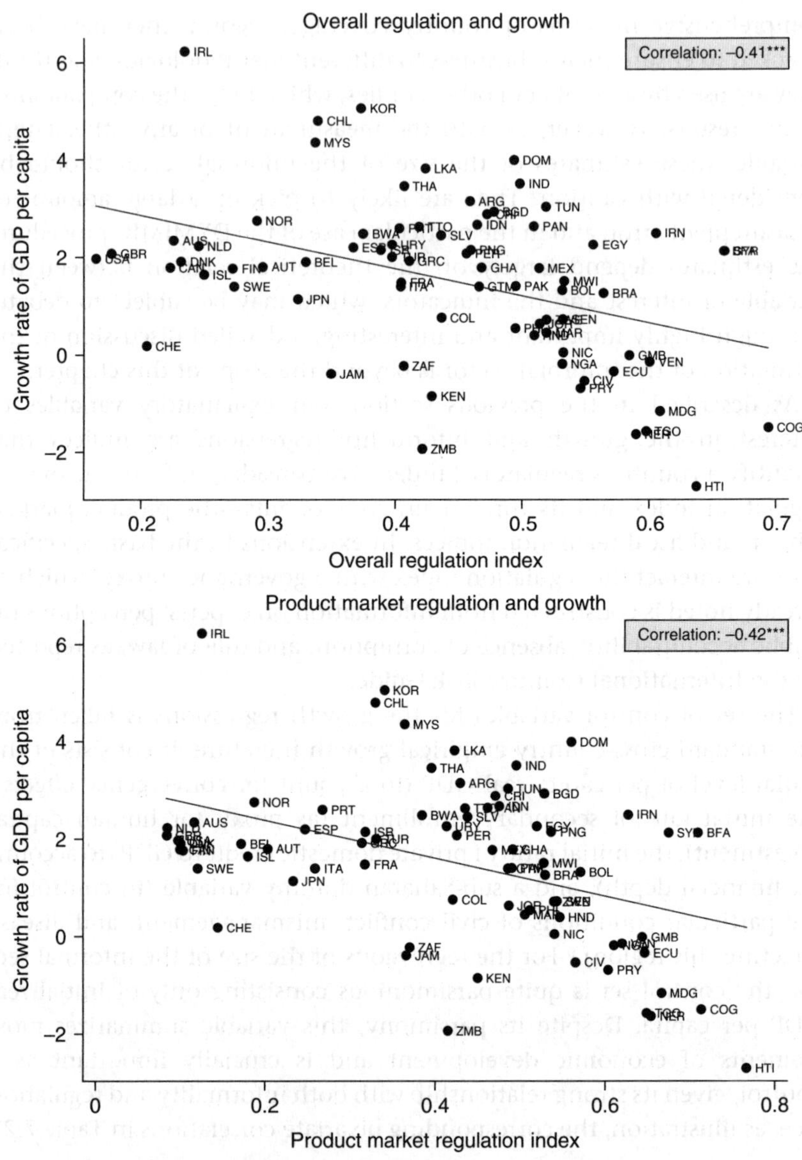

Figure 7.2. Growth of GDP per capita versus regulation indices

Note: ***denotes significance at the 1% level.

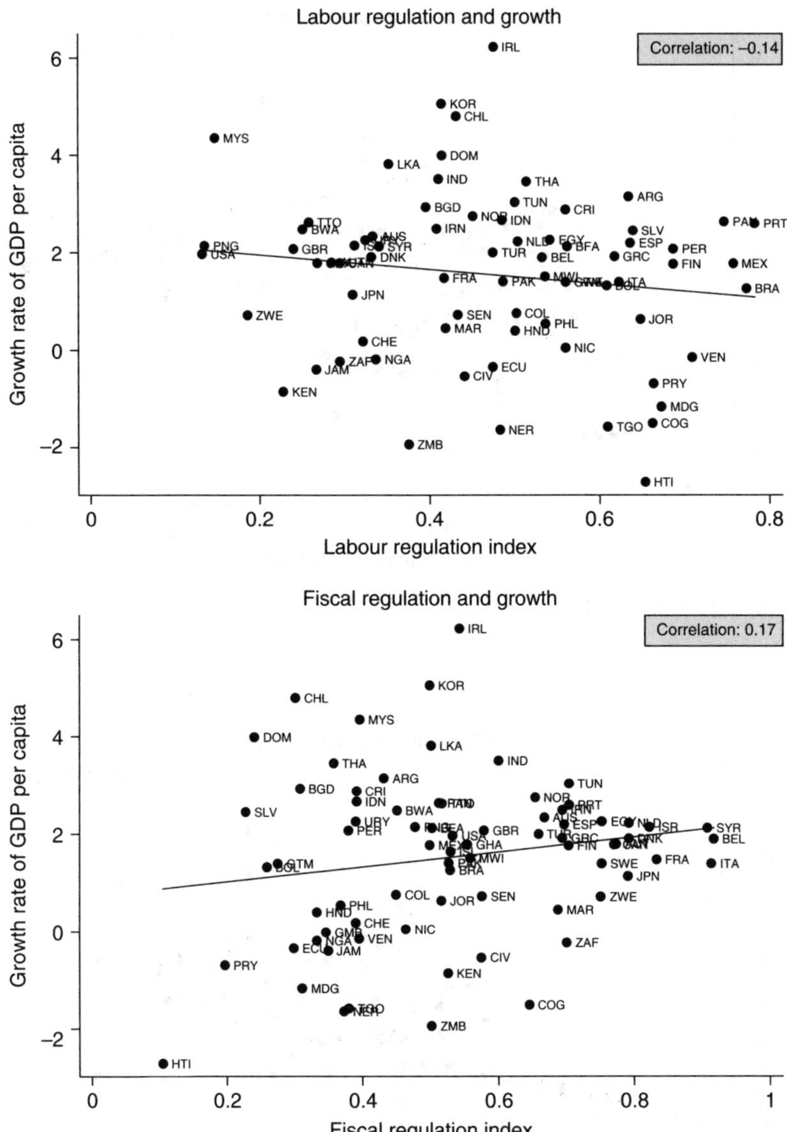

Figure 7.2. (*Continued*)

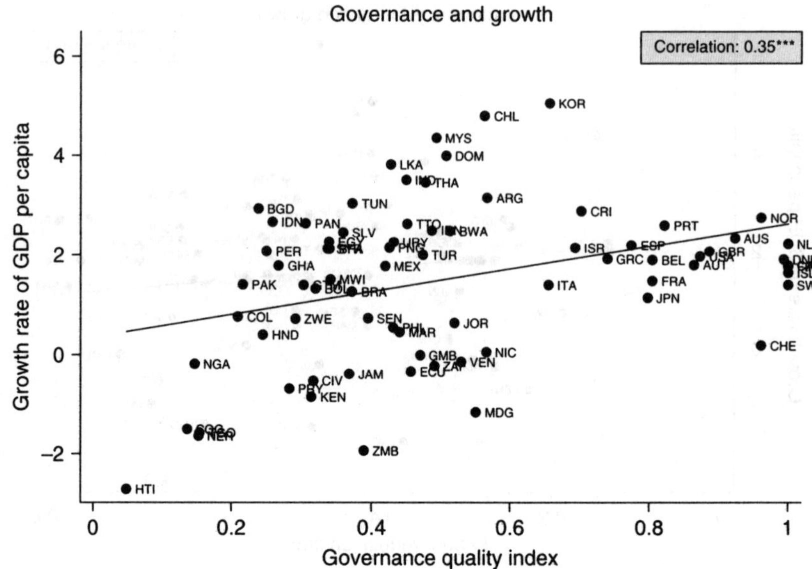

Figure 7.2. (*Continued*)

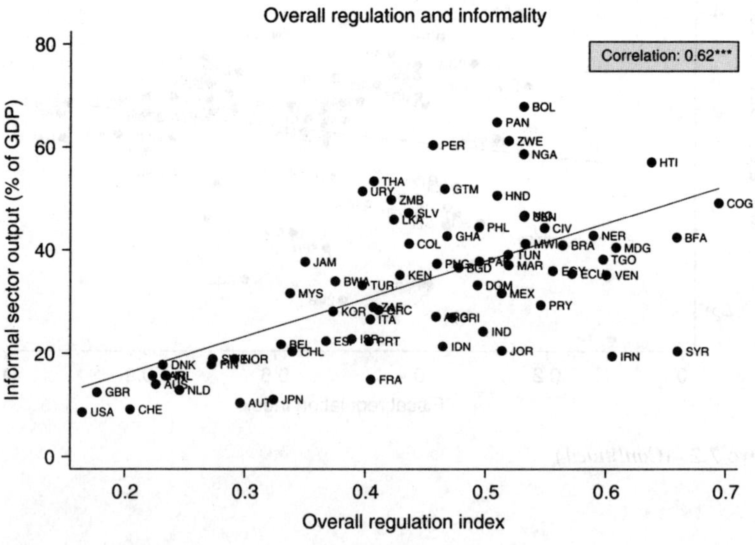

Figure 7.3. Informality versus regulation indices

Note: ** and *** denote significance at the 5% and 1% level respectively.

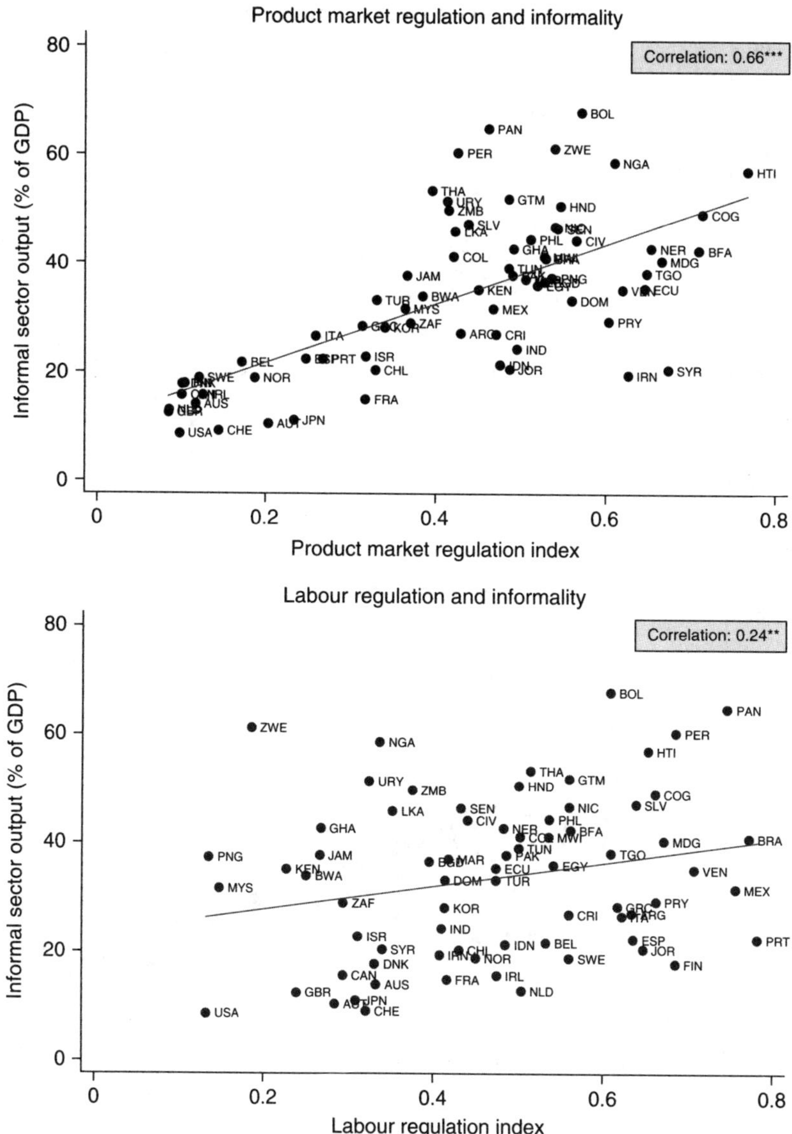

Figure 7.3. (*Continued*)

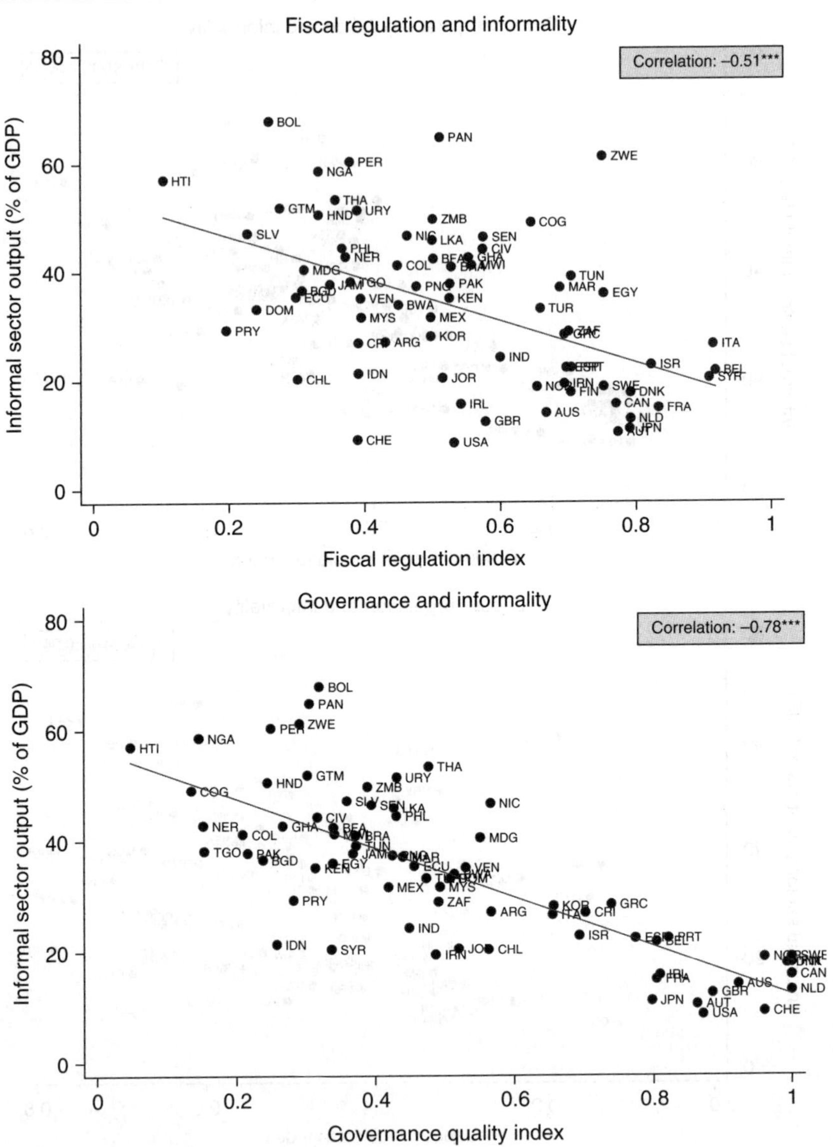

Figure 7.3. (*Continued*)

respectively, economic growth and the size of the informal sector. The graphs using overall regulation consistently suggest that more heavily regulated economies tend to grow less and be more informal. Observations reflecting poor economic growth, large informality, and high overall regulatory burden belong mostly to developing countries, while developed economies tend to occupy the other end of the distribution. These links with overall regulation seem to be driven by product market regulation and, to a lesser extent, labour regulation. Conversely, the connection with fiscal regulation appears to go in the opposite direction, so that economies with larger fiscal regulation show somewhat better economic growth and smaller informal sector. We shall see if the opposite behaviour of fiscal regulation survives the scrutiny of regression analysis. Finally, Figure 7.4 connects directly our two dependent variables, plotting per capita GDP growth against informal production (relative to GDP) for our cross-section of countries. The correlation coefficient is negative and significant, suggesting that countries where the relative size of the informal sector is larger tend to grow at a slower pace.

A more formal evaluation of the link between the regulation indices, growth, and informality requires multiple regression analysis, to which we turn now. As forewarned in the introduction, we should note that the

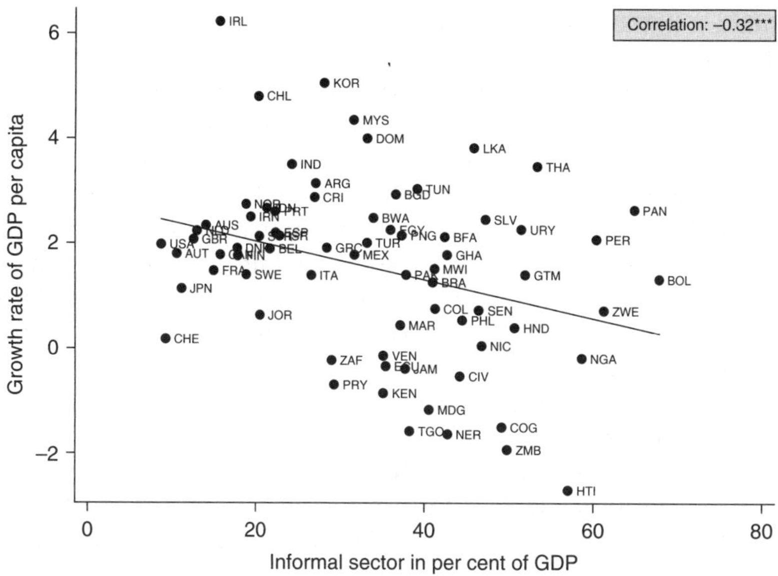

Figure 7.4. The informal economy and growth

Notes: *** denotes significance at the 1% level.

evidence we offer is only suggestive—and not definitive or detailed proof—of the causal links underlined in the theoretical discussion and the following empirical analysis. The regression results are organized in such a way that we first present the results on economic growth and then those on the relative size of the informal sector as dependent variables. For each of them we start with a basic specification where the effect of regulation is unrelated to governance. Then, we allow for the effects of regulation to vary with the quality of governance.[10]

Table 7.3 Panel (A) presents the basic specification results on economic growth. The overall index of regulation has a negative and significant association with economic growth, and so do the product market and labour regulation indices, while the index of fiscal regulation has no significant relation.

Panel (B) presents the estimation results when we allow for the effect of regulation on growth to vary with the quality of governance. The overall, product market, and labour regulation indices all carry significantly negative signs and their interaction terms with governance show a positive and significant coefficient. Thus, the negative association of these regulation indices with economic growth appears to be mitigated when the quality of governance rises. As to fiscal regulation, neither its direct coefficient nor the coefficient on the interaction term is statistically significant in the growth regression.

How large or economically important are the growth effects of regulation? Using the point estimates of the regression that accounts for governance interactions, we can perform some illustrative exercises. If a country's index of labour regulation were increased by one standard deviation in the cross-country sample (0.16) and its level of governance is equal to the world median (0.46), then its annual rate of per capita GDP growth would decrease by 0.3 percentage points. More remarkably, if a typical developing country were to decrease its product-market regulation to the median level of industrial countries (that is, from 0.51 to 0.17) while maintaining its level of governance (equal to the median of developing countries, 0.37), then its annual growth rate would rise by about 1.7 percentage points.

The point estimates of the coefficients are such that if the quality of governance is sufficiently high, the negative growth effect of an increase in regulation can be nearly cancelled. For product-market regulations this

[10] We also ran all regressions using a weighed least squares procedure, using the square root of the (log) of population for each country observation as weights. The results from these procedures are virtually the same as those presented.

Table 7.3. Economic growth and burden of regulation
Method of estimation: Ordinary least squares
Sample: 73–75 countries, 1990–2000
Dependent variable:
Economic growth: Average annual growth rate of GDP per capita, 1990–2000

	Type of regulation index			
	Overall [1]	Product Market [2]	Labour [3]	Fiscal [4]
Panel A: Basic specification				
Regulation	−5.71	−5.37	−1.71	0.75
(index ranging from 0 to 1, higher meaning more regulated)	−2.43	−2.67	−1.86	0.61
Control Variables:				
Initial GDP per capita	−0.52	−0.67	−0.17	−0.26
(in logs)	−2.22	−2.65	−0.78	−1.15
Initial education	0.53	0.46	0.47	0.52
(log of secondary enrollment rate in 1990)	1.23	1.14	1.02	1.03
Initial financial depth	0.22	0.22	0.24	0.34
(log of private domestic credit/GDP in 1990)	0.80	0.75	0.84	1.21
Sub-Saharan Africa dummy	−1.71	−1.80	−1.80	−1.71
(1 if country belongs to sub-Saharan Africa and 0 otherwise)	−3.59	−3.86	−3.53	−3.12
Constant	5.70	6.91	1.44	0.34
	2.78	3.03	1.06	0.24
No. of observations	75	75	73	75
R-squared	0.34	0.36	0.29	0.28
Panel (B): With governance interactions				
Regulation	−7.68	−7.70	−4.14	0.63
(index ranging from 0 to 1, higher meaning more regulated)	2.13	−3.69	−2.79	0.39
Governance–Regulation interaction	6.80	7.45	5.02	0.21
(Governance index * Regulation index) (Gov. index ranges from 0 to 1, higher meaning better governance)	2.13	2.64	2.31	0.12
Control Variables:				
Initial GDP per capita	−0.81	−0.87	−0.47	−0.28
(in logs)	−3.11	−3.51	−1.95	−0.92
Initial education	0.57	0.47	0.44	0.53
(log of secondary enrollment rate in 1990)	1.51	1.33	1.09	1.07
Initial financial depth	0.27	0.29	0.22	0.34
(log of private domestic credit/GDP in 1990)	0.86	0.90	0.68	1.20
Sub-Saharan Africa dummy	−1.71	−1.72	−1.94	−1.71
(1 if country belongs to sub-Saharan Africa and 0 otherwise)	−3.75	−3.78	−4.31	−3.09
Constant	7.10	7.83	3.98	0.46
	3.26	3.32	2.57	0.22
No. of observations	75	75	73	75
R-squared	0.39	0.43	0.35	0.28
P-value of Ho: sum of regulation coefficients = 0	0.79	0.92	0.52	0.57

Notes:
(a) Standard errors are robust to heteroscedasticity (Newey–West).
(b) t-Statistics are presented below the corresponding coefficient.
Source: Authors' estimation.

threshold level is quite high and could only be approximated by countries like Switzerland, Sweden, or Canada. For labour market regulations, the threshold is somewhat smaller and comparable to that of Ireland or Portugal.

We now turn to the regressions where the dependent variable is the relative size of the informal sector (in terms of informal production as percentage of GDP). Table 7.4 Panel (A) presents the basic specification

Table 7.4. Informality and burden of regulation
Method of estimation: Ordinary least squares
Sample: 72 countries, 1990–2003
Dependent variable:
Informal sector output (% of GDP), 2000–2003

	Type of regulation index			
	Overall [1]	Product market [2]	Labour [3]	Fiscal [4]
Panel (A): Basic specification				
Regulation	21.67	21.61	17.03	−16.62
(index ranging from 0 to 1, higher meaning more regulated)	1.39	1.74	2.10	−1.96
Initial GDP per capita	−5.04	−4.28	−6.25	−5.40
(in logs)	−4.65	−3.20	−10.08	−6.10
Constant	63.49	58.07	74.45	84.69
	4.32	3.80	10.37	15.83
No. of observations	72	72	72	72
R-squared	0.49	0.50	0.52	0.52
Panel (B): With governance interactions				
Regulation	41.21	37.87	39.39	7.73
(index ranging from 0 to 1, higher meaning more regulated)	2.55	2.87	3.51	0.63
Governance-Regulation interaction	−65.84	−50.16	−48.76	−42.91
(Governance index * Regulation index)	−3.37	−3.03	−3.74	−3.03
(Gov. index ranges from 0 to 1, higher meaning better governance)				
Control Variables:				
Initial GDP per capita	−2.52	−3.01	−3.31	−1.93
(in logs)	−1.93	−2.22	−3.09	−1.33
Constant	48.41	50.18	52.45	57.50
	3.28	3.38	5.13	5.53
No. of observations	72	72	72	72
R-squared	0.56	0.54	0.59	0.57
P-value of Ho: sum of regulation coefficients = 0	0.22	0.44	0.25	0.00

Notes:
(a) Standard errors are robust to heteroscedasticity (Newey–West).
(b) t-Statistics are presented below the corresponding coefficient.
Source: Authors' estimation.

results. The product-market and labour regulation indices carry positive and significant coefficients, suggesting that these types of regulation lead to more extensive informality. The coefficient on overall regulation is also positive but fails to be statistically significant. This weakened effect is apparently due to the inclusion of fiscal regulation in the overall index; indeed, fiscal regulation by itself carries a significantly negative coefficient. This last result may seem rather puzzling, and we return to it. Regarding the control variable, as expected, the level of income per capita carries a significantly negative coefficient. This indicates that, other things being equal, informality is more prevalent in poorer countries.

Panel (B) presents the results of the informality regressions when we include the interaction between regulation and governance as an additional explanatory variable. The coefficients on overall, product-market, and labour regulation indices are positive and statistically significant. Their corresponding interaction terms with the governance index carry a statistically negative coefficient. Taken together, these results have a similar interpretation as those related to the growth regression: For low levels of governance (implying poor regulatory quality), an increase in product-market or labour regulation leads to an expansion of the informal sector. As governance improves, the amplifying effect of these types of regulation on informality diminishes until it disappears. This happens at moderately high levels of governance, that is, the threshold value corresponding roughly to those of Greece, Spain, and Japan. Regarding fiscal regulation, its direct coefficient is positive, changing signs with respect to that in the basic specification; it, however, fails to be statistically significant, and now it is the interaction term with governance which carries a significantly negative coefficient. This indicates that for low levels of governance (up to those roughly corresponding to Colombia and Pakistan), the impact of fiscal regulation on the size of the informal sector is zero; but as governance improves, higher fiscal regulation actually leads to a reduction in informality. We can understand the puzzling negative relationship between fiscal regulation and informality by considering that the increase in fiscal burden not only makes evasion more attractive (which implies a positive relationship) but can also generate better public services and more resources for enforcing tax compliance (both of which make formality attractive). When governance is sufficiently good, the formality-inducing effect of fiscal regulation prevails.

As in the case of growth, we can use the estimated coefficients to ascertain how economically important the informality effects of regulation are. Using the point estimates of the regression that accounts for governance interactions, let's consider the changes in the size of the informal sector brought about by changes in labour and product-market regulations. If a country's index of labour regulation were increased by one standard deviation in the cross-country sample and its level of governance is equal to the world median, then the size of the informal sector relative to GDP would increase by nearly three percentage points. If a typical developing country decreased its product-market regulation to the median of industrial countries while keeping its level of governance, then its informal sector would decrease by close to seven percentage points of GDP.

7.4 Concluding Remarks

Regulation is becoming a core policy factor to explain the bottlenecks to economic growth in many countries around the world. Using a large sample of industrial and developing countries, this chapter provides an evaluation of the impact of business regulation on economic growth and informality.

Our regression analysis suggests that high levels of regulation are associated with lower growth. This is clearly the case for product and labour market regulation. However, the quality of regulation—as captured by the overall institutional framework—makes a big difference: in most instances we find that better institutions help mitigate, and even eliminate, the adverse impact of regulation on economic growth.

The literature indicates two main channels through which regulation can have a negative impact on economic growth. The first—and most popular—is the distortionary effect of regulation on the Schumpeterian process of firm dynamics. The second—to which we devote our attention in this chapter—is the incentive that regulation may create for firms to work outside the legal framework. We start an exploration of the informality channel by assessing the effect of regulation on the size of the informal sector (in terms of production relative to GDP). We find that an increase in either product-market or labour regulation leads to an expansion of informality. As in the case of growth, this pernicious effect is gradually mitigated as governance—and thus regulatory quality—improves. Fiscal regulation has a different effect on informality (which may explain why we do not find a clearly negative impact of fiscal regulation on economic growth): when the level of governance is not too low, an increase in fiscal regulation brings about a decrease in informality. This can be explained by considering that an increase in fiscal regulation not only makes evasion less attractive but can also generate better public services and more resources for enforcing tax compliance (which makes formality more attractive). Theoretically, analogous positive effects could also apply to other product-market and labour regulation, but they are not discernible in the cross-country sample we study.

Does the negative growth effect of regulations imply that they should be eliminated altogether? This chapter does not intend to assess the impact of regulation on social goals that could be beyond the strict sphere of economic growth—broad goals such as social equity and peace, or narrow ones such as worker safety, environmental conservation, and civil security, which typically motivate specific regulations. Thus, our conclusions on the role of regulation must necessarily be evaluated in a more comprehensive context before drawing definitive social welfare implications. At any rate, to the extent that economic growth is quite an important goal, our findings imply that streamlining regulation and strengthening governance in highly regulated countries could have a significant payoff.

References

Claessens, S. and L. Klapper (2002). 'Bankruptcy Around the World: Explanations of its Relative Use'. World Bank Working Paper No. 2865. Washington, DC: World Bank.

de Soto, H. (1989). *The Other Path: The Invisible Revolution in the Third World.* New York: Harper and Row.

Djankov, S., R. La Porta, F. López-de-Silanes, and A. Shleifer (2002). 'The Regulation of Entry'. *Quarterly Journal of Economics,* 117: 1–37.

Doing Business. Washington, DC: World Bank. http://rru.worldbank.org/doingbusiness. Accessed 22 March 2006.

Easterly, W. and R. Levine (1997). 'Africa's Growth Tragedy'. *Quarterly Journal of Economics,* 112: 1203–50.

Gerxhani, K. (2004). 'The Informal Sector in Developed and Less Developed Countries: A Literature Survey'. *Public Choice,* 120: 267–300.

International Country Risk Guide—*ICRG, Brief Guide to the Rating System,* ICRG (1999) http://www.icrgonline.com. Accessed 22 March 2006.

KPMG, Corporate Tax Rate Survey, March 1998–January 2003.

Loayza, N. (1996). 'The Economics of the Informal Sector: A Simple Model and Some Empirical Evidence from Latin America'. *Carnegie-Rochester Conference Series on Public Policy,* 45: 129–62.

Loayza, N., A. M. Oviedo, and L. Servén (2005a). 'Regulation and Macroeconomic Performance'. World Bank Policy Research Working Paper No. 3469, Washington, DC: World Bank.

Loayza, N., A. M. Oviedo, and L. Servén (2005b). 'Regulation and Firm Dynamics'. Mimeo. Washington, DC: World Bank.

Maloney, W. (2004). 'Informality Revisited'. *World Development*, 32(7): 1159–78.

Nicoletti, G., S. Scarpetta, and O. Boylaud (2000). 'Summary Indicators of Product Market Regulation With an Extension to Employment Protection Legislation'. Economics Department Working Paper No. 226. Paris: OECD.

O'Driscoll, G., E. Feulner, and M. O'Grady (2003). *Index of Economic Freedom*. The Heritage Foundation and The Wall Street Journal.

Rama, M. and R. Artecona (2002). 'A Database of Labor Market Indicators Across Countries'. Unpublished. Washington, DC: World Bank.

Schneider, F. (2004). 'The Size of the Shadow Economies of 145 Countries all over the World: First Results over the Period 1999 to 2003'. IZA DP No. 1431.

Schneider, F. and D. H. Enste (2000). 'Shadow Economies: Size, Causes, and Consequences'. *Journal of Economc Literature*, 38: 77–114.

8

Financial liberalization in Vietnam: impact on loans from informal, formal, and semi-formal providers

Robert Lensink, Mark McGillivray, and Pham Thi Thu Trà

8.1 Introduction

Since 1986 Vietnam has gone through a process of economic reforms—a so-called *doimoi*. One of the targets of this transformation is to build a strong and efficient financial system that can play an active role in mobilizing resources and allocating them to investments. The financial sector has been diversified in terms of type, size, and ownership. In 1988–89 the government initiated banking reforms that transformed the mono-bank system into a two-tier banking system including the State Bank of Vietnam (SBV, henceforth) and a system of commercial banks. During the 1990s, the government stimulated the entry of new players into the financial sector. This policy led to a substantial increase in the number of joint-stock commercial banks as well as branches of foreign banks and joint-venture banks. Non-bank financial institutions, such as finance and insurance companies, have also come to exist. The stock market establishment in July 2000 is still elementary. In line with other developing economies, Vietnam also has a vibrant informal financial sector, in the form of, for example, moneylenders and rotating savings and credit associations (ROSCA), and a substantial semi-formal financial sector.

The authors are grateful to Basudeb Guha-Khasnobis and the conference participants for many useful comments and to Anne Ruohonen for invaluable editorial support. The usual disclaimer applies.

The most important financial sector reform in Vietnam took place in 1995. Since 1995, commercial banks are allowed to freely set deposit rates to enhance competition in raising funds. In the literature on financial liberalizations, the effectiveness of interest rate deregulations is an important point of discussion. The standard references are McKinnon (1973) and Shaw (1973) who are strongly in favour of interest rate deregulations. They argue that interest rate deregulations will lead to an increase in savings, and consequently higher investments. There are, however, also several papers by so-called neostructuralists, in which it is argued that financial liberalization may not be that positive. An important reason for this may be the existence of an informal financial sector. It may then be the case that the increase in savings in the formal financial sector is nullified by a decrease in savings in the informal financial sector, so that the total supply of funds will stay constant or may even decline (see e.g. Van Wijnbergen 1983a, b; Buffie 1984). Bencivenga and Smith (1992), who plea for financial liberalizations, show that the neostructuralists' results hold if financial liberalization is not expansionary.

This chapter contributes to the small empirical evidence on the effectiveness of financial reforms in the presence of informal lenders. We take a closer look at financial liberalizations in Vietnam by presenting a descriptive survey of the main liberalizations. Moreover, and more importantly, we examine to what extent the interest rate deregulations have affected loans from formal, informal and semi-formal lenders. We perform a descriptive analysis to compare some key characteristics of borrowing and savings activities pre and post-financial reforms, using the *Vietnam Living Standard Surveys* of 1992/93 and 1997/98. In addition, we conduct an econometric analysis of the determinants of loans from different types of lenders, and examine to what extent this has been affected by the financial reforms.

8.2 The Financial System in Vietnam and the Financial Liberalizations

8.2.1 *Overview of the Vietnamese Financial System*

The Vietnamese financial system can be divided into formal, informal, and semi-formal financial sectors. In September 2002 the formal financial sector contained:

(1) 4 state-owned commercial banks (SOCBs);
(2) 36 joint-stock banks (JSBs);

(3) 60 branches and representative offices of 27 foreign banks;
(4) 4 joint-venture banks (JVBs);
(5) 9 financial lease companies (FLCs);
(6) a lesser number of securities and insurance companies; and
(7) one stock exchange, established in July 2000 in Ho Chi Minh city.

The informal sector contained:

(1) moneylenders, relatives, friends, and neighbours;
(2) rotating savings and credit associations (ROSCA); and
(3) agricultural input shopkeepers.

The semi-formal sector contained:

(1) Vietnam Bank for the Poor (VBP) (currently known as the Vietnam Bank for Social Policy (VBSP));
(2) credit operatives;
(3) various national development programmes (such as the poverty alleviation programme and the job creation programme); and
(4) savings and credit schemes supported by NGOs and donors.

The formal financial sector is characterized by the dominance of SOCBs. They account for more than 70 per cent of the total assets of the whole system. Not surprisingly, SOCBs dominate the credit market with 73.5 per cent of total lending to the economy as of 2002 (ADB 2003). The dominance is also mirrored in the mobilization of funds where the SOCBs captured 76 per cent of all resources mobilized through formal institutions. In addition, SOCBs have advantages in providing banking services and credit to customers, given their better technical equipment, highly qualified staff, and better means of communication. The main customers of SOCBs are the state-owned enterprises (SOEs) which contribute 75 per cent of the economic output and hold 53 per cent of the banks' loans (*Vietnam Investment Review* 2003). The heavy credit concentration on SOEs exposed SOCBs to a high credit risk due to great volumes of bad loans and soft budget constraint problems. In addition, this lending policy effectively crowded out the private sector, which comprises primarily small and medium-sized enterprises and individual households. Recently, SOCBs have been more inclined to shift their loan portfolio to household borrowing in line with the policy of boosting the private sector.

JSBs are supposed to fill the gap in serving the private sector. However, their position appears to be modest. Despite a considerable growth in number, JSBs were exposed to high competition and high risk due to their characteristics: low capital base, a small number of branches, inadequate banking services and, concentration in two host business centres. With 15 per cent of the lending market, JSBs primarily serve the private sector, particularly local businesses and small enterprises. However, rapid loan growth and weak capacity to assess credit risk could result in non-performing loan problems, and JSBs may not have adequate access to external sources of recapitalization.

Foreign banks in Vietnam are far from becoming full fledged participants in the Vietnamese financial sector due to the current regulatory structures and costly acquisition of information. As a result, they are mainly engaged in lending to foreign-invested enterprises.

In general, SOCBs tend to keep their traditional trend in lending. Loans to SOEs capture a high share of total loan portfolio. However, SOCBs have recently exerted efforts to shift their credit focus to the private sector, especially SMEs (small to medium enterprises) and households. JSBs concentrate on SME lending and individual consumers whereas JVBs primarily serve foreign-owned firms and joint-ventures. The formal sector appears to be underdeveloped and cannot fully serve the credit needs of the economy.

In developing countries, informal financial sectors exist mainly because of the underdevelopment of the formal financial sector. Likewise, Vietnam has a relatively large informal financial sector. It is, however, difficult to exactly measure the size of this sector in terms of financial services provided. The informal financial sector in Vietnam is estimated to account for around 60–70 per cent of total credit in the early 1990s. As implied, the major actors of the informal financial sector include moneylenders, relatives, friends, rotating savings and credit associations (ROSCA), and agricultural input shopkeepers.

Moneylenders are usually wealthy families who live in the communities or villages where their clients reside. This gives moneylenders an advantage in acquiring intimate knowledge about clients. As a result, they often do not need any collateral but have mutual trust. Loans can be made in both cash and kind, typically of short duration and at enormously high interest rates.

Households in Vietnam also rely on a credit source coming from relatives and friends, and neighbours. An interest free loan is typically provided if a household suffers from difficulties due to for example, disease or floods, or if a household is facing a major event such as a wedding or building a house.

Another alternative of informal credit comes from ROSCAs, which are known in Vietnam as *hois* in the North and *huis* in the South. Like other forms of ROSCA, a *hoi/hui* refers to a setting in which a group of individuals who know and trust each other get together to formulate simultaneously the saving and the borrowing process. *Hois/huis* are a way of circumventing the difficulties in getting access to other sources of finance in Vietnam. According to an estimate, around 60 per cent of credit in the urban areas was provided by *hois/huis* (*Far Eastern Economic Review*, 4 March 1993).

Agricultural input shopkeepers are currently a very popular form of rural credit in Vietnam. Lenders are agricultural input shopkeepers. They sell agricultural input such as pesticides, fertilizers, and seeds on credit, and receive payment after the harvest. Interest rates vary, depending on the relationship between buyers and shopkeepers.

Generally, all forms of the informal credit sector currently fill in part of the credit gap left by the formal credit sector. Although they are subject to resource constraints, high default risks, and the lack of legal protection, they continue to play a role in the Vietnamese financial system, especially serving individuals, households, and small private enterprises.

The semi-formal financial sector is important in Vietnam, providing subsidized credit to target groups of borrowers. By 2002, as a dominant actor in the semi-formal sector, VBP has offered credit at a substantial outreach, totalling US$452 million, to some 2.7 million households (World Bank 2002a). In March 2003, VBP has been recognized as a new policy bank, Vietnam Bank for Social Policy (VBSP).

8.2.2 *Financial Liberalization*[1]

In the wave of *doimoi*, the financial sector also went through a number of remarkable reforms. This section highlights the major aspects of the financial sector reforms and anticipates the impact on the development of the formal and informal financial sectors.

Following the establishment of a two-tiered banking system in 1988–89, a number of banking reforms have been carried out. Notably, banking regulations have been improved in both content and form to support the more distant supervision and inspection. With the main focus on recapitalization and resolving non-performance, restructuring of the commercial banks has made considerable progress. Most commercial banks have greatly increased their chartered capital. As officially estimated by the World Bank, more than 43 per cent of all non-performing loans of

[1] Information presented in this sub-section is taken from World Bank (2002a,b and 2003).

the banking system have been worked out, bringing the ratio of non-performing loans in total outstanding loans from 12.7 per cent (31 December 2000) to 5 per cent (31 December 2002). Gradually, policy-oriented lending is separated from the commercial credit in SOCBs.

As a core issue of the financial sector reforms, interest rate liberalization commenced in 1995 and went through various key steps. From 1990, the SBV imposed a ceiling on lending rates for both domestic and foreign currency loans, discriminating by sectors. That is, different ceilings were applied to loans for agriculture, industry, and trading and services. Different deposit rates were set for households and firms as well.

In 1993, the discrimination in lending rates between sectors was abolished, but lending rates still varied across working capital loans and fixed capital loans. However, the lending rates on fixed capital loans were lower than on working capital loans, creating a reversed structure of interest rates. This policy discouraged banks from making long-term loans.

From 1995, the SBV allowed commercial banks to freely set deposit rates to enhance competition in raising funds. However, the maximum spread between lending rates and deposit rates allowed was 0.35 per cent per month given that the SBV continuously maintained a ceiling on lending rates. The primary reason for keeping interest rate ceilings was to restrict adverse selection, or prevent the banks from over-increasing deposit rates, and then using the funds raised in risky lending. Despite a certain deregulation in deposit rates, the persistence on a ceiling-based lending rate continued to discourage formal lenders from extending small loans to the rural poor and low-income households, due to high transaction costs for small loans.

Under the 1997 Asian financial crisis, the Vietnamese banking sector started to suffer a strong (though indirect) impact on the quality of bank assets. In other words, many borrowing firms fell into difficulty due to decreased income, export, and FDI (foreign direct investment) growth, making it tricky for their loans to be collected. On the other hand, the SBV did not tighten interest rate controls in 1997 and early 1998, rather, it relaxed them. Interest rate ceilings were raised so that commercial banks, especially JSBs, were able to increase deposit rates in 1997. As a response to this policy, the 1998–99 period witnessed an explosion in domestic credit in the economy through the banking system. The government's domestic credit promotion policy aimed at two objectives: (i) helping the SOEs sustain production and employment in a difficult period; and (ii) implementing an investment stimulation policy (instead of undertaking structural reforms) with the hope that income growth would recover. As a matter of fact, the 1998–99 expansionary credit policy did not stimulate economic growth, given that the growth rates slowed down from 5.8 per cent in 1998 to 4.8 per cent in 1999.

The year 2000 was marked by a number of further reforms concerning the interest rate policy. In August 2000, the SBV adopted a new interest rate mechanism in which the domestic currency lending rates offered by commercial banks could be adjusted according to a base interest rate announced by SBV. However, lending rates charged by commercial banks were not allowed to exceed the base interest rate plus 0.3 per cent per month for short-term loans or 0.5 per cent for medium and long-term loans.

Moving towards a full interest rate liberalization, the lending rate ceiling on foreign currency loans was abolished in November 2001. Since then domestic borrowers in foreign currencies have been allowed to negotiate interest rates with domestic and foreign banks. Interest rates were entirely liberalized in June 2002. Banks are now free to set lending rates conditional upon their own appraisal and negotiation with their customers including firms and individuals. With the official liberalization of interest rates, the base interest rate announced by the SBV has become just a reference.

8.3 The Dataset and a Descriptive Analysis of the Impact of Interest Rate Deregulations

8.3.1 *The Dataset*

Our data are drawn from two surveys on living standards in Vietnam, namely the *Vietnam Living Standard Surveys—VLSS* 1992/93 and *VLSS* 1997/98. The first survey was conducted in 1992/93 by the State Planning Committee, known now as the Ministry of Planning and Investment and the General Statistical Office (GSO). The second was conducted by the GSO in 1997/98. Both surveys were funded by UNDP and Swedish International Development Cooperation Agency (Sida) and supported with technical assistance from the World Bank.

VLSS 1992/93 covered a sample of 4,799 households, of which, 3,839 were rural households, accounting for 80 per cent of the overall sample. *VLSS* 1997/98 was designed to provide up-to-date data on households. It covered a sample of 6,002 households, including all households surveyed in 1992/93. The proportion of rural households was 71.1 per cent (4,269 households).

Both surveys include information on households: household expenditures and consumption; educational level of the household's members;

health, fertility, and nutrition; employment and earnings; demography including migration; housing and durable assets; agricultural activities; non-agricultural self-employment; credit and saving, and general community characteristics. For our research objectives, we focus on the financing activities, that is, borrowing and saving of households. The dataset provides information on 3,837 and 5,851 households engaged in financing activities in 1992/93 and 1997/98, respectively. Among them, 2,728 households are present in both years. Our sample sketches an interesting picture of household borrowing and savings in Vietnam regarding the sources of credit, contract characteristics, and borrower-related characteristics. We define formal credit as credit supplied by the private and government commercial banks. The providers of informal credit include private moneylenders, relatives, revolving credit associations, and other individuals. The source of semi-formal credit refers to the VBP, credit cooperatives, poverty alleviation programmes, job creation programmes, and other development programmes. Similarly, informal savings refer to the amount of lending by households to relatives and friends. Formal savings of a household take one of the three following forms: real savings, liquidity savings, and financial savings.

8.3.2 *Descriptive Statistics on the Quantity Effects of the Interest Rate Deregulation*

Figure 8.1 and Table 8.1 depict some key characteristics of the financing activities in the periods before and after the interest rate deregulation. As shown in Figure 8.1, the year 1998 was marked with a substantial increase in both credit extension and savings compared to the year 1993, suggesting positive effects of the interest rate deregulation. The supply of funds from all lenders increased. The same holds for savings in the formal and informal financial sectors (we do not have information on savings in the semi-formal sector).

In both years, the informal sectors captured the largest share in household borrowing, making up 73.96 per cent and 52.73 per cent in 1993 and 1998, respectively. This reflects the important role of the informal sector in the Vietnamese credit market. In contrast, the informal sector appears minor in savings activities, given the small portion of 13 per cent and 14 per cent of total savings in 1993 and 1998, respectively.

Table 8.1 also indicates the differences among the three financial sectors in terms of loan size, loan interest rate, loan maturity, and savings. While these figures do not reveal a strong disparity in credit volume between

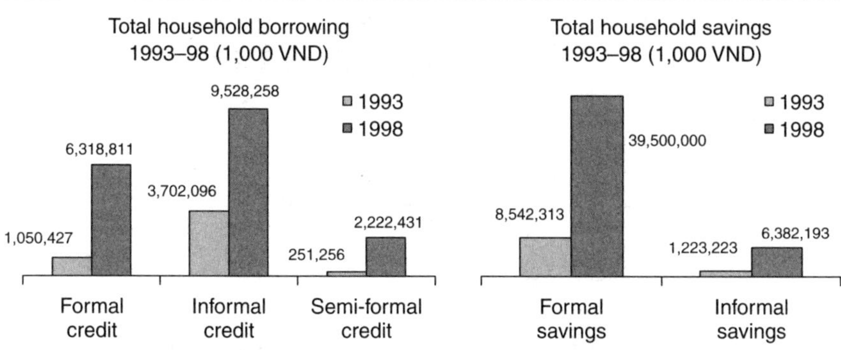

Figure 8.1. Household financing activities in 1993 and 1998

different credit providers, they represent substantial increases in an average amount of borrowing per household over time. By comparing medians, the average loan size is only slightly higher for formal sources than informal sources of credit, and the loan size of semi-formal credit remains at the lowest level in both years. Concerning the loan interest rate of borrowing cost, one can see the divergence of loan interest rates with respect to three credit sources and the remarkable decline over time. Interest rates are considerably lower for formal loans and semi-formal loans than for informal loans. Household savings also increase in time with respect to both formal and informal sectors. On average, informal savings/household is lower than formal savings/household in 1993 and reaches a comparable level in 1998.

Table 8.2 illustrates the access to credit of different sources in 1993 and 1998. Although the proportion of access to credit of the overall survey remains relatively stable over time, the complete access to formal credit has increased considerably, from 16.99 per cent in 1993 to 28.27 per cent in 1998. Regarding the other two financial sectors, we can also observe some transformation in credit. It appears that households tend to shift their loans from informal sources to semi-formal sources of finance. Whereas the complete access to informal credit has decreased dramatically from 61.74 per cent in 1993 to 37.19 per cent in 1998, the complete access to semi-formal credit has gone up from 5.21 per cent in 1993 to 16.22 per cent in 1998.

8.4 Econometric Analysis and Empirical Results

Our interest now turns to econometrically estimating key borrowing behavioural relationships and the impact of liberalization on household

Table 8.1. Key characteristics of household financing in 1993 and 1998

	Size of loan/household (1000 VND)			Loan interest rate/household (%/month)			Loan maturity (months)	Savings/household (1000 VND)	
	Formal credit	Informal credit	Semi-formal credit	Formal credit	Informal credit	Semi-formal credit		Formal	Informal
1992/93									
Mean	1,526.78	2,046.49	934.04	2.69	8.12	2.55	9.98	3,691.58	1,550.35
Median	635.00	500.00	250.00	2.50	7.00	2.10	6.00	830.00	500.00
Max	80,000.00	1,150,000.00	20,000.00	31.0	32.50	8.00	185.00	1,001,000.00	50,000.00
Min	16.00	2.00	1.00	0.03	0.03	0.09	0.50	1.00	20.00
SD	4,543.76	27,215.06	2,667.25	2.80	5.54	1.69	12.74	27,718.71	3,586.86
1997/98									
Mean	5,345.86	5,966.35	3,036.11	0.99	3.92	0.89	17.15	7,121.39	7,661.70
Median	3,000.00	2,000.00	1,500.00	1.20	3.00	0.80	12.00	1,050.00	2,000.00
Max	100,000.00	215,000.00	650,000.00	2.85	20.00	6.00	371.00	1,069,000.00	252,000.00
Min	100.00	2.00	70.00	0.01	0.07	0.01	1.00	–	40.00
SD	8,914.91	16,185.16	24,095.08	0.46	3.48	0.55	16.80	34,696.29	22,593.68

Table 8.2. Access to credit of different sources

	1993		1998	
	No. of households	%	No. of households	%
% access to credit of total households in survey	–	49.18	–	49.10
Access to credit	2360	100	2947	100
Complete access to formal credit	401	16.99	833	28.27
Partial access to formal of which	287	12.16	349	11.84
Access to formal and informal	233	9.87	286	9.70
Access to formal and semi-formal	27	1.14	39	1.32
Access to all the three	27	1.14	24	0.81
Non access to formal of which	1672	70.85	1765	59.89
Complete access to informal credit	1457	61.74	1096	37.19
Complete access to semi-formal credit	123	5.21	478	16.22
Access to informal and semi-formal credit	92	3.9	191	6.48

borrowing behaviour in Vietnam. Cognizant of the data provided by the *VLSS*, our current objectives are therefore, confined to modelling household borrowing from providers in the informal, formal, and semi-formal sectors. We are in particular interested in the impacts of Vietnam's financial sector liberalization on this borrowing. We therefore posit the following reduced-form loan functions:

$$B_{f,i} = \alpha_0 + \alpha'_1 s_i + \alpha_2 y_i + \alpha'_3 c_i + \alpha'_4 h_i + \alpha'_5 l_i + \mu_i; \tag{8.1}$$

$$B_{n,i} = \beta_0 + \beta'_1 s_i + \beta_2 y_i + \beta'_3 c_i + \beta'_4 h_i + \beta'_5 l_i + \varepsilon_i; \tag{8.2}$$

$$B_{s,i} = \gamma_0 + \gamma'_1 s_i + \gamma_2 y_i + \gamma'_3 c_i + \gamma'_4 h_i + \gamma'_5 l_i + v_i; \quad \text{and} \tag{8.3}$$

$$B_{o,i} = \delta_0 + \delta'_1 s_i + \delta_2 y_i + \delta'_3 c_i + \delta'_4 h_i + \delta'_5 l_i + \upsilon_i. \tag{8.4}$$

$B_{f,i}$, $B_{n,i}$, $B_{s,i}$ are the level of household *i*'s borrowing from the formal, informal, and semi-formal sectors, respectively, and $B_{o,i}$ is other borrowing of this household. s_i is a vector of variables measuring the amount of savings, y_i is income (proxied by expenditure), c_i is vector of measures of the amount of collateral, and h_i is a vector of household characteristics, each for household *i*. l_i is a vector of financial sector liberalization variables, capturing differences between the pre- and post-liberalization periods, as they apply to household *i*. Each of these variables is treated as exogenous. α_0, β_0, γ_0, and δ_0 are constants and the remaining αs, βs, γs, and δs are slope coefficients, showing the relationship between each category of borrowing and their respective empirical determinants captured within equations (8.1) to (8.4). μ_i, ϵ_i, ν_i and υ_i are residual terms and $i = 1, \ldots, j$. Equations (8.1) to (8.4) do not contain interest rate variables. While there might be a case for treating formal sector interest rates during the pre-liberalization period as exogenous, we believe, on balance, that interest rates in all sectors are endogenous. Thus we depart from the assumption of our illustrative model. Since equations (8.1) to (8.4) are defined as reduced-forms (a necessary treatment—given the data at our disposal), we exclude all interest rates from these equations.

It is reasonable to assume that the amount of borrowing that household i obtains from one sector will be linked to the amount it borrows from other sectors. If that be the case, it follows that $B_{f,i}$, $B_{n,i}$, $B_{s,i}$, and $B_{o,i}$ will be jointly determined. This in turn will mean that the residual terms of (8.1) to (8.4) will be correlated. It is well-established in the econometrics literature that failing to account for this correlation in the estimation of the equations in question, will yield inefficient estimates of the standard errors for each slope coefficient. As a result, the corresponding t ratios will be underestimated and erroneous conclusions will be drawn. Equations (8.1) to (8.4) need, therefore, to be treated as a system and estimated simultaneously (equation (8.4) is the omitted equation). An appropriate estimation method, given that we treat the variables on the right hand side of (8.1) to (8.4) as exogenous, is the well-known Zellner Seemingly Unrelated Regressions (SUR) approach. This method is still valid even if the dependent variables are not jointly determined.

Equations (8.1) to (8.3) were estimated using either the 1993 survey data alone, the 1998 survey data alone and using combined or pooled 1993 and 1998 data. The savings variable vector s_i contains i's financial savings and liquidity savings as separate variables. The collateral variable c_i contains the value of i's durable assets and predicated house value as separate variables. The vector of household characteristics h_i contains the following variables: the gender of the household head, the age of the household head, whether the household is a farm household, and the household size defined by the number of family members living in the house.[2] The gender, marital status, and farm status are each binary dummy variables. The financial liberalization vector l_i, used only in the estimates obtained from the combined 1993 and 1998 data, consists of a number of variables. The first is a financial liberalization dummy variable taking the value of

[2] Careful consideration was given to including a measure of land ownership in the collateral vector c_i and interacting that variable with the liberalization dummy. While one might expect that land ownership would, in general, increase credit availability, there is strong anecdotal evidence to suggest that this is not the case in Vietnam.

one for 1998 and zero for 1993. It serves as an intercept dummy, and plays an important role in our econometrics, exploring further the effects of the liberalization on household borrowing. This dummy picks up the effects on borrowing of exogenous changes in the levels of the variables on the right hand side of equations (8.1) to (8.3). The liberalization, if resulting in higher interest rates, could increase household savings then, this will increase one or more of the constants in our equations. The liberalization dummy empirically captures such effects. We attribute these changes to the financial liberalization, but of course acknowledge that there could be many other causes. The remaining variables are interactive variables. They have been obtained by taking the liberalization dummy and multiplying it by the above-mentioned non-binary variables. These variables capture changes in the responsiveness of borrowing to these variables between the pre- and post-liberalization periods, evident from changes in their respective slope coefficients.

These results are shown in Table 8.3. Our main interest concerns the coefficient attached to the liberalization dummy, $\alpha_{5,1}$, $\beta_{5,1}$, and $\gamma_{5,1}$. The descriptive statistics shown in Section 8.3 reveal an increase in formal, informal, and semi-formal borrowing, following Vietnam's financial liberalization. What does our econometric analysis tell us? It tells us that the introduction of the financial liberalization programme increased the level of household borrowing from the informal sector. This conclusion is based on the significance of $\beta_{5,1}$, obtained from fitting the informal sector borrowing equation to the combined 1993 and 1998 dataset. Such an effect is not observed for the other borrowing categories, as $\alpha_{5,1}$ and $\gamma_{5,1}$ are statistically insignificant.

Another feature of our results is that, while a number of parameters appear not to be significantly different from zero when estimated using 1993 data, the opposite appears to be the case when estimated using the 1998 data. For example, the parameters attached to the financial savings, house value, household size, and farm status variables are significantly different from zero in 1998, but not in 1993. Behavioural relationships appear to have altered between the two periods, and this might be due to liberalization. We formally test for this, through the inclusion of the above mentioned interaction variables in the equations fitted to the combined 1993 and 1998 data. These interactive variables model for changes in behaviourial relationships, evident from changes in slope coefficients, due to the introduction of the liberalization programme. They are constructed by multiplying the chosen dependent variable by the liberalization dummy.

Table 8.3. SUR estimation results

		Formal sector loans			Informal sector loans			Semi-formal sector loans		
		1993	1998	1993 and 1998	1993	1998	1993 and 1998	1993	1998	1993 and 1998
Constant	(α_0, β_0, orγ_0)	−706.28	−1960.30	−1252.42	−1937.54	3176.36	−750.20	−81.38	−5499.5*	−2804.35
		(−0.65)	(−0.23)	(−1.05)	(−0.32)	(1.10)	(−0.27)	(−0.38)	(−2.33)	(−1.46)
Financial savings	($\alpha_{1,1}$, $\beta_{1,1}$, or$\gamma_{1,1}$)	−0.04	−0.03*	−0.03	−0.20	0.07*	−0.22	−0.01	0.87*	−0.00
		(−0.94)	(2.01)	(−0.40)	(−0.88)	(2.07)	(−1.12)	(−1.17)	(30.68)	(−0.03)
Liquid savings	($\alpha_{1,2}$, $\beta_{1,2}$, or$\gamma_{1,2}$)	−0.05	0.34*	−0.06	18.51*	0.47*	18.46*	−0.01	0.06	−0.02
		(−0.69)	(16.57)	(−0.43)	(50.65)	(11.42)	(58.68)	(−0.80)	(1.63)	(−0.07)
Income	(α_2, β_2, orγ_2)	0.16*	0.03	0.16*	0.16	0.37*	0.17*	−0.01*	−0.23*	−0.01
		(9.26)	(1.58)	(4.38)	(1.68)	(11.28)	(2.04)	(−1.97)	(−8.80)	(−0.20)
Durable assets	($\alpha_{3,1}$, $\beta_{3,1}$, or$\gamma_{3,1}$)	0.07*	0.84*	0.06	−0.34*	−0.41*	−0.32*	0.02,*	−0.34*	−0.00
		(2.93)	(14.44)	(1.20)	(−2.60)	(−3.54)	(−2.84)	(4.45)	(−3.56)	(−0.05)
House value	($\alpha_{3,2}$, $\beta_{3,2}$, or$\gamma_{3,2}$)	−1.63	−11.54*	−1–14	106.74*	35.27*	106.52*	−0.07	103.69*	0.89
		(−0.73)	(−4.71)	(−0.24)	(8.62)	(7.17)	(9.97)	(−0.16)	(25.79)	(0.12)
Gender	($\alpha_{4,1}$, $\beta_{4,1}$, or$\gamma_{4,1}$)	135.10	261.19	273.32	4807.89*	662.68	1584.12*	46.45	588.97	545.35
		(0.49)	(0.75)	(0.99)	(3.16)	(0.95)	(2.49)	(0.86)	(1.04)	(1.23)
Age	($\alpha_{4,2}$, $\beta_{4,2}$, or$\gamma_{4,2}$)	−59.13	54.04	27.42	−91.92	−56.01	−41.13	2.71	102.84	71.13
		(−1.20)	(0.89)	(0.57)	(−0.34)	(−0.46)	(−0.37)	(0.28)	(1.04)	(0.92)
Age^2	($\alpha_{4,3}$, $\beta_{4,3}$, or $\gamma_{4,3}$)	0.69	−0.59	−0.30	1.36	0.95	0.12	−0.03	−0.93	−0.64
		(1.35)	(−0.97)	(−0.61)	(0.48)	(0.08)	(0.11)	(−0.27)	(−0.93)	(−0.82)
Marital status	($\alpha_{4,4}$, $\beta_{4,4}$, or $\gamma_{4,4}$)	−31.86	−304.07	−264.73	−4101.5*	−1469.90	−2170.0*	16.06	142.90	108.88
		(−0.09)	(−0.73)	(−0.79)	(−2.18)	(−1.76)	(−2.82)	(0.24)	(0.21)	(0.20)
Household size	($\alpha_{4,5}$, $\beta_{4,5}$, or $\gamma_{4,5}$)	32.25	204.10*	659.13*	−262.34	−396.64*	−131.14	−2.74	283.27*	−56.77
		(0.67)	(3.13)	(3.35)	(−0.99)	(−3.03)	(−0.61)	(−0.29)	(2.65)	(0.37)

Farm	($\alpha_{4,6}$, $\beta_{4,6}$, or $\gamma_{4,6}$)	−53.97	606.21*	15.27	536.87	−1018.4*	−737.39	59.50	1900.68*	1493.62*
		(−0.27)	(2.68)	(0.16)	(0.48)	(−2.07)	(−1.63)	(1.51)	(4.72)	(4.74)
Liberalization	($\alpha_{5,1}$, $\beta_{5,1}$, or $\gamma_{5,1}$)			46.96			2924.54*			−1606.30
				(−0.08)			(2.06)			(−1.63)
Liberalization-financial savings	($\alpha_{5,2}$, $\beta_{5,2}$, or $\gamma_{,5,2}$)			0.00			0.29			0.88*
				(0.01)			(1.45)			(6.23)
Liberalization-liquid savings	($\alpha_{5,3}$, $\beta_{5,3}$, or $\gamma_{5,3}$)			0.40*			−17.99*			0.07
				(2.91)			(−56.65)			(0.33)
Liberalization-income	($\alpha_{5,4}$, $\beta_{5,4}$, or $\gamma_{5,4}$)			−0.13*			0.20*			−0.23*
				(−3.45)			(2.23)			(−3.61)
Liberalization-durable assets	($\alpha_{5,5}$, $\beta_{5,5}$, or $\gamma_{5,5}$)			0.78*			−0.09			−0.34*
				(10.84)			(−0.56)			(−2.90)
Liberalization-house value	($\alpha_{5,6}$, $\beta_{5,6}$, or $\gamma_{5,6}$)			−10.83*			−70.50*			102.00*
				(−2.11)			(−5.96)			(12.40)
Liberalization-household size	($\alpha_{5,7}$, $\beta_{5,7}$, or $\gamma_{5,7}$)			196.77			−286.66			359.96*
				(1.79)			(−1.13)			(2.05)
N		688	2663	3351	688	2663	3351	688	2663	3351
R^2		0.18	0.24	0.24	0.90	0.23	0.73	0.04	0.47	0.47
X^2		150.16*	828.17*	1078.34*	6355.61*	783.20*	9175.21*	27.90*	783.20*	956.7*
B–P Test		6.79*	195.99*	184.86*	6.79*	195.99*	184.86*	6.79*	195.99*	184.86*

Note:
* denotes significant at the 95 per cent level or greater. Numbers in parentheses are *t*-ratios.

Evidence of statistically significant structural or behavioural changes is shown for all categories of borrowing under consideration. These changes occur, for at least one of the borrowing categories, with respect to financial savings, income, durable assets, house value, and household size. These changes are however, not uniform. For instance, prior to or in absence of liberalization, there appears to be a positive relationship between income and borrowing in both the formal and informal sectors. This is based on the estimates of α_2 and β_2, both of which are positive and statistically significant. The positive relationship between income and informal sector borrowing remains after liberalization, given $\beta_{5,4}$ is positive and significant. Moreover, since $\beta_{5,4}$ is slightly higher in value than β_2 (0.20 compared to 0.16), informal sector borrowing appears slightly more responsive to income levels in a liberalized environment. Quite different results were obtained for formal sector borrowing, with its relationship with income becoming negative after the financial liberalization. This is evident from the estimated value of $\alpha_{5,4}$, which is negative and significantly different from zero. A possible reason for this is that, households with lower incomes have turned to the formal sector after the liberalization.

Finally, we note that our assumption, that borrowing decisions are linked, and thus that the error terms of equations (8.1) and (8.4) are cross-correlated, appears valid. This is based on the Breush–Pagan (B–P) Test shown in Table 8.3. It tests for the independence of these error terms. The null hypothesis (of zero dependence) is rejected in all instances. The use of the SUR modelling approach appears valid, therefore.

8.5 Conclusion

This chapter surveys financial sector liberalization in Vietnam during the 1990s. Using the *VLSS* 92/93 and 97/98, we compare loans from providers in the formal, informal and semi-formal sectors. We first show, in a descriptive analysis, that loans from all three sectors increased after liberalization—that is, household loan amounts in 1998 are higher than in 1993. These results are consistent with the view that financial liberalization has positive quantity effects. To further examine the quantity effects of financial liberalization, we simultaneously estimate the parameters of a system of reduced-form borrowing (loan amount) equations using econometric methods. These equations allow for changes in behavioural relationships due to financial liberalization. They also allow for the detection of direct effects of this liberalization on loan amounts, after controlling for a range of other effects. Evidence in support of the view that financial liberalization changes borrowing amounts was presented, with informal sector borrowing being higher after liberalization. There is an element of 'voting with feet' implicit to this result. That is, borrowers have responded to the liberalization by 'walking towards' the informal sector. Our econometric results show no evidence of borrowers 'walking away' from the formal sector, although implicit to these results is a decrease in the relative importance of the formal sector owing to the liberalization. Evidence of diverse change in a number of behavioural relationships, consistent with the financial liberalization, was also presented.

Finally, a brief word on future research is warranted. The data provided in the *Vietnam Living Standard Surveys* of 1993 and 1998 can facilitate much more investigation of borrowing behaviour. More exploration of these data for this purpose would appear to be warranted, including further econometric work. The fact that the amount of borrowing a household obtains from one sector, will be linked to the amount it borrows from other sectors, does very much complicate further econometric analysis. In particular, it requires a systems estimation approach and this does limit what can be done. There is still room, however, for further econometric research on a range of issues relating to household borrowing. We highlight three possible directions for future research. The first is to treat interest rates not as endogenous, as the current paper has, but to treat them as exogenous. Ultimately the status of these variables should not rest on an assumption, but on actual empirical testing. The second is to model the ratio of formal to informal borrowing, formal to semi-formal borrowing and so on, testing *inter alia* whether these ratios have changed over time, especially between the pre- and post-liberalization periods. The third is to test for differences in household borrowing behaviour between Vietnam's regions, or between farm and non-farm borrowers. In particular, it is not beyond the realms of imagination to posit that liberalization will have had a non-uniform impact on borrowing behaviour across these regions, or indeed that in certain regions these reforms have had little or no impact on such behaviour. This chapter has made a start at modelling household borrowing using *VLSS*; subsequent research could pick up this mantel and run with it further.

References

Asian Development Bank (ADB) (2003). *Key Indicators 2003: Education for Global Participation*. Manila: Asian Development Bank.

Bencivenga, V. R. and B. D. Smith (1992). 'Deficits, Inflation and the Banking System in Developing Countries: The Optimal Degree of Financial Repression'. *Oxford Economic Papers*, 44: 767–90.

Buffie, E. F. (1984). 'Financial Repression, The New Structuralists, and Stabilization Polices in Semi-Industrialized Economies'. *Journal of Development Economics*, 14: 305–22.

Far Eastern Economic Review (1993). 4 March.

McKinnon, R. (1973). *Money and Capital in Economic Development*. Washington, DC: Brookings Institute.

Shaw, E. (1973). *Financial Deepening in Economic Development*. New York: Oxford University Press.

Van Wijnbergen, S. (1983a). 'Credit Policy, Inflation and Growth in a Financially Repressed Economy'. *Journal of Development Economics*, 13: 45–65.

Van Wijnbergen, S. (1983b). 'Interest Rate Management in LDCs'. *Journal of Monetary Economics*, 18: 433–52.

Vietnam Investment Review (2003). 21 August.

World Bank (2002a). *Vietnam Development Report 2002*. Washington, DC: World Bank.

World Bank (2002b). *Banking Sector Review: Vietnam*. Washington, DC: World Bank.

World Bank (2003). *Vietnam Development Report 2003*. Washington, DC: World Bank.

9

Blocking human potential: how formal policies block the informal economy in the maputo corridor*

Fredrik Söderbaum

9.1 Introduction

This chapter deals with one of the most interesting cross-border regions in Africa, the Maputo corridor. The aim is to relate the formal policies of the much-talked about Maputo Development Corridor (MDC) with the underlying informal social fabric of the corridor, in order to determine whether the formal project blocks or unlocks the human potential, inherent in the informal economy of the micro-region.

There are many different views about the nature and impact of the informal economy and its linkages to the formal sector and policies. The study rests on three general points of departure; first, that the informal economy constitutes an important part of African reality and deserves more attention; second, that sometimes the informal economy provides opportunities for development, but that under certain conditions it is also detrimental; and, third, that the linkages between the formal sector and the informal economy are complex, and should therefore not be generalized and determined *a priori*. It is undisputed that many parts of Africa are characterized by myriads of informal and non-institutional interactions and activities between a mosaic of informal workers and self-employed agents, families, business networks, petty traders, migrant labour, refugees, and so forth. In fact, the size of the informal economy in

* Thanks to the Swedish International Development Cooperation Agency (Sida) for generous research support, and to an anonymous reviewer for constructive comments.

Africa relative to the formal economy is the highest in the world. Furthermore, informal employment as a percentage of non-agricultural employment is about three quarters in large parts of Africa, including Mozambique, but for South Africa it is just over 20 per cent (ILO 2002, Table 2.1). The informal sector's GDP is nearly half of total non-agricultural GDP in sub-Saharan Africa, and much higher with agriculture included, and for the informal economy as a whole. In 1994, informal sector's GDP as a percentage of total non-agricultural GDP was almost 40 per cent for Mozambique (ILO 2002: 22).

The Maputo corridor is a particularly relevant case for studying how the formal and the informal economy impact and relate to one another. There is a long history and strength of the informal economy in the area. In fact, the Maputo corridor has been an informal cross-border micro-region for more than a century, constructed by millions of migrants, extensive informal trading as well as dense socio-ethnic interactions. Since the mid-1990s, there is a formal project in the making, officially known as the MDC, which seeks to reconstruct and revitalize this rather informal cross-border relationship that effectively has existed for more than a century. The MDC is seen as a key component of the economic development policy in this part of Africa, built as it is around private investment in infrastructure and industry. Its architects believe that the remaking of this territorial space offers considerable opportunities for diminishing the spatial and social imbalances created during the apartheid era in particular, emphasizing instead the mutuality of benefits that can be realized and for reaping the benefits of globalization. What makes the case of the Maputo corridor particularly relevant for the purposes of this volume is the fact that, whereas there is an intense debate on how the MDC impacts on the formal economy, there is silence concerning the linkages and effects on the informal economy. Given the size and importance of the informal economy, especially in Mozambique, this is a critical issue well worthy of further scrutiny.

The analysis proceeds as follows. Section 9.2 outlines the informal and historical corridor, which is centred on labour migration and informal trade. Section 9.3 describes the objectives, institutions, and planning strategies of the formal MDC initiative. In Section 9.4, the formal policies are analysed in regard to how they relate and impact on the informal economy, and to what extent the former contribute to unlocking human potential of the latter. A conclusion summarizes the main points and also discusses ways and policy options whereby the formal and informal can become mutually reinforcing.

9.2 The Informal Corridor

The Maputo corridor covers the eastern part of the Republic of South Africa, the northern part of Swaziland, and southern Mozambique, and has constituted a 'real' regional space for the last two centuries. Migrant labour and informal trade are the key components of this corridor.

Since far back in history there exists a migratory tradition in Africa, *inter alia* documented by the spread of people of Bantu origin to cover all of southern Africa. This migratory pattern created new ethnicities, social and cultural structures and spaces, as well as more bureaucratic and organized political entities than the previously co-existing smaller chiefdoms, for instance the Shangans and the Empire of Gaza in Mozambique. The migratory pattern extended all the way to the frontiers of current Malawi, but it has also particularly concentrated around the Maputo 'corridor' (in a broad sense). These migrations of indigenous people were followed by the *voortrekkers*, the Dutch-speaking descendants of the European settlers in the Cape, which together marks the beginning of the creation of southern Africa as a region.

From the late nineteenth century, there was also a pattern of migration from south of the Save River in Mozambique to work on the plantations in KwaZulu-Natal and the diamond mines in Kimberley. After the so-called pacification campaign carried out by Portugal in Mozambique in 1895, the colonial powers in Mozambique and Transvaal signed the first accord to regulate the afflux of labour to the mines in Transvaal in 1897. In return for the right to recruit black labour in southern Mozambique, almost half of the export traffic from the Witwatersrand in South Africa was directed through the port of Lorenco Marques, present-day Maputo (Taylor 1999: 4). The migrant and export linkage rested on the transport spine, which together consolidated the Maputo corridor. In addition to this, later in the century hundreds of thousands of white tourists annually went to visit Mozambique.

Throughout the twentieth century, there was a steady flow of migrant labour along the corridor, from Mozambique to South Africa, and also from Lesotho, Swaziland, and Botswana, and in the past, significant numbers also from Malawi and Zimbabwe. A considerable portion of the miners have always originated from Mozambique, although the figures have fluctuated substantially over time, for reasons such as the apartheid regime's infamous 'carrot and stick' strategy. For instance, in January 1976, substantially more than a hundred thousand miners came from Mozambique, but at the end of the year this number had decreased by more than half. The number remained about approximately 30–40,000 from the mid-1970s to the mid-1980s, and then increased again by about 50 per cent only a few years later (Davies 1990). Regulated labour migration has decreased in the 1990s for all involved countries. In 1996, there was approximately a total of 340,000 formal labour migrants in South Africa (Niemann 1998). But this has not implied an end to migration, which has increased for purposes other than mining and formal contracts. There are now an estimated number of between one to three million so-called 'illegal aliens' in South Africa, many of whom come from Mozambique.

For more than a hundred years labour migration has constituted part of the ritual of passage to adulthood in southern Mozambique. In general most migrants are not settling permanently in South Africa. In fact, in the countryside of the provinces of Inhambane, Gaza, and Maputo, there exists a 'migrant culture', whereby young males are supposed to migrate to work in South Africa and stay away sufficiently long enough to accumulate enough money to be able to buy a house, pay the brideswealth and get married (Lundin and Söderbaum 2002). The migratory patterns and other cultural and socioeconomic linkages have gradually transformed social life and resulted in a dramatic increase of imported goods. Goods are sent to the family in rural zones, where, even at present, the miner is recognized when back home to visit or returning to stay longer, for instance by the clothing and special manners acquired from compound-life.

Of the Mozambicans who do not manage to get work in the mines, many are seeking agricultural work at plantations around KwaZulu-Natal, Mpumalanga and the Northern Province. These migrants can either be legal or illegal, but often they tend to 'crowd out' South African workers, since they are willing to work for lower wages and poor working conditions compared to the South African workforce. Other Mozambicans are engaged in a rich mix of informal trade or selling on the streets of Johannesburg, or small towns in Mpumalanga and Gauteng, often 'illegally' without proper documents.

The second main facet of the informal Maputo corridor is the extensive amount of informal trading. This has increased during the last few decades, above all, when the socialist experience was abandoned in

Mozambique and the old safety net provided by the state gradually disappeared as a consequence of structural adjustment and economic reforms. This implied that many men and women left the traditional occupation of agriculture and embraced the market sector for commerce and petty trade in the cities. The informal market expanded in Maputo, throughout the country and also to neighbouring countries. This marks the beginning of the institution of *mukhero*, informal trading of all types of goods, vegetables, fruits, clothes, and small home appliances along the Maputo corridor (Lundin and Söderbaum 2002). Initially, it was mainly a question of acquiring agricultural products to supply a market in need, because the situation of war had cut off Maputo from the countryside. Agricultural products were brought in from other parts of Mozambique and sold in Maputo, and revenues were used to buy goods in South Africa and Swaziland and other neighbouring countries, which were then brought to the informal market in Maputo. Subsequently, other products have been incorporated into the *mukhero*. This movement and trading has created a never-ending circle of new types of business, hawking, trading, and interaction, increasing the flux of people along the corridor. In this way, Maputo attracts people from all over Mozambique and sometimes even from other neighbouring countries. Many people stay in Maputo and take part in the informal market activities. Often this requires being engaged in a regular or daily informal cross-border trade.

Although several of the mainly female traders are ending up building viable business enterprises, the *mukhero* constitutes a basic and small-scale survival strategy. In the words of one *mukherist*:

> none of us hold a valid passport or visa, we cross the border under the fence. We have special arrangements with some officers, 'we pay and they don't see us'. However, the agreement is not always respected because many times we pay and they catch us anyway. When that is so we have no choice other than either to pay again, many times with sexual services to more than one of them, or to loose our goods risking also being arrested. *Mukhero* is not an easy business, but as far as I see it is at the moment the only alternative for us to survive (quoted in Lundin and Taylor 2003: 99).

Various attempts have been made to regulate and control borders, smuggling, informal trading, hawking, and migration, but people have often found other ways to get around these restrictions. The movement has decreased from time to time, but the city of Maputo continues to be supplied with all types of goods from neighbouring countries and other imports acquired from or via South Africa.

9.3 The Formal MDC Initiative

The MDC has become known as the 'flagship' of the Spatial Development Initiative (SDI) programme. The SDIs programme was launched by the central government in South Africa in 1995 as targeted and short-term interventions in order to facilitate global competitiveness, access to global capital, infrastructural development, and job creation in areas which have unrealized economic potential due to a range of historical and political reasons (Jourdan 1998: 718). This has resulted in the implementation of a substantial number of SDIs in South Africa, and more recently also in the broader southern African region (see Söderbaum and Taylor 2003; and www.africansdi.com).

The basic idea behind the MDC initiative is the implementation of a large number of private investment projects and public–private partnerships (PPPs). A rough distinction can be made between infrastructural projects and the major economic development projects. With regard to the rehabilitation of primary infrastructure, the following projects, with a total estimated value of US$661.5 million, were of crucial importance. Firstly, the Witbank-Maputo N4 toll road. This was the first major PPP in southern Africa. Other projects included the rehabilitation of the port of Maputo, the establishment of a public/private company to manage, operate, and maintain the southern Mozambique rail network, and a single facility/one-stop border post at Ressano Garcia/Komatipoort.

The most comprehensive economic development projects, the so-called 'mega-projects', include the US$1.3 billion Mozambique Aluminium Smelter (Mozal), which in the second phase was supplemented, making it worth a total of more than US$2 billion in investment (Hentz 2003). The Maputo Iron and Steel Project (MISP) (US$1.5 billion) and the Pande/Temane gas pipeline (US$250 million) are among the most important. In addition to these gigantic projects there are a significant number of other investment projects included in the MDC's investment portfolio, in fields such as mining, energy, chemicals, manufacturing, agriculture, forestry, commerce, and tourism (de Beer and Arkwright 2003). It needs saying that many of the smaller private investment projects included in the portfolio were merely wishes and will never materialize, whereas on the other hand, other projects may be added along the way. It is also important to underline that the investment projects must be commercially viable, and depend solely on private rather than public financing. The main role of the public sector and the institutional structure of the MDC is to promote and fast-track implementation of the private investment projects—a characteristic which negatively impacts on the informal economy (see more below).

Although each SDI has to adjust to the different conditions under which it operates, there is a generalized 'SDI methodology'.[1] According to this methodology, the institutional structure should be kept to a minimum. The initial phases of planning and project implementation are driven by a loose and fluid network consisting of the political champions, central government institutions, the different line departments (mainly transport, trade, and industry), the project manager, and the technical teams. An important task of the project manager is to identify local 'champions' and stakeholders in order to provide the programme with legitimacy, and to ensure that there is an organization that can secure implementation upon the decentralization of functions to provincial and local authorities, particularly their investment promotion agencies, whose main brief is to facilitate new investment in the region (Jourdan 1998). An important component in the decentralization phase (or 'exit strategy' as it is officially called) is the establishment of clusters for selected sectors in the MDC area, which is supposed to bring firms across the supply chain together, in order to promote their collective efficiencies and various types of upstream and downstream linkages, in the economies in the corridor area.

9.4 The MDC and the Informal Economy

When analysing the links between the formal policies of the MDC and the informal economy, it is important to recognize that the MDC is based not only on infrastructural development and large industrial investment projects, but officially also contains a third and a fourth objective: to maximize social development, employment opportunities, and the participation of historically disadvantaged communities; and to ensure a holistic, participatory, and environmentally sustainable approach to development. These objectives are supposed to be promoted by the 'cluster' processes mentioned above, and various types of support programmes, such as a strategic environmental management plan (SEMP); local economic development (LED); and institution building (de Beer and Arkwright 2003).

[1] See Söderbaum and Taylor (2003) and Söderbaum (2004) for a detailed account of the key institutions and agents in the institutional landscape surrounding the MDC.

This is a rather promising point of departure as far as the large masses of people living in the corridor and engaged in the informal economy are concerned. The problem is that in sharp contrast to the stated objectives, the 'actually existing' MDC is heavily geared towards infrastructural development and the implementation of gigantic industrial investment projects, with the result that the broader developmental objectives and the support programmes claimed to enhance social development, employment, and participation have not received much attention. There is hardly any emphasis on, and very little financial resources devoted to, a people-centred development path. As a matter of fact, economic development is assumed, rather naively, to be created through the crowding in of global capital to mega-projects and there is no strategy to mobilize and utilize the human resources and entrepreneurship inherent in the informal economy.

Needless to say, with a total stated investment portfolio valued at more than US$7 billion, all the mega-projects in the MDC are bound to have enormous direct and indirect effects on the economy as a whole. Mozal is clearly the most important of all the investment projects, so it can be seen as a test-case of whether it is unlocking or blocking human potential. A recent assessment shows that, other things equal, Mozal contributes directly and indirectly to more than 3 per cent to Mozambique's GDP (up to 5 per cent when construction is included); to nearly half of Mozambique's total manufacturing output; and that in 2003 Mozal's net trade gains alone may reduce Mozambique's trade deficit by about one quarter (Castel-Branco and Goldin 2003: 6, 8, 11). Given that we are talking about a single company, this is a dramatic contribution to the economy.

Mozal's links to the domestic economy are crucial in order to assess whether it unlocks human potential. The opportunity cost and relative efficiency of implementing such a capital-intensive mega-project in one of the poorest countries in the world is certainly problematic. Thus, mega-projects such as Mozal can be questioned not merely by their extreme size and capital-intensity, but also by the fact that they have only limited effect on permanent employment opportunities. Mozal in itself creates only just over 1,000 jobs (excluding the construction phase) and then another 400 indirect jobs in related firms and in the Mozal Community Development Trust (MCDT). In addition, there are an additional 2,000 jobs through contractors and subcontractors on-site at Mozal (Castel-Branco and Goldin 2003: 32). Thus, one of the more important weaknesses of Mozal is that there is no evidence of a sharp increase in new employment opportunities.

A related problem is that the links to firms in the domestic economy are too few, and result primarily from foreign firms (mainly South African) that have relocated to Mozambique, or formed partnerships between foreign and Mozambican firms (Castel-Branco and Goldin 2003: 6). In addition, almost 50 per cent of Mozal's purchases in Mozambique is water and energy, which has little spread effect on the Mozambican domestic economy. Hence, there are few linkages to other Mozambican firms, one important reason being that they lack the capacity and experience to deal with a world-class multinational corporation such as Mozal. This means that the much-talked about downstream linkages in the economy are still to be seen. 'At this time... one cannot even forecast the dynamics of potential downstream production in Mozambique because there are not... concrete data and projects to look at... no concrete projects have been proposed' (Castel-Branco and Goldin 2003: 21).

According to Castel-Branco and Goldin (2003: 10), 'Mozal's ability to be a growth engine is short lived'. In an interview in August 2004, Carlos Nuno Castel-Branco, a Mozambican professor in economics and the most well-known analyst of the Mozal, concluded that 'Mozal is by far the most professional and best company that has ever operated in Mozambique, but it represents the worst possible development strategy for the country'. This means that the main problem is not Mozal in itself, but the fact that Mozambique's economic development strategy is obsessed with the mega-projects. This strategy is designed for serving foreign and 'big business', with exclusionary effects on most people living in the corridor, and with very little positive links to the informal economy. There are many problematic aspects of this industrialization strategy, such as, the Mozambican economy is too weak and fragmented to be able to absorb the mega-projects, that the mega-projects are insufficiently employment-intensive, and they are overly focused on capital-intensive industrialization instead of agriculture which is the poor's primary income source.

According to formal policies of the MDC and two of its most important projects, the Mozal and the N4 toll road, it is as if there is no informal economy in Mozambique or that it is an impediment to development rather than a resource which needs to be promoted and reconciled with formal policies. The negligence of the informal economy—which constitutes between half and two-thirds of the total economy in Mozambique—can be seen in the gigantic financial resources devoted to large investment and infrastructure projects with only a small fraction devoted to local development and community participation, and hardly anything that targets the informal economy in itself. But even if a few million US$ out of a multi-billion US$ MDC investment portfolio are earmarked for local development and local communities, it is perhaps even more problematic that the funds are focused on formal businesses and initiatives very closely linked to the interests of the agents controlling the mega-projects, such as small business training (for suppliers to the mega-projects), malaria programme (because many employees are infected with malaria), a local school (in the community situated around Mozal) or the creation of a Mozal football club (www.mozal.com/). In other words, there are hardly any formal policies or initiatives that targets the informal economy as such or seeks to unlock the human potential vested in it.

Hence, the MDC is designed first and foremost for 'big business' in the formal sector, and above all from South Africa and further afield, rather than the masses of people engaged in the informal economy along the corridor. What this means is that all effort is devoted to trying to make the formal economy grow through external investment capital and 'commercially viable solutions' and not by reconciling the formal and informal economy as part of an economic development strategy.

A key component in the MDC strategy is to build so-called PPPs, which are mechanisms for involving the private sector and broadening the ownership base, especially in order to enhance the delivery of infrastructure. The point of departure of this strategy is that when the public sector has difficulty raising funds for investment in infrastructure, with PPPs 'the private sector can play an active role in financing, managing and maintaining large infrastructure projects that would traditionally have been seen as purely the public sector's responsibility' (Driver 1999: 18). The Witbank-Maputo N4 toll road is the most comprehensive PPP within the MDC project. It is certainly a risky strategy when conventional state functions and investment projects are being privatized and must be 'commercially viable' and profitable in order to stand the test of being implemented. But such market solution favours the strongest actors in the formal economy and hurts the weakest segments of society disproportionally. The toll road places a big financial burden on poor people and informal traders using the corridor. With no alternative route available, small-scale traders, informal businesses, and hawkers are losing out in the competition with large-scale and organized traders and businesses, especially from Gauteng and South Africa more generally.

In the MDC, local participation occurs on a rather arbitrary basis or under favourable conditions and it is not an integral part of the strategy as such. That is, the SDI methodology, and the MDC in particular, is founded on a capital-intensive, 'big business' and top-down development strategy, with the real intention of increasing export growth and foreign exchange rather than people-centred development and unlocking human potential of the informal sector. The so-called holistic, environmentally sustainable, and people-centred development goals proudly stated in the official declarations of the MDC are simply rhetoric and cannot be seen in practical implementation. In this sense, the MDC strategy therefore conforms with neo-liberal trends towards 'jobless growth', which we can see in many other parts of the world. This is particularly devastating for the agents in the informal economy since there are no mechanisms for integrating them into the project. Instead, there seems to be a lot of wishful thinking regarding how this development paradigm can be positive for the disadvantaged communities, and the people engaged in the informal economy along the corridor.

In this context, it needs saying that the MDC contains a rather innovative governing structure. The SDI management team is to identify obstacles and then speedily mobilize political support from the political champions in order to enforce implementation. However, this particular governance mechanism works only for a small group of politicians, government officials, and big business within the formal decision-making structure and is not designed to deal with the ordinary citizens or affected people on the ground, particularly not those engaged in the informal economy.

The exclusionary effects are magnified by a general lack of institutions on both sides of the border, although it is particularly deep on the Mozambican side. This is illustrated by the failure to establish the Maputo Corridor Company (MCC), which was supposed to be part of the decentralization strategy and bring people-centred development to the corridor. The establishment of the MCC did not work, *inter alia* due to a lack of capacity and commitment at both local and provincial levels, both amongst public and private actors, particularly in Mozambique and also in Mpumalanga. Today, both the South African and the Mozambican governments have largely withdrawn from the MDC, claiming that the project is implemented and self-sustaining. More or less the only institution left to deal with the corridor is the Maputo Corridor Logistics Initiative (MCLI), which is a membership organization, composed of private infrastructure investors and service providers, and with minor representation from public actors in South Africa. According to its stated purpose, the MCLI should promote the logistical development of the MDC and the interests of its members, and also promote the broader objectives of the MDC, which among other things includes, 'creating an increasingly favourable climate for investment and new opportunities for communities along the length and breadth of the Corridor' as well as 'represent[ing] the combined views of all users of the Corridor and all parties involved in the provision of services in the Corridor' (www.mcli.co.za). The MCLI is clearly professionally managed and has already had an impact on networking between formal agents and businesses. The fundamental problem is that the MCLI has a narrow understanding of who the corridor is for, and how development can be achieved. The MCLI does not deal with informal communities and agents in the informal sector. This failure is reflected in that it is difficult for informal sector and other types of bottom-up forces to become organized and integrated into the formal project, in a context when the state and other institutions in the MDC such as the MCLI are doing very little.

The difficulties to reconcile formal decision-makers with the agents in the informal economy is to a large extent, a consequence of the failure of the former to acknowledge the potential of the latter. In fact, the informal economy is seen as a problem rather than a resource. This negative attitude towards the informal sector is seen in the statement by the MCLI:

> The MCLI is not against informal trading *per se*, only the black market part of it, but it needs to be better organized. The Lebombo border-post ... looked like a pig sty because of the vendors. People lived there and traded there. Vendors were in danger, any moment they could get hit by a truck. Vendors need to be capacitated about rules and regulations connected to trading etc., there are bodies for that. From a logistical point of view, the squatters/vendors living at the border-post had to be evacuated, which is a good thing. Now they reside in a place with good facilities and better infrastructure some km's away from the border-post.[2]

This view contrasts sharply with that of Patricia Horn from StreetNet International alliance of street vendors who argues that the proponents of the MDC are bad at recognizing street vendors and informal traders: 'they try to pretend that they do not exist by dealing with what they call the SMME's ... if the government continues to do their planning without any consultation with the organizations of informal traders, it will be a matter of pot luck whether they happen to benefit the vendors or not.'[3] Furthermore, the vendors operating around at the Lebombo border-post, were seen as stumbling blocks to the improvement of the post and were finally removed in September 2004 to an old, isolated airport area far away from the main road. According to Horn, this is just another sign of bad communication between the MDC policymakers and informal traders.

[2] Telephone interview, CEO of MCLI, December 2004.

[3] E-mail interview, StreetNet, December 2004. SMME: Small, medium, and micro enterprises.

She adds that '[i]t is appalling that they think that a roadside free of vendors is more desirable than an active trade along the roadsides with traders who come from the local communities'.[4]

The spread of HIV/AIDS along the corridor is another important issue with links to the informal sector. Needless to say, HIV/AIDS is not a consequence of the transport route as such, but on the whole the corridor certainly fuels the pandemic. The virus is being spread along the Maputo corridor by truck-drivers and others utilizing the transport route, and certain key-points have been established along the corridor where prostitutes and truck-drivers gather. The MCLI agrees that there are great problems with sex-workers at the border-posts and along the corridor. According to MCLI, 'Truck-drivers need to be discouraged to engage with these sex-workers. But this is not the role of MCLI. MCLI focuses on logistics and does not have the resources to deal with HIV/AIDS-issues, this is the job of other stakeholders.'[5] The fundamental problem is not that the MCLI is unwilling to address the problem, but that the policy-makers behind the MDC do not deal with the negative repercussions of the formal project. This is yet another illustration of an uneasy relationship between the formal policies and informal economy in the Maputo corridor.

9.5 Conclusion: From Blocking to Unlocking Human Potential

In the mid-1990s, the governments of South Africa and Mozambique agreed to reconstruct the Maputo corridor through the implementation of the MDC and its gigantic portfolio of large-scale private investment projects. There are undoubtedly many intriguing and fascinating features about the MDC, both positive and negative. This chapter has drawn particular attention to the fact that the MDC policies have not been designed in order to utilize and unlock the human potential and entrepreneurship of the vivid informal economy along the corridor. On the contrary, the MDC is designed for the purpose of crowding-in external capital in order to build industrial and infrastructural mega-projects. It is externally driven, and the endogenous and informal capacities in the corridor are neglected or even seen as problematic. Hence, the fundamental problem with the MDC lies in that it is based on a development

[4] E-mail interview, StreetNet, December 2004.
[5] Telephone interview, MCLI, December 2004.

strategy, which emphasizes a capital-intensive industrialization strategy which fails to utilize and unlock the human potential of Mozambique's population.

The future of the corridor seems to develop along one of the following two scenarios: One scenario is a strengthening of the neoliberal project, which is designed for large-scale capital and foreign business, existing in isolation and with few positive links to the informal economy. In this scenario, the informal region will continue to exist and even expand, since it provides an escape route and opting out from the negative impacts created by formal policies.

There is, however, a chance of the consolidation of the corridor in a more positive and developmental sense, whereby the formal and informal corridors become mutually reinforcing and build on the strengths of a combination of formal policies and informal potential. That is, the development strategy as well as the governance mechanisms of the formal region *can* be redesigned, to promote the welfare and needs of the people inhabiting the area and engaged in the informal economy. On a general level, this requires formal policies that also build on the endogenous capacities of people rather than restrict the creativity and entrepreneurship in the informal economy.

For this to happen, it is necessary to acknowledge that informal activity is a reality and will not simply disappear in the foreseeable future. It can be detrimental, or at least less productive than the formal sector, but more often than not informal activities in the corridor arise, in order to search for economic opportunities in a situation where the formal economy has little to offer. Seen from this perspective, the challenge for formal policies is to unlock rather than block the potential inherent in the informal economy. Some of the policy implications that stem from this study are:

Build knowledge. We need to increase our knowledge of how the informal economy can contribute to economic development, and reinforce the positive impact of formal policies. One of the main challenges is to understand more about the negative impact that formal policies have on informal economy, how they could be recrafted in order to stimulate human potential locked in the informal economy, and also to understand the negative effects of the informal economy (an aspect which has received little attention in this chapter).

A change of attitude towards the informal sector. Informal activities should not simply be seen as impediments to development, which often is the case today, as illustrated by this study of the MDC. The informal sector has a huge potential that needs to be unlocked (although its role in the economy should by no means be romanticized).

Policy change. Formal policies need to be recrafted for them to be relevant for the informal economy and to unlock its inherent potential. The MDC has been a failure in this regard, since it was designed only to deal with big businesses and a small network of policymakers and parastatals, rather than the masses of peoples and groups in the informal economy.

References

de Beer, G. and D. Arkwright (2003). 'The Maputo Development Corridor: Progress Achieved and Lessons Learned', in F. Söderbaum and I. Taylor (eds), *Regionalism and Uneven Development in Southern Africa: The Case of the Maputo Development Corridor*. Aldershot: Ashgate, pp. 19–31.

Castel-Branco, C. N. and N. Goldin (2003). 'Impacts of the Mozal Aluminium Smelter on the Mozambican Economy'. Final report submitted to Mozal, September.

Davies, R. (1990). 'Reconstructing South-Southern African Economic Relations after Apartheid: Some Key Issues'. *Southern African Perspectives* No. 2. Centre for Southern African Studies. Bellville: University of the Western Cape.

Driver, A. (1999). 'Infrastructure, Corridors, and Regional Integration in Southern Africa. *Trade and Industry Monitor.* 9 March. Cape Town: University of Cape Town.

Hentz, J. J. (2003). 'The Mozambique Aluminium Smelter: Partnership for Exploitation or Development?', in F. Söderbaum and I. Taylor (eds), *Regionalism and Uneven Development in Southern Africa: The Case of the Maputo Development Corridor*. Aldershot: Ashgate, pp. 83–96.

ILO (2002). 'Women and Men in the Informal Economy: A Statistical Picture'. Geneva: International Labour Office.

Jourdan, P. (1998). 'Spatial Development Initiatives (SDIs)—The Official View'. *Development Southern Africa*, 15(5): 717–25.

Lundin, I. B. and F. Söderbaum (2002). 'The Construction of Cross-Border Regions in Southern Africa: The Case of the Maputo Corridor', in M. Perkmann and N.-L. Sum (eds), *Globalization, Regionalization and the Building of Cross-Border Regions*. Basingstoke: Palgrave Macmillan, pp. 241–62.

Lundin, I. B. and I. Taylor (2003). 'A View from Maputo', in F. Söderbaum and I. Taylor (eds), *Regionalism and Uneven Development in Southern Africa: The Case of the Maputo Development Corridor*. Aldershot: Ashgate, pp. 97–105.

Niemann, M. (1998). 'Regional Labor Migration in Post-Apartheid Southern Africa'. Paper presented at the Workshop: Globalisms and Regionalisms of the IPSA Study Group III, New World Orders? 6–8 August. Oslo: University of Oslo.

Söderbaum, F. (2004). *The Political Economy of Regionalism: The Case of Southern Africa*. Basingstoke: Palgrave Macmillan.

Söderbaum, F. and I. Taylor (eds) (2003). *Regionalism and Uneven Development in Southern Africa: The Case of the Maputo Development Corridor*. Aldershot: Ashgate.

Taylor, I. (1999). 'The Maputo Development Corridor: Whose Corridor? Whose Development?'. Mimeo, University of Stellenbosch. Published in (2003) in S. Breslin and G. Hook (eds), *Micro-Regionalism and World Order*. Basingstoke: Palgrave Macmillan, pp. 144–65.

10

Microinsurance for the informal economy workers in India

Basudeb Guha-Khasnobis and Rajeev Ahuja

10.1 Introduction

'Microinsurance' refers to insurance for low-income people, extended with the involvement of various civil society associations who either negotiate with formal insurance providers or self-manage the risks for which insurance is provided. Typically, microinsurance deals in a low value product (involving modest premium and benefit package), requires different design and distribution strategies such as premium based on community risk rating (as opposed to individual risk rating), and seeks active involvement of an intermediate agency representing the target community. In India, microinsurance is fast emerging as an important risk management strategy for the low-income people engaged in a wide variety of income generation activities, and who remain exposed to a variety of risks mainly because of absence of cost-effective risk hedging instruments.

Risks play an important role in the lives of the poor. Although the type of risks faced by the poor such as that of death, illness, injury, and accident, are no different from those faced by others, they are more vulnerable to such risks because of their economic circumstance. In the context of health contingency, for example, a World Bank study (Peters *et al.* 2002) reports that about one-fourth of hospitalized Indians fall below the poverty line as a result of their stay in hospitals. The same study reports that more than 40 per cent of hospitalized patients take loans or sell assets to pay for hospitalization.[1]

[1] Such high percentage is also noted by some MFIs in the utilization pattern of loans advanced by them (see for e.g. SHEPHERD 2003).

Providing security to the workers against various contingencies is essential for their economic and social well-being.[2] Indeed, enhancing the ability of the poor to deal with various risks is increasingly being considered integral to any poverty reduction strategy (Holzmann and Jørgensen 2000; Siegel *et al.* 2001).

Of the different risk management strategies,[3] insurance that spreads the loss of the (few) affected members among all the members who join insurance schemes, and also separates time of payment of premium from time of claims is considered an important strategy. It is particularly beneficial to the poor who have limited ability to mitigate risk on account of imperfect labour and credit markets.[4]

In the past, insurance as a prepaid risk managing instrument was never considered as an option for the poor. The poor were considered too poor to be able to afford insurance premiums. Often they were considered uninsurable, given the wide variety of risks they face. However, recent developments in India, as elsewhere, have shown that not only can the poor make small periodic contributions that can go towards insuring them against risks but also that the risks they face (such as those of illness, accident and injury, life, loss of property, etc.) are eminently insurable as these risks are mostly independent or idiosyncratic.[5] Moreover, there are cost-effective ways of extending insurance to them. Thus, insurance is fast emerging as a prepaid financing option for the risks facing the poor.

In this chapter, we analyse the early evidence on microinsurance already available in this regard, highlight the current debate on strengthening microinsurance activity in the country, and suggest ways that can help promote insurance to the target segment. The chapter is organized as follows. In Section 10.2 we analyse the factors leading to the development of microinsurance in India. In Section 10.3 we analyse the

[2] According to the ILO (2000), social security includes at least the following types of contingencies: those relating to unemployment, sickness, employment injury, maternity, invalidity, old age, and death. In addition, the ILO considers medical care and family benefits also to be an essential part of social security. In developing countries like India social security has a much wider connotation. Besides including the ILO type of security, it must also include basic needs as well as interventions designed to raise income of the poor.

[3] Depending on an individual response to dealing with risks, the literature classifies all risk management practices into three broad groups: risk reduction (RR), risk mitigation (RM) and risk coping (RC) strategies. The first two are *ex ante* risk management strategies (that is, used before a risky event takes place) whereas the third is an *ex post* strategy (that is after the event takes place). Insurance, similar to savings and borrowings, is a part of risk mitigation strategy (Brown and Churchill 1999; Holzmann and Jørgensen 2000).

[4] According to Zeller and Sharma (1998), in spite of vibrant informal markets that can be observed in many [developing countries], financial services for the poor remain inadequate. For credit market imperfections see Besley (1995).

[5] Insurability of risks depends on the characteristics of risk (see Brown and Churchill 1999; Siegel and Alwang 1999; Jütting 2002).

developments on the supply and demand sides of microinsurance. In Section 10.4, we bring out the current debate on extending insurance to low-income people; focusing on two specific issues, namely the effect of flexibility of insurance premium and of combining microinsurance with microfinance. Section 10.5 concludes.

10.2 Development of Microinsurance in India

Historically in India, a few microinsurance schemes were initiated, either by non-governmental organizations (NGOs) due to the felt need in the communities in which these organizations were involved or by the trust hospitals. These schemes have now gathered momentum partly due to the development of microfinance activity, and partly due to the regulation that makes it mandatory for all formal insurance companies to extend their activities to rural and well-identified social sector in the country (IRDA 2000).[6] As a result, increasingly, microfinance institutions (MFIs) and NGOs are negotiating with the for-profit insurers for the purchase of customized group or standardized individual insurance schemes for their clients/members. The clients of MFIs are primarily low-income people who take credit for livelihood purposes (Sa-dhan 2005).[7] Likewise, many NGOs provide a range of services, including credit, to their members with the view to provide socioeconomic security. These clients/members constitute a section of informal economy workers. Although the reach of microinsurance schemes is currently very limited—anywhere between 5 and 10 million individuals—their potential is viewed to be considerable (ILO 2004).

However, microinsurance is not the only phenomena through which the informal economy workers in India are getting insurance cover. Several central and state government programmes also provide some risk cover to the workers in the informal sector. One good example of this is the National Agricultural Insurance Scheme (NAIS), which was introduced

[6] The concept of social/universal obligation is not new in India. It has been applied in other sectors as well such as aviation, telecommunications etc. In aviation, for example, all domestic airlines in India have the obligation to serve the unprofitable segments and this obligation is defined in terms of their service to the most profitable segments.

[7] The information compiled by Sa-dhan suggests that 11 per cent, 24 per cent, 51 per cent, and 14 per cent of outstanding credit was for agriculture, animal husbandary, non-agricultural income generation, and 'other' purposes respectively. Similarly, 20 per cent, 23 per cent, 47 per cent, and 10 per cent of total clients who received credit were in agriculture, animal husbandary, non-agricultural income generation, and 'other' purposes respectively.

in 1999–2000.[8] From 1999–2000 to 2003–04, the scheme has (cumulatively) covered around 46.2 million farmers and paid claims to around 16 million. Around 80 per cent of farmers covered under the scheme have been small and marginal farmers having a farm size of less than 2 ha (20,000 m^2).[9] In this chapter we do not cover all government initiatives aimed at covering different sections of the informal economy workers. Some of these initiatives have been around for a number of years and, therefore, have already been well documented. The focus of the chapter is on this new and emerging phenomenon of microinsurance only.

Insurance market in India was a public monopoly for a number of years. There was one insurer in the life insurance segment and four in the non-life segment.[10] Under government pressure in the early 1980s, these public insurance companies started offering insurance to the poorer segments of the population especially in rural areas where the majority of the poor live. However, the performance of public insurers was far from satisfactory. Loan arrangements for which banks required insurance cover from the borrowers still accounted for most of the rural business. In 2000 when the Indian insurance industry was opened to entry of private firms, the insurance regulator made it mandatory for all insurance companies to serve both the rural and socially disadvantaged sections of the society (IRDA 2000). To fulfill their obligation, the insurance companies in the liberalized, competitive market are offering insurance to the low-income population.

According to the ILO (2004), 'The simultaneously engagement in India, of both public and private insurance companies in the provision of a wide spectrum of microinsurance products aiming to protect the disadvantaged groups is to be considered as a unique experience in the world...'.

The insurance regulator defines rural sector as consisting of (1) a population of less than 5,000, (2) a density of population of less than 400

[8] NAIS was not totally a new scheme. In fact, it replaced an earlier scheme called Comprehensive Crop Insurance Scheme which was introduced as early as in 1985.

[9] Although the premium under the scheme is subsidized for small and marginal farmers to the extent of 10 per cent (which is shared equally by the central and state government), effective subsidy is much higher as the scheme is loss-making. The scheme is being implemented by one of the non-life public insurance companies called Agriculture Insurance Company of India Limited (AIC), formed in 2002–03. Prior to its formation the scheme was implemented by another public company called General Insurance Corporation of India. Being a new company, AIC's own crop insurance schemes have a very limited reach and coverage at present.

[10] In the life segment the public insurer is the Life Insurance Corporation of India (LIC) with its head office in Mumbai, and in the non-life segment, the 4 public non-life insurers are National Insurance Company Limited, New India Assurance Company Limited, Oriental Insurance Company Limited, and United India Insurance Company Limited with their head offices in Calcutta, Mumbai, Delhi, and Chennai respectively.

per km^2, and (3) more than 25 per cent of the male working population is engaged in agricultural pursuits and includes cultivators, agricultural labourers, and workers in livestock, forestry, fishing, hunting and plantations, orchards and allied activities.

The social sector as defined by the insurance regulator consists of (1) unorganized sector, (2) informal sector, (3) economically vulnerable or backward classes, and (4) other categories of persons, both in rural and urban areas.[11]

The social obligations are in terms of number of individuals to be covered by both life and non-life insurers in certain identified sections of the society.[12] The rural obligations are in terms of certain minimum percentage of total policies written by life insurance companies and, for general insurance companies, these obligations are in terms of percentage of total gross premium collected. Some aspects of these obligations are particularly noteworthy. First, the social and rural obligations do not necessarily require (cross) subsidizing insurance. Second, these obligations are to be fulfiled right from the first year of commencement of operations by the new insurers. Third, there is no exit option available to insurers who are not keen on servicing the rural and low-income segment. Finally, non-fulfillment of these obligations can invite penalties from the regulator.

In order to fulfil these requirements, all insurance companies have designed products for the poorer sections and low-income individuals. Both public and private insurance companies are adopting similar strategies of developing collaborations with the various civil society associations. The

[11] (1) Unorganized sector includes self-employed workers such as agricultural labourers, *beedi* workers (*beedi* is an unfiltered cigarette made by rolling tobacco in a dry leaf; it is an inexpensive substitute for cigarettes and is used mostly by poorer smokers), brick workers, carpenters, cobblers, construction workers, female tailors, handicraft artisans, handloom workers, leather and tannery workers, street vendors, primary milk producers, rickshaw pullers, salt producers, sericulture workers, sugarcane cutters, washerwomen, working women in the hills, or such other categories; (2) informal sector includes small scale, self-employed workers typically at a low level of organization and technology, with the primary objective of generating employment and income, with heterogeneous activities, with the work being mostly labour intensive, having often unwritten and informal employer–employee relationship; (3) economically vulnerable or backward classes persons who live below the poverty line; and (4) other categories of persons include persons with disabilities and who may not be gainfully employed, as well as persons who tend to the disabled.

[12] Social sector obligation is applied to all insurers and it includes covering 5,000 lives in the first financial year, 7,500 lives in the second, 10,000 lives in the third, 15,000 lives in the fourth, and 20,000 lives in the fifth year. In case of a general insurer, the obligations specified include insurance for crops also. Rural sector obligation for life insurers is set in terms of percentage of total policies written: 7 per cent in the first financial year, 9 per cent in the second, 12 per cent in the third, 14 per cent in the fourth, and 16 per cent in the fifth year. Such obligations for general insurers are in terms of total gross premium income written in a year. It is 2 per cent in the first financial year, 3 per cent in the second, and 5 per cent thereafter.

presence of these associations as a mediating agency, or what we call a nodal agency, that represents, and acts on behalf of the target community is essential in extending insurance cover to the poor. The nodal agency helps the formal insurance providers overcome both informational disadvantage and high transaction costs in providing insurance to the low-income people. This way microinsurance combines positive features of formal insurance (prepaid, scientifically organized scheme) as well as those of informal insurance (by using local information and resources that helps in designing appropriate schemes delivered in a cost-effective way).[13]

In the absence of a nodal agency, the low resource base of the poor, coupled with high transaction costs (relative to the magnitude of transactions) gives rise to the affordability issue. Lack of affordability prevents their latent demand from expressing itself in the market. Hence the nodal agencies that organize the poor, impart training, and work for the welfare of the low-income people play an important role in generating both the *demand* for insurance as well as the *supply* of cost-effective insurance.

10.3 Supply and Demand Side Developments

10.3.1 *Supply of Microinsurance*

Recently, the International Labour Organization (2005) prepared a list of products of all insurance companies, public as well as private, for the disadvantaged groups in India. Some of the observations made on the basis of the list are presented below:

- Out of 83 listed insurance products, 46 (55 per cent) cover only a single risk. The other products, covering a package of risks, mostly focus on two (20 per cent) or three (18 per cent) risks.
- The available products cover a wide range of risks. However, the broad majority of the insurance products cover life (42 products or 52 per cent) or accident-related risks. The health coverage remains very limited (14 products).
- Most life insurance products (24 out of 42) are addressed to individuals. However, some products may be bought both by individuals and groups.
- Most life insurance products (55 per cent) have been designed to cover extended duration of contract—ranging from 3 to 20 years.

[13] For more on the role of nodal agency in extending microinsurance see Ahuja (2004).

- Out of 42 life insurance products, 23 are pure risk products. The other 19 products propose various types of maturity benefits.
- Out of the 14 currently available health insurance products, eight have been designed and are restricted to groups; nine products propose the reimbursement of hospitalization expenses while the other five have chosen to narrow down the coverage to some specific critical illnesses.
- Most of the health insurance products specifically exclude deliveries and other pregnancy-related illnesses. Most of these products also mention amongst their exclusion clauses, HIV/AIDS.
- Most products whether life or non-life require a single payment of premium (i.e. a one-time payment) upon subscription.
- Private insurance companies have three times more products than the public companies.

As per the Insurance Regulatory and Development Authority (IRDA) statistics, the public insurance companies still play a predominant role in the present coverage of the rural and social sectors. This is only to be expected since the incumbent public insurers have been in the market for a number of years now.

10.3.2 *Demand for Microinsurance*

On the demand side too, the ILO (2004) has recently prepared an inventory of microinsurance schemes operational in India. Based on this list some of the observations are made below:

- The inventory lists 51 schemes that are operational in India.
- Most schemes are still young, having started their operations during the last few years. Of the 39 schemes for which this information is available, around 24 schemes came up during the last 4 years, and about seven schemes have operated for more than a decade.
- As regards the beneficiaries, the 43 schemes for which the information is available cover 5.2 million people.
- Most insurance schemes (66 per cent) are linked with microfinance services provided by specialized institutions (17 schemes) or non-specialized organizations (17 schemes). Twenty-two per cent of the schemes are implemented by community based organizations, and 12 per cent by health care providers.
- Life and health are the two most popular risks for which insurance is demanded: 59 per cent of schemes provide life insurance and 57 per

cent of them provide health insurance.[14] In SEWA's[15] experience health insurance tops the list of risks for which the poor need insurance.

- Twenty-five out of 37 schemes received some external funds to initiate their schemes. Twenty out of 32 schemes received external technical assistance in the form of advisory services, technical services, training, or even referral services for their schemes.
- In the majority of the schemes special staff had been recruited to manage the insurance activities. The other schemes relied on their regular staff and gave them the additional responsibilities linked to the management of the scheme.
- Most schemes (74 per cent) operate in four southern states of India: Andhra Pradesh (27 per cent), Tamil Nadu (23 per cent), Karnataka (17 per cent) and Kerala (8 per cent), and the two western states, Maharashtra (12 per cent), and Gujarat (6 per cent) account for 18 per cent of the schemes.
- 56 per cent of schemes deal with one single risk.
- Most schemes require single yearly premium at the time of subscription. Of the 43 schemes, six use a monthly payment for their contribution, while two others have linked the contributions to some other activities developed with their members (disbursement of loan etc.).
- Most of the schemes (27) rely on voluntary contribution, while 10 schemes imposed compulsory contributions, and seven adopted a mix of voluntary and compulsory contributions (based on the type of service provided).

Any nodal agency keen on buying insurance for its members now has a choice of insurers and approaches those who offer it the best deal. According to the ILO inventory, eight schemes have already entered into partnerships with at least two insurance companies (public or commercial), and three schemes have already entered simultaneous partnerships with both public and commercial insurance companies.[16]

Clearly, health and life are the two most important risks for which insurance is demanded. Indeed, at low-income level, where much of the income goes into meeting basic needs, the scope of having varying priority needs is very limited. On the supply side we observe that out of

[14] Many MFIs and NGOs are in the process of introducing health insurance.

[15] SEWA is a labour union of informal economy women workers based in Ahmedabad city of Gujarat. Its operations now run in other states such as Madhya Pradesh and Delhi.

[16] Twenty schemes have already developed partnerships with public insurance companies and 14 schemes have already developed partnerships with commercial insurance companies.

about 80 products only seven products are health insurance products that provide for reimbursement of hospital expenses. Admittedly, compared to life insurance, which is a relatively straightforward business, health insurance is a much more complex service as it involves addressing the provision of healthcare that is location specific. The design and sale of products is currently driven by the objective of meeting the regulatory obligation, and the making of profits or reducing losses. In this situation, there is a danger of certain priority needs getting neglected by the insurance companies.

Most products require a single yearly premium at the time of subscription. It is well known that rural incomes are irregular and not assured of enabling payment of a premium in one go; more so when only part of the remuneration is paid in cash. In the above, we find only a few schemes offering flexibility in paying a premium, which could act as a serious drawback in increasing membership.

We find that most of the schemes are concentrated in the southern region of the country. The southern regions are well known for the social mobilization of low-income people. In contrast, the northern region is bereft of such mobilization as the nodal agencies are either non-existent or dysfunctional. Creating and nurturing nodal agencies can be quite involved and can take a long time to develop. Local government, that can also perform the role of nodal agency, will take a long time to strengthen as a result of decentralization process currently underway in most Indian states. There have to be alternative approaches to extending insurance in regions where nodal agencies do not exist.

Even before insurance is bought for all important contingencies, affordability constraint is likely to kick in, especially for the low-income people. The issue then is how to cover for these other important contingencies. One of the ways suggested is to impose a tax at industry level (this could be on the turnover of the industry), and use the tax proceeds for the benefit of informal economy workers working in the same industry.

Finally, the type of contingency and the number of people covered under it are important parameters, but so is the extent of benefit provided should the contingency happen. Currently, the benefit or protection provided under some insurance schemes is quite shallow.

The attitude of insurers towards these obligations has been mixed. Some have taken a positive view of the regulatory obligations and have made a genuine attempt to understand the rural and low-income segment of the market. Indeed, a few insurers have actually surpassed their obligations by a wide margin. These companies have realized that there is potential in the rural and low-income segment but tapping that potential requires a different kind of approach. In some cases, insurance companies have actually cross-subsidized their microinsurance products while in other cases insurers have been able to find a donor for paying premium, at least in part, on behalf of the low-income people.

The impact of rural and social obligations on extending insurance to the intended people has been positive. However, development of microinsurance needs further guidance from the insurance regulator by way of supplementary provisions. Sensing this, the insurance regulator has already come out with a concept paper on microinsurance[17] in which it has spelled out its thinking on what these supplementary provisions could be.

10.4 The Current Debate

Prior to the introduction of social and rural obligations, insurance to the low-income people took the form of (1) a nodal agency tying up with one of the public insurance companies (the intermediate model), and (2) a nodal agency itself underwriting risk, that is, performing the role of an insurance company (the insurer model). However, with the social and rural obligations the insurer model is becoming less common and is getting subsumed in the intermediate model.

For many MFIs, underwriting insurance is one of the profitable avenues which they would want to undertake themselves instead of letting this opportunity go to formal insurers. Many NGOs and microfinance organizations have been wanting to underwrite risk themselves by providing insurance to their members/clients and, therefore, have been pressing with the government and the insurance regulator (IRDA) for lowering the minimum capital requirement which at present stands at Rs. 1 billion. Currently, the minimum capital requirement is the same for all insurance companies. According to the nodal agencies, microinsurance involves modest premium and benefit package, and therefore, merit lower capital requirement. However, IRDA does not want itself to be involved with regulating numerous entities that lowering of the capital requirement may give birth to. Instead of lowering the minimum capital requirement, for which there may be some rationale, IRDA has adopted a different

[17] The concept paper on microinsurance can be downloaded from: www.irdaindia.org.

approach. It has not debarred the NGOs and MFIs from underwriting risks, but such programmes are outside the ambit of IRDA, and hence, do not enjoy the benefit of legal protection available to individuals who buy insurance from a formal, recognized insurance provider. To that extent individuals who partake in insurance schemes run by NGOs and MFIs will be exposed to the risks inherent in running these programmes.

Minimum capital requirement is just one of the issues. IRDA will have to have a separate set of regulations on a range of issues such as agents' commission, solvency margins, underwriting margins, investments, administrative expenses and so forth. Another issue that comes up relates to composite insurance. Currently, life insurance business is kept separate from non-life insurance. If permitted, the NGOs may want to underwrite both classes of business.

The soft stand adopted by IRDA is also motivated by the fact that there is scope for a few genuine, large grass root agencies to be capable of running their own insurance schemes. IRDA does not want to scuttle the attempts of such agencies that have a potential of providing protection to the poor.

In fact, regulating insurance activities of NGOs and MFIs touches on a broader issue of regulating these diverse entities, with varying motives, commitment, and legal status. Even the credit and savings activities of most MFIs are at present not regulated. The banking regulator has been facing the same dilemma for quite some time now. Given the complexity in regulating these grass root level organizations, there has been some discussion on having a separate regulator for all finance activities—credit, savings and insurance—of the MFIs.

The route favoured by IRDA is that of the intermediary or principal-agent model. For this, the IRDA has come up with a concept note on microinsurance in which it has defined 'microinsurance' and 'micro-insurance agent'. The concept note suggests how a single insurance company can offer composite insurance product to the low-income people, sets a ceiling on the commission that can be paid to insurance agents, minimum coverage to make insurance meaningful, and so forth.[18]

At a time when the supplementary provisions on microinsurance are still under consideration by IRDA, two aspects that need to be considered are: (1) the role of flexibility in premium collection, and (2) micro-insurance taken up by MFIs as distinct from non-MFIs. We elaborate each of these two points below.

[18] Discussions on several provisions under the concept note are already underway and the regulator has an open mind on the subject. A noteworthy point is that the concept paper is very much in line with promoting insurer-agent model.

10.4.1 *Flexibility in Premium*

In the IRDA's concept note on microinsurance there is no provision that explicitly calls for allowing flexibility in premium collection which is necessary for extending the reach of microinsurance. Although some microinsurance products allow for half-yearly, quarterly, and even monthly payment of premium, most products, whether life or non-life require single, yearly payment of premium upon subscription. This can be a serious drawback in extending the reach of insurance to low-income people, especially in rural areas. Often nodal agencies adopt several methods to facilitate premium collection. These methods may take the form of soft loans for paying premium, collecting premium in kind, collecting smaller amounts but more frequently, having insurance contract of shorter durations, and so forth. Where a nodal agency collects annual premium in one go, there is not much involvement of the agency.

Rural incomes display seasonality. Moreover, for the low-income people premium constitutes a significant proportion of their income. Therefore, flexibility in premium collection has a bearing on their joining or not joining an insurance scheme, and hence, on the membership size. The literature on microinsurance cites the importance of appropriate 'timings' for premium collection. In particular, premium collection schedule should match with the cash flows. The cash flow varies for different categories of workers. For example, the cash flows in the case of farmers would depend on the number of crop cycles in a year as well as on the timings of harvest, whereas a self-employed household worker may have a more stable income stream. Therefore, synchronizing premium collection with the harvest time is necessary for farmers, whereas for self-employed household workers paying premium in small but regular instalments may be easier. Also, cash flows for the rural poor may be different from those of the urban poor.[19]

The 'type' of flexibility needed in premium collection would depend very much on (1) the pattern of income stream of the target population, and (2) the spread of risk for which insurance is sought. As noted above the former is necessary for increasing the membership. The latter is needed to induce the insurance company to allow for flexibility in premium collection. To elaborate on this, supposing for a 1 year insurance contract, the premium is collected twice a year in equal instalments. If the risks for which insurance is bought are unevenly distributed between the

[19] Rural poor get lump sums in the agricultural season, whereas urban poor get small amounts frequently (Sinha 2002).

two sub-periods that make up a year, then the interest of the insurance company needs to be protected against the possibility of greater outflow (on account of higher claims) than the premium inflow in the first sub-period. The protection could come when either the nodal agency provides for some implicit guarantees or when the insurance contract is initiated in a sub-period having lower risk or when flexibility in premium collection is built taking this fact into account.

Thus, flexibility in premium collection needs to be appropriate from the viewpoint of both the insurer and the insured.[20] An explicit provision in this respect in the concept note would be a significant step forward.

10.4.2 *Microinsurance and Microfinance*

Microfinance activity in the country is leading to the spread of micro-insurance among its members/clients. For MFIs, integrating insurance with their credit and savings activities makes logical sense, as it helps them to reap scale economies in financial management, provides them with a captive market, and enables them to use their existing network and distribution channels to sell insurance. Besides, linking microinsurance with microcredit makes it cheaper for the borrower to have both these financial services.

Indeed, the natural linkage between microinsurance and microfinance is well reflected in the ILO inventory referred to earlier. Not only are the specialized microfinance organizations the most numerous in initiating the microinsurance schemes, but many organizations involved in other activities are also providing microfinance services to their target groups. Since most of the larger microfinance organizations operate in the three southern states of Andhra Pradesh, Tamil Nadu, and Karnataka, the existence of microinsurance schemes in the south appears directly proportional to the growth of microfinance activities in that part of the country.

Insurance helps in reducing interest rate charged on credit. With insurance, interest rate together with the premium may be lower than interest rate charged in the absence of insurance. The intuition runs as follows: contingencies such as illness, accident, life, etc. have a bearing on project performance and thereby on loan recovery. Health insurance, for example, by improving financial access to medical care of the insured who

[20] According to Tenkorang (2001), several studies on Africa show that demand for health care services is often hindered by immediate cash payments involved.

takes loan/credit, reduces disruption in the economic activity for which loan is taken, and thereby enables the borrower to repay loan. Higher loan recovery is an important determinant of interest rate charged by a lending agency. The higher the loan recovery, the lower is the interest rate charged by a lender. Thus, insurance, by reducing the risk of loan default due to the contingency against which insurance is bought, reduces interest rate charged by the lender. For this reason it makes better sense for microcredit organizations to introduce microinsurance. It is important here to stress that when insurance is integrated with credit, the total amount charged (i.e. interest plus premium) may be lower than the interest charged in the absence of insurance.

Given the beneficial outcome of integrating microinsurance with microfinance, it is necessary to have a pro-active policy that would promote such integration. Currently, the MFIs are not even regulated and therefore the scope of public policy in promoting this integration or even promoting microinsurance in general is very limited. Furthermore, besides MFIs, microcredit is also being extended by the government through several programmes. It becomes imperative for the government to have a clear thinking on how to promote microinsurance on the one hand and microcredit with its positive impact on poverty reduction and empowerment on the other. At present, the concept note does not make any distinction between microinsurance through microfinance institutions and microinsurance through other agencies.

10.5 Conclusions and Recommendations

Policy-induced and institutional innovations are promoting insurance among the informal economy workers who form a sizable group in total work force and who are mostly without any social security cover. Although the current reach of 'microinsurance' is limited, the early trend in this respect suggests that the insurance companies, both public and private, operating with commercial considerations, can insure a significant percentage of the informal economy workers. Serving the informal economy workers who can pay the premium certainly makes for sound business proposition. To that extent, imposing social and rural obligations by insurance regulator (IRDA) is helping all insurance companies appreciate the vast untapped potential in serving the lower end of the market.

However, it is becoming increasingly clear that microinsurance needs a further push and guidance from the regulator as well as the government. IRDA has already come up with the concept note on microinsurance, which suggests the regulator's favour for only insurer-agent model. Even so, two areas in which having explicit provisions would aid the development of microinsurance are: one, flexibility in premium collection, and two, encouraging microinsurance among MFIs.

Given irregular and uncertain income stream of informal economy workers, flexibility in premium collection is needed to extend the reach of microinsurance net far and wide among informal workers. Moreover, MFIs are playing a significant role in improving the lives of poor households. Quite apart from this, linking microinsurance with microfinance makes better sense as it helps bring down the cost of lending. Given this, there is a case for strengthening the link between microinsurance and microcredit. At present MFIs are without any regulation. Regulation of MFIs is needed not only to promote microfinance activity in the country but also to promote linking of microinsurance with microfinance.

Microinsurance, the way it is developing in India, should at best be considered as one of the strategies of extending protection to the informal economy workers. The insurance regulator needs to experiment with alternate models of extending insurance, especially in areas where an intermediate or nodal agency is difficult to identify or is non-existent. For example, taxing different industries and then using tax proceeds for the welfare of informal workers engaged in the same industry could be another model. Similarly, even where a nodal agency exists, people may not be able to afford buying protection against all major contingencies or buying adequate coverage for such contingencies. How best to ensure adequate coverage against major contingencies remains an open public policy issue.

References

Ahuja, R. (2004). 'Health Insurance for the Poor'. *Economic and Political Weekly*, XXXIX(28): 3171–8.

Besley, T. (1995). 'Savings, Credit, and Insurance', in J. Behrmann and T. N. Srinivasan (eds), *Handbook of Development Economics*, Vol. 3. Amsterdam: North-Holland, pp. 2123–2207.

Brown, W. and C. Churchill (1999). 'Providing Insurance to Low-Income Households'. Part I: Primer on Insurance Principles and Products (November). Washington, DC: USAID—Microenterprise Best Practices Project.

Holzmann, R. and S. Jørgensen (2000). 'Social Risk Management: A New Conceptual Framework for Social Protection, and Beyond'. *Social Protection Discussion Paper* 0006. Washington, DC: World Bank.

ILO (2000) 'World Report 2000: Income Security and Social Protection in a Changing World'. Geneva: ILO.

ILO (2004). 'India: An Inventory of Community-based Micro-insurance Schemes, Strategies and Tools Against Social Exclusion and Poverty (STEP)'. (February) Geneva: ILO.

ILO (2005). 'India: Insurance Products Provided by Insurance Companies to the Disadvantaged Groups, Special Studies, Global Campaign on Social Security and Coverage for All'. Geneva: ILO.

IRDA (2000). 'Insurance Regulatory and Development Authority (Obligations of Insurers to Rural Social Sectors) Regulations'. IRDA Notification dated 14 July. New Delhi. Downloaded from: http://www.irdaindia.org/ December 2004.

Jütting, J. (2002). 'Social Risk Management in Developing Countries. An Economic Analysis of Community Based Health Insurance Schemes'. Monograph and 'habilitation thesis'. Germany: University of Bonn.

Peters, D. H., A. S. Yazbeck, R. R. Sharma, G. N. V. Ramana, L. H. Pritchett, and A. Wagstaff (2002). 'Better Health Systems for India's Poor: Findings, Analysis, and Options'. Washington, DC: World Bank.

Sa-dhan (2005). 'Side-by-Side: A Slice of Microfinance Programs in India'. March. Sa-dhan: New Delhi: The Association of Community Development Finance Institutions.

SHEPHERD (2003). 'Insurance—A Safety Net to Poor, Self-Help Promotion for Health and Rural Development (SHEPHERD)'. Tamil Nadu: Trichy.

Siegel, P. and J. Alwang (1999). 'An Asset-based Approach to Social Risk Management: A Conceptual Framework'. *Social Protection Discussion Paper* 0116. Washington, DC: World Bank.

Siegel, P., J. Alwang, and S. Canagarajah (2001). 'Viewing Micro-insurance as a Risk Management Tool'. *Social Protection Discussion Paper* 0115. Washington, DC: World Bank.

Sinha, S. (2002). 'Strength in Solidarity: Insurance for Women Workers in the Informal Economy, Self-Employed Women's Association (SEWA)'. Ahmedabad, Gujarat.

Tenkorang, D. A. (2001). 'Health Insurance for the Informal Sector in Africa: Design Features, Risk Protection, and Resource Mobilisation'. *CMH Working Paper Series*, Paper No. WG3: 1.

Zeller, M. and M. Sharma (1998). 'Rural Finance and Poverty Alleviation, Food Policy Report'. Washington, DC: International Food Policy Research Institute.

11

Turning to forestry for a way out of poverty: is formalizing property rights enough?

*Krister Andersson and Diego Pacheco**

11.1 Introduction

Most of the existing studies on the issue of how public policies affect the performance of actors who operate in the informal economy focus on the urban context. Surprisingly few studies analyse the links between policy and the informal rural economy (but see Usher 1983; Apedaile and Harrington 1995). Yet, if policy reforms are to help reduce poverty, the rural context—where the poorest people in most developing countries live—needs to be analysed and brought into the public policy debate. This chapter seeks to do just that.

The core public policy question is essentially the same for both urban and rural contexts: How can formal, national-level policies be structured so that they enhance citizens' capabilities and possibilities for sustained improvements of their quality of life? This chapter analyses this question, drawing upon first-hand observations of the consequences from a recent public policy reform in Bolivia's forestry sector.

* The authors wish to thank the ninety-four members of the six communities in the Bolivian Lowlands who agreed to participate in the study. We also benefited from constructive input from several participants at the EGDI-WIDER Conference on 'Unlocking Human Potential: Linking the Informal and Formal Sectors' in Helsinki, Finland on 17–18 September 2004 as well as from the editors in this volume. Thanks also to David Price and Patty Lezotte for editing the paper. Financial support from the National Science Foundation (NSF) grant SES0004199, and the Center for the Study of Institutions, Population, and Environmental Change (CIPEC) at Indiana University (NSF grant SBR9521918) is gratefully acknowledged.

The 1996 Bolivian forestry reforms decentralized the governance of the country's forests and redistributed considerable forest property rights among the country's many resource users. For the first time in the country's modern history, smallholder farmers and indigenous peoples gained the possibility of formal management rights to forest resources. Because of the importance of a variety of forest products for the livelihood of the majority of Bolivia's large rural population, rural development analysts and practitioners saw the reforms as a big step forward. A growing body of empirical literature, however, shows that the results are quite mixed and far from clear-cut successes. Whereas the reforms have given smallholders the possibility of acquiring formal rights, getting actual access to such rights has proven to be quite an ordeal. Only a small number of farmers have actually acquired forest property rights for forest exploitation due to the difficulties of complying with the many formal requirements in the forestry regulation.

In areas with high rates of in-migration and perceived resource scarcity, insecure *de facto* forest property rights weaken the incentives for the smallholder farmers to invest in forest management activities (Knox *et al.* 1998; Gibson *et al.* 2000; Barbier 2004). Under such uncertainty, forest users face the risk of losing part or all of the future benefits from the forest management system to outsiders, and they are therefore likely to discount the perceived profitability of forest management. Without the distortions introduced by tenure insecurity, it may make more economic sense for rural smallholder farmers[1] to increase the proportion of land used for forestry rather than other land uses, such as agriculture or raising cattle. In theory, then, rural people could increase overall incomes from their land uses if they had more secure forest property rights. In this 'best case scenario', forestry could make a more significant contribution towards the alleviation of rural poverty. In this chapter, we examine this possibility in a concrete field setting: the forest-rich, tropical lowlands of Bolivia.

We analyse two principal questions: (1) Have the forest property-rights reforms altered forest users' incentive structures in favour of forest management practices? and (2) For communities that have acquired formal forest property rights, what factors help explain why some are more successful than others with regards to generating benefits from forest use?

To answer these questions, we use the tools of institutional analysis, studying how the incentive structures of local forest users change in the

[1] Hereafter referred to as 'smallholders'. In this chapter, no distinction is made between whether such smallholders are of indigenous, Spanish, or mestizo descent.

face of recent policy reforms and how these incentives influence decisions and actions in the forest. We conceptualize local forest user decisions as a function of local institutional arrangements for self-governance that filters the influence of the external legal, socioeconomic and biophysical environment. We propose that the effectiveness of the formalization policy depends to a large extent upon how the local institutions respond to the different combinations of these external factors. These institutional responses, in turn, shape the incentives that forest users perceive in the interactions with other forest governance actors. Hence, the critical factor is not just the particular policy content or even its institutional design but rather the *fit* between the formal policy and the local institutional arrangement.

11.2 Background

The tropical lowlands of Bolivia is a vast geographical area with diverse ecological, ethnic, and socioeconomic characteristics. Despite this diversity, lowland smallholder farmers share many of the predominant realities of small-scale, subsistence farmers in other parts of tropical Latin America. Like other rural populations throughout the region, rural lowland communities rely on forests to satisfy essential subsistence needs. Forests provide products such as fuelwood, fruits, nuts, fibres, medicinal plants, and wood for construction. According to the 2001 national census, 41.7 per cent of the country's entire population—rural and urban—rely on firewood as their primary source of energy for cooking (Government of Bolivia 2002).

Smallholder agricultural production constitutes a very important part of agricultural activities in Bolivia's total agricultural production, more so than in any other country in Latin America (FAO 1988). The typical smallholder farmer practices slash-and-burn agriculture to produce mainly maize, rice, and yuca and also clears forests for pastures to graze cattle. A common livelihood strategy for small-scale farmers is to produce enough crops to satisfy two primary objectives: to produce enough food crops to feed their families; and to produce enough excess crops to sell these for a profit, which is then used for the family's nonfood needs such as school fees and healthcare items (Thiele 1995). Once the basic livelihood objectives are met, households will invest any remaining residuals in alternative activities that yield the highest possible return for their scarcest resources, which is often cash and family labour (Davies *et al.* 2000).

Cattle has proven to be the most popular investment object, regarded by many as a comparatively low-risk placement option for excess resources in the lowlands (Davies *et al.* 2000). Despite the 1996 reforms, forestry has not been able to stir up much of an interest as a prospective area of investment for risk-averse, smallholder farmers, even in the forest-rich tropical lowlands.

Lowland farmers who practice slash-and-burn agriculture often keep a large proportion of their land under forest cover, as they clear only small areas of forest each time they rotate their crops. Because forest clearing is very labour intensive and family labour is a scarce resource for many smallholders, it is common practice to rotate the crops every two years between three to four different fields rather than clearing new forest areas every year. Over a 20-year-period, the average lowland farmer uses about 10 to 15 hectares of land for agricultural production (Maxwell and Pozo 1981). The remaining land is usually used for a combination of housing, pastures, and forest. Godoy (2001) shows that smallholder farmers often reduce old-growth forest cover over time unless there are economically viable alternatives to slash-and-burn agriculture.

Through the 1996 forestry law, the commercial extraction of forest resources became a possible source of income for all lowland settlers. While timber extraction is often mentioned as the most significant income-enhancing activity, the law also provides for the possibility to acquire alienation rights for a variety of other, nontimber forest products such as nuts, grasses, and medicinal plants. In an increasingly specialized market economy, rural settlers need cash to acquire many essential household items, such as food, farming equipment, healthcare, and school fees. Unlike household consumption, however, the commercial extraction of forest resources requires the forest users to comply with a large number of government regulations.

The problem for many smallholder farmers in the Bolivian lowlands is that it can be both costly and complicated to obtain the necessary government permits. As a result, even the smallholder communities that have vast forest resources on their lands tend to view forest management as an uncertain and costly land use activity—an obstacle to agriculture and pasture. Evidence of such behaviour is prevalent in Bolivia. For example, a study in the Department of Pando found that the price of one hectare of forested land was about US$4–US$20, compared to about US$200–US$300 for land in the same region—a price difference that roughly corresponds to the costs of clearing the forest, failing to reflect the value of the forest resources on the land (Tratado de Cooperación Amazónica 1997).

In the Bolivian forestry legislation there is a clear distinction between forest management and forest clearing for agricultural purposes. An individual (or a group of individuals) who has private ownership of a piece of land with forest on it cannot clear forest areas for agricultural purposes, including smallholder subsistence agriculture, without a government permit for forest clearance. Permits, in turn, may require a specially developed land use plan signed by an authorized agronomist that the land is apt for agriculture as well as an advance payment of a flat administrative fee.[2] For all other household uses of the forest—including extraction of timber, firewood, fruits, and plants—the proprietor has the authority to define rules of access, withdrawal, management, and exclusion with respect to the forest. However, they do not hold the alienation rights that would authorize them to sell some of the forest products that they harvest from the resource.

In order to acquire alienation rights, proprietors need a series of special government permits. According to one recent study, applicants need to fulfil twenty-six different administrative requirements defined by the central government—a process that involves providing proof of land possession or title, an official forest management plan, as well as an advance payment of a tax representing 17 per cent of the commercial value of the products that will be harvested and sold (Contreras-Hermosilla and Vargas 2001). An individual or a group that acquires the government permits is a conditional owner of the resource since he or she is authorized to make decisions with regards to rules of access, withdrawal, management, exclusion, and alienation, as long as these rules do not break the forestry law and the regulations of the forest management plan.

Once a group has obtained the formal rights for commercial forestry activities, it faces an array of operational challenges, such as learning how to operate a commercially efficient forest management operation, developing market contacts, and organizing the participating forest users in the day-to-day forest management activities.

11.3 Are Formal Property Rights Enough?

The farmer's decision to dedicate a piece of his or her land to formal forest management activities, with all the necessary government permits, boils down to weighing the likely costs against the projected income from future forest product sales along with the estimated value of potential

[2] Land areas inferior to three hectares are exempt, but local users must still obtain an official permit from the municipal government and the agrarian superintendence.

nonmonetary benefits. Even if local users are able to acquire formal forest property rights, there are several potential pitfalls that hamper the potentially positive effect of formal property rights on incentives for sustainable forest management. For instance, for forest users who have high discount rates and value short-term income much more than long-term returns to investments, formal forest property rights may not do much to strengthen the incentives for forest management, even if the implementation of such rights should provide effective forest tenure security. Other public policies, including formal property regimes, land reform initiatives, agricultural subsidy programmes, and trade policies, can also counteract the incentives to invest in forestry. Public policies that are biased in favour of agriculture have contributed to make agricultural activities artificially more profitable than investments in forest management, even in places where agriculture is not an ecologically sustainable land use (Solorzano 1994; Stewart and Gibson 1995).

The introduction of a formal property-rights system that recognizes the rights of rural smallholders may be a necessary policy reform for improving forest tenure security for smallholders, but it is hardly sufficient. The degree to which a new formal regime is actually able to deliver the promise of forest tenure security, we argue, depends to a great extent on how local forest users are able to organize themselves, to respond to the constraints and opportunities represented by the existing biophysical conditions, socioeconomic characteristics, and the social structure embodied in government policies and governance tradition. We articulate the relationship between these concepts in the theoretical framework in Figure 11.1.

In this view, the bundles of forest property rights form a part of the social structure in which local forest users carry out their forestry activities. The way local forest users respond to government policies, and the particular property rights that are available to them, also depend on other factors such as their previous knowledge and experience related to forest management, existing equipment and technology, the availability of valuable forest products, market opportunities, and social networks connecting local users to market actors, among other intervening factors. Local landowners tend to filter, modify, adapt, and sometimes even ignore the formal *de jure* rules of the government, especially if the government lacks an effective enforcement mechanism at the local level (Gibson *et al.* 2000). In this sense, local forest user institutions interpret the meanings of the forestry reforms and transform the *rules-in-form* (i.e. formal property rights) into *rules-in-use*. We posit that the degree to which these rules-in-use conform or not with the rules-in-form depends on whether the new rules

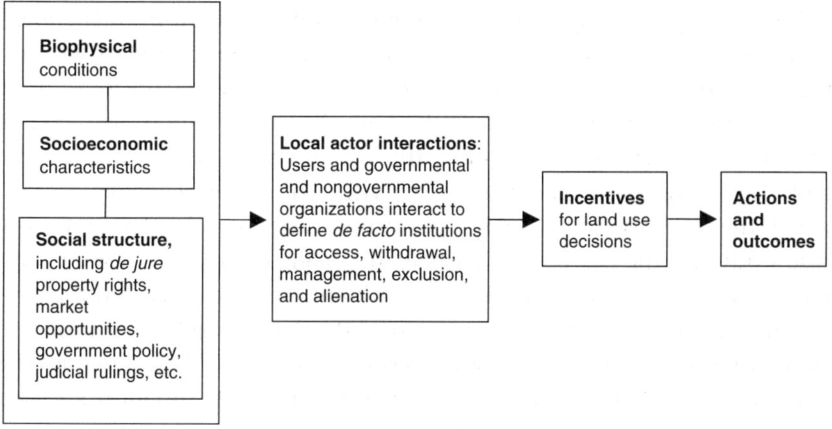

Figure 11.1. Linking context, institutions, incentives, and outcomes
Source: Authors' elaboration based on the Institutional Analysis and Development (IAD) framework (Ostrom *et al.* 1994).

are beneficial to local users, combined with the intensity with which governmental organizations enforce the rules of the new property regime.

The empirical analysis assesses this proposition by first looking at the extent to which smallholders' access to *de jure* property rights have raised their likelihood to choose forest management over alternative land uses. We then analyse the conditions that seem conducive for successful community forest management by comparing two communities' experiences after acquiring formal forest property rights.

11.4 Empirical Analysis

The empirical research aims at explaining local land use decision making with respect to how the introduction of *de jure* alienation rights affects the probability of a typical smallholder farmer to opt for forest management as a viable land use alternative. Case studies of forest user communities were carried out to study the factors that influence the formation of forest user incentive structures in the Bolivian lowlands. A total of six cases were selected, according to a three-step selection procedure.

Based on the results of a survey with the mayors of fifty randomly selected municipalities in the lowlands (see Andersson 2002; 2003), three municipalities were identified in which the municipal governments had worked actively to promote the new formal forest property regime and another three municipalities in which such efforts had not materialized.

A workshop was organized with representatives of all forest-dependent rural communities in each of the six municipalities. During the workshops, the costs and benefits of forest management were discussed for forest users in the municipality in general. At the end of each workshop, participants were asked to identify a community that represented typical characteristics with regards to forest management activities in the municipality, and on which the research team would be able to conduct an in-depth community case study. On the basis of the participants' suggestions, the research team selected a community where the predominant land uses included forestry, agriculture, and cattle-raising and spent 7–15 days in each community to study the communities' land use decision making. Table 11.1 describes the main land use characteristics and forest property-rights situation for each of the six communities. To protect the anonymity of the community members, we use fictitious community names.

The analysis compares the effects of formal forest ownership rights on land use decisions in forest-dwelling communities. The analytical approach for this exercise draws on the earlier work by Davies *et al.* (2000), who have developed a benefit-cost analysis tool to assess local landholders' economic payoff for a variety of land uses. Our gross marginal analysis compares the benefits and costs of forest management for two different sets of communities. The first set includes three communities in which formal property rights authorize logging activities by community members according to an approved forest management plan. The second set consists of three communities in which forest logging is also prominent, but primarily without formal logging permits.

Table 11.1. Main characteristics of selected case study sites

Community	Main income	Land uses	Forest property rights
'Castaña' Filadelfia, Pando	Nuts	Forestry, agriculture, and cattle	Informal *de facto* rights, conditional proprietors
'Ganado' San Borja, Bení	Maize, yuca, and cattle	Agriculture, cattle, and forestry	Informal *de facto* rights, conditional proprietors
'Carbón' El Torno, Santa Cruz	Charcoal, maize	Forestry, agriculture, and cattle	Formal harvesting rights, conditional owners
'Café' San Ignacio, Santa Cruz	Cattle	Pasture, forestry, coffee, and agriculture	Formal harvesting rights, conditional owners
'Maíz' San Rafael, Santa Cruz	Maize	Agriculture, cattle, and forestry	Formal harvesting rights, conditional owners
'Arroz' Buena Vista, Santa Cruz	Rice, maize	Agriculture, cattle, and forestry	Informal *de facto* rights, conditional proprietors

Source: Authors' elaboration based on International Forestry Resources and Institutions (IFRI) database information.

11.5 Results

In the six sites, smallholder community representatives were first asked about the differences in existing market prices of timber harvested with and without the required logging permits. In areas where there are markets for both legal and illegal timber, local forest users received between 28 and 65 per cent lower prices for illegal than for legal products, all species considered. We found that the stricter the control against illegal logging, the larger the differences between prices of legal and illegal products. These findings would suggest that the timber markets in our study put a premium on legally harvested products.

We asked forest users to specify the most important nonmonetary benefits of acquiring formal property rights to forest products. A majority of users agreed that having *de jure* logging rights could increase the market value of the property where the timber extraction takes place; speed up the land title regularization process; and increase institutional support for forest management from municipal governments, NGOs, and forestry superintendence. Although such benefits are not trivial, farmers who had formalized their forest management activities said such benefits had not been important in their decision because, so far, most of these expected benefits were hearsay that had not yet been validated by experience. There was consensus among the interviewed smallholders that the most important consideration of whether or not to apply for logging permits was the prospects for increasing economic profitability of their production system.

Table 11.2, which displays the comparison of the economic costs and benefits between formal and informal forest management activities, shows that users with formalized forest management rights generally receive higher economic returns than users without such rights.

During the first year of community-based forest management activities in 'Maíz', the net income increased by an average of US$320 per family for all of the thirteen families that constituted the community members. Only one of these families had incomes related to forestry activities previous to obtaining the community logging permits. In 'Café', total incomes from community forest management were slightly higher than in 'Maíz', reaching almost US$6,000, but this amount was divided between forty-eight families, providing a forest management-related net household income of US$125. Previous to acquiring alienation rights, forestry activities were not part of the community-organized production activities but were carried out by a subgroup of six individuals. These individuals

Table 11.2. Returns for forest management with and without formal rights

Forest management *with* logging permits[a]	Average annual US$/ha	Forest management *without* logging permits	Range average annual US$/ha
Benefits		**Benefits**	
Timber sales (at farm gate)		Timber sales (at farm gate)[b]	
–hardwoods per hectare	43.64	– hardwoods per hectare	18.54–28.80
–softwoods per hectare	94.55	– softwoods per hectare?	31.23–52.27
		– 10% risk of losing timber through inspections[c]	−6.91
Total benefits	138.18	Total benefits	42.86–74.16
Costs		**Costs**	
–planning	21.82		
–logging (including hired labour)	18.18	–logging (including hired labour)	21.99
–training, taxes, depreciation of equipment	13.45	–depreciation of equipment	9.00
Total costs	53.45	Total costs	30.99
Family labour average 15 days per year/ha		N/A	
Net income/year/family/ha	**84.73**	**Net income/year/family/ha**	**11.67–43.17**
Returns to cash	**1.59**	**Returns to cash**	**0.38–1.39**

Notes:

[a] Costs and benefits for legal and illegal logging activities are calculated averages from the six selected municipalities and communities, respectively, and do not take into consideration non-monetary items such as increased property values, higher probability of acquiring regularized land titles, or lower management costs because of the legal back-up and assistance from the municipal authorities.

[b] Illegal timber sales vary greatly from one area of the country to another, depending on a combination of factors such as local demand for wood products and the rigour of law enforcement agencies.

[c] The 10 per cent risk is based on the analysis of Stocks (1999), who estimates that the central government is able to confiscate about 10 per cent of all illegally extracted wood in Bolivia.

Source: Authors' elaboration.

estimated their annual net incomes from these formally illegal forestry activities to be about US$400 per person.

In 'Café', getting formal logging permits has produced a more equitable distribution of the benefits from forest management activities and has increased average household incomes and diversified production for a majority of community members. The effect of formal property rights is less conclusive in the community of 'Carbón'. There, formal alienation rights were given to community members authorizing them to produce and sell charcoal from hardwoods. Household incomes have increased somewhat after formal permits were granted, but production has not diversified and the same number of households engage in forestry activity today as when this activity was formally illegal.

These results suggest a predominantly positive effect of the introduction of formal forestry alienation rights on smallholders' incentives to engage in forestry activities. For these communities, the acquisition of formal ownership rights to forest resources—although conditional in nature—has increased average household incomes compared to previous levels of incomes. In smallholder communities where formal forest property rights exist, land use based production is more diversified compared to communities that do not possess government permits to commercial forest management. However, this result requires some further discussion.

The comparison between legal and illegal logging activities is complicated by the fact that actors in these types of activities often follow fundamentally different strategies. While legal logging activities take place in a specific area according to the approved management plan, such area specificity does not apply to many illegal logging activities. Organized illegal logging often takes place on *de facto* open-access lands outside community boundaries, which makes a per hectare comparison of net benefits skewed in favour of formalized management. Another extremely important factor that was not held completely constant in the comparison was the availability of valuable timber species. At the individual farm level, the potential net gains derived from formalizing forest management activities are likely to vary with the values of available species. Nevertheless, the comparison does give a powerful testimony about the *potential* economic benefits from acquiring *de jure* forest property rights.

Another caveat of this comparative analysis has to do with the possibility that the formal property rights are endogenous to our explanation. The high barriers to access formal property rights imply that only communities that are motivated enough to pay this high price have been able to acquire formal property rights. In other words, the communities with formal rights may be quite different from those that have not acquired such rights. This possible bias should be kept in mind when interpreting the results.

The economic benefits being substantial, why is it that more Bolivian smallholders do not apply for formal forest user rights? The case studies point to three plausible explanations. First, for smallholders to acquire formal forestry rights, they must first produce a valid land title to the forested land in question. The legalization of such a right can be undertaken either by the state or the private forestland owners. If the latter is the case, however, the private owner must pay the costs of the entire legalization procedure, which can be very costly. This procedure is headed by the National Institute of Agrarian Reform, which determines the order in which particular areas go through the legalization procedure.

Second, smallholders in the three municipalities where forestry activities were not a priority for the municipal government were of the opinion that forest management was not really interesting for most rural communities because of the high costs associated with the development of a forest management plan, the government permits, taxes and fees. None of the interviewed forest users in these municipalities had ever heard of the possibility of avoiding these costs with the assistance of the municipal staff. What is even more surprising is that none of the municipal staff in these municipalities knew about this possibility.

Finally, forestry is a relatively new land use alternative for many Bolivian smallholders and although its proponents claim that it may generate increased household income to farmers who engage in such activities, farmers still do not perceive these benefits as reliable as the more traditional land uses, such as agriculture and cattle-raising. Even if formalizing forest management can increase the net benefits from forestry, this increase may not be enough to motivate smallholders to shift their investments from the activities that have proven to be secure, albeit low-yielding investments over time. Smallholder farmers are often extremely cautious and risk-averse when it comes to decisions about their income portfolio. In order for risk-averse farmers to decide to change their present investment strategies, they are likely to want to see a proven, successful track record of formalized forest management because such a change would involve considerable costs for the farmer.

To start, a forest management operation would require substantial financial investments in terms of new production hardware as well as time and effort to learn effective forest management techniques, develop market contacts, and if management is not individual, to create institutional arrangements that allow for effective collaboration with fellow community member forest managers. Interviewed smallholder farmers who were sceptical about starting forest management activities mentioned the high opportunity costs as a major constraint, together with a general lack of trust towards governmental authorities.

11.5.1 *What Makes Formalized Forest Management Profitable?*

Once communities acquire formal property rights to forest resources, the central question becomes: What factors influence their performance as commercial forest managers? To find answers to this question, we went back to two of the communities that were visited just after receiving formal forest property rights in 2001 to see what had happened to them three years later. The communities we visited in January of 2004 were 'Maíz' and 'Café', both located in the Chiquitanía region of the Department of Santa Cruz, Bolivia. Focus groups and interviews with key informants were carried out to gain a better understanding of the processes involved in community forest management in the two sites.

Even though these communities have been pioneers in the development of commercial community forestry in the region, they have achieved dramatically different results in timber production. For instance, the 'Café' community has had only one timber harvesting, while the 'Maíz' community is preparing for its third annual harvesting. Families of 'Maíz' identified a timber buyer who paid a 20 per cent higher price than the 'Café' got for their timber. 'Maíz' had a net benefit from timber management that was US$6,618 higher than that of 'Café'.

We find that a combination of different natural endowments, social networks, and community institutions for collective action explain the differences in economic performance between the two communities. Forest management has become an alternative source of income for the entire population of both communities, something that would not have been possible without the introduction of formal property rights. The commercial success, however, is by no means any guarantee just because formal rights now exist.

According to the forest inventories carried out in connection with the forest management plans for the two communities: 'Maíz' has a larger quantity of high-value timber species. 'Maíz', therefore, has a higher potential for commercial forest management than 'Café'. One of the factors limiting the development of timber extraction in 'Café' is the relative lack of valuable forest species to be sold in the local markets, something that community members did not find out until after their first harvest. As a result, the income from the first timber harvest barely covered the costs, leaving each family with about US$125. Community leaders told us that the results from the first harvest were so disappointing that the community council decided that it would be better to protect the forest and wait a few years to anticipate better market conditions for the species that exist in their forest. One of the benefits from the introduction of formal forestry property rights is that the community now controls its territory to a greater extent than before, and can therefore afford to think longer term about when to harvest.

While most socioeconomic characteristics are very similar in the two communities, they do differ in one crucial aspect: population size. The 'Café' community is larger and therefore pays higher transaction costs to coordinate and reach agreements about collective activities, such as forest management decisions.

Finally, in relation to the social structure, both communities are in a similar situation. Both have formal forestry property rights for carrying out commercial forest management. What is to some extent different are the interactions between the local community and external actors who deal with forestry, including municipal authorities, the central government's forestry service, and timber buyers. We call these contacts the external networks of commercial forest management. We find that the strength of this external network is a key factor in explaining the different outcomes in the two communities.

The 'Maíz' community can more easily mobilize internal networks because of its smaller population. They do not have difficulties in organizing timber production that includes all community members. The expectations of the 'Café' community's members are more diverse, since productive activities are more diversified and families rely on long traditions of cultivating cash crops (coffee) for export. Regarding the development of external networks, the 'Maíz' community has developed more opportunities to create linkages with market actors, much because of the closer distance between their community and an urban dwelling with timber-market outlets. In 'Maíz', we found the personal contacts of the community leaders to be quite crucial in the development of favourable timber-purchasing contracts.

11.6 Conclusions

The empirical evidence from six selected municipalities suggests that the acquisition of *de jure* alienation rights can strengthen forest users' incentives to engage in sustainable forest management. The benefit-cost analysis suggests that, all other factors equal, the profitability of forest management increases if users have *de jure* alienation rights for forest products. Nevertheless, existing farming knowledge, skewed policies in favour of agriculture and cattle-raising, as well as more advantageous subsidies and technical assistance for such land uses, may potentially weaken the perceived feasibility of commercial forest management, even if *de jure* alienation rights exist.

The qualitative case study analysis also found that simply getting *de jure* alienation rights to timber products is not sufficient to make forestry a successful commercial undertaking. The comparison of two communities that recently acquired formal forest management rights points to the importance of the community's connectivity with external governance actors and markets, the community capacity for organizing collective enterprises, and the availability of valuable timber species as key factors that help explain differences in commercial performance. For analysts interested in the impacts of formal property-rights reform, these findings illustrate the value of considering the fit between existing local institutional arrangements and the formal government policies.

These results confirm earlier research findings that forest management in the tropics can be economically viable, although the traditional policy bias towards agricultural activities tends to distort farmers' decision making at the cost of forestry investments. Based on data from Costa Rica, Stewart (1994) estimated that without distortions, well-managed tropical forests can yield yearly incomes of US$270 to US$450 per year and per hectare. Most competing agricultural crops yield much less. In Ecuador, for instance, Southgate *et al.* (1989) estimated agricultural income of no more than US$20 per year and hectare. Income from cattle ranching can be as low as US$2.50 to US$3.00 per year and hectare (Stewart 1994). Profits for all agricultural crops for all three countries were less than US$100 per year and hectare, except for potato in the Bolivian highlands (Stewart and Gibson 1995).

The results of the economic importance of forest management in this study are less dramatic, but they nevertheless show that forest management can, under some circumstances, compete with agriculture and cattle-raising, even with a policy that favours these traditional land uses. Larger studies are needed to test these results more rigorously.

The observed methodological limitations notwithstanding, our study unequivocally identifies that substantial barriers remain for smallholders to engage in commercial forest management activities, even when the trees that they would like to manage, grow in their own backyards. Even after receiving titles for the forestlands, communities are required to request government permits to exploit the forest on their land commercially. To date, very few communities have been able to fulfil these requisites—and only after a great deal of struggle. Simplifications of the existing procedures—and keeping the smallholder farmers in mind—have been introduced, but further modification is needed to make commercial forest management a more attractive form of land use for the rural poor.

References

Andersson, K. (2002). 'Can Decentralization Save Bolivia's Forests? An Institutional Analysis of Municipal Governance of Forest Resources'. Ph.D. dissertation. Bloomington, IN: Indiana University.

Andersson, K. (2003). 'What Motivates Municipal Governments? Uncovering the Institutional Incentives for Municipal Governance of Forest Resources in Bolivia'. *Journal of Environment and Development*, 12(1): 5–27.

Apedaile, L. P. and D. Harrington (1995). 'Implications of Agricultural Structural Change in the United States and Canada for Policy, Performance and Trade Harmonization'. *Canadian Journal of Agricultural Economics*, 43(1): 241–53.

Barbier, E. B. (2004). 'Explaining Agricultural Land Expansion and Deforestation in Developing Countries'. *American Journal of Agricultural Economics*, 86(5): 1347–53.

Contreras-Hermosilla, A. and T. M. Vargas (2001). *Dimensiones Sociales, Ambientales y Económicas de las Reformas en la Política Forestal de Bolivia*. Santa Cruz: Proyecto de Manejo Forestal Sostenible and the Center for International Forestry Research.

Davies, J., E. Magariños, E. Osinaga, and A. Bojanic (2000). 'Is Natural Forest Management a Viable Land Use Option in a Colonization Zone in Bolivia?' ODI Working Paper. London: Overseas Development Institute.

FAO (Food and Agriculture Organization) of the United Nations (1988). *La Participación Campesina en el Desarrollo* Rural. Santiago: La Oficina Regional de la FAO para America Latina y el Caribe.

Gibson, C., M. McKean, and E. Ostrom (2000). *People and Forests: Communities, Institutions and Governance*. Cambridge, MA: MIT Press.

Godoy, R. (2001). *Indians, Rain Forests, and Markets: Theory, Methods, and Analysis*. New York: Columbia University Press.

Government of Bolivia (2002). Censo Nacional 2001. La Paz: Instituto Nacional de Estadísticas (INE).

Knox, A., R. Meinzen-Dick, and P. Hazell (1998). 'Property Rights, Collective Action and Technologies for Natural Resource Management'. CAPRi Working Paper 1. Washington, DC: IFPRI.

Maxwell, S. and M. Pozo (1981). 'Farming Systems in the Colonization Crescent of Santa Cruz, Bolivia: Results of a Survey'. Working Document No. 22. Santa Cruz: CIAT.

Ostrom, E., R. Gardner, and J. Walker (1994). *Rules, Games, and Common-Pool Resources*. Ann Arbor, MI: University of Michigan Press.

Solorzano, R. (1994). 'Incentivos al Desarrollo del Sector Forestal en Bolivia'. *Informe final de consultoría*. La Paz: Proyecto FAO PAFBOL.

Southgate, D., R. Sierra, and L. Brown (1989). *The Causes of Tropical Deforestation in Ecuador: A Statistical Analysis*. Paper No. 89. London: London Environmental Economics Centre.

Stewart, R. (1994). 'Economic Impacts of Forest Sector Trade Policies: The Case of Costa Rica'. Report Prepared by Stewart Associates for USAID-Costa Rica.

Stewart, R. and D. Gibson (1995). 'Environmental and Economic Development Consequences of Forest and Agricultural Sector Policies in Latin America: A Synthesis of Case Studies of Costa Rica, Ecuador, and Bolivia', in H. Cortes-Salas, R. de Camino, and A. Contreras (eds), *Readings of the Workshop on Government Policy Reform for Forestry Conservation and Development in Latin America*. San Jose, Costa Rica: IICA, pp. 5–38.

Stocks, A. (1999). *Iniciativas Forestales Indígenas en el Trópico Boliviano: Realidades y Opciones*. Documento Técnico 76/1999. Santa Cruz: Proyecto BOLFOR.

Thiele, G. (1995). 'The Displacement of Settlers in the Amazon: The Case of Santa Cruz, Bolivia'. *Human Organization*, 54: 273–82.

Tratado de Cooperación Amazónica (TCA) (1997). *Estrategia para Implementar las Recomendaciones de la Propuesta de Pucallpa sobre el Desarrollo Sostenible del Bosque*. Caracas: Secretaría Pro-Témpore del Tratado de Cooperación Amazónico.

Usher, P. (1983). 'Property Rights: The Basis of Wildlife Management', in *National and Regional Interests in the North*, 3rd National Workshop on People, Resources, and the Environment North. Ottawa: Canadian Arctic Resources Commission.

12

Voluntary contributions to informal activities producing public goods: can these be induced by government and other formal sector agents? Some evidence from Indonesian posyandus

*Jeffrey B. Nugent and Shailender Swaminathan**

12.1 Introduction

The purpose of this chapter is to determine the extent to which, and how, government or other formal sector contributions may induce informal sector and voluntary contributions by individuals in such a way as to produce important local public goods. The study is motivated by the extreme scarcity of funding by government and external donors and the dearth of private providers, of local public goods and services, or even markets for such services in developing countries. Given the rather dismal prospects for formal sector provision of local public goods, the informal sector is a potentially important vehicle for unlocking the human potential by producing appropriate kinds of public goods, especially health and education services.

One important set of informal sector activities are those involving voluntary activities, such as time and money volunteered to various kinds of informal community associations. These associations are typically not

* The authors express their appreciation to Tomoya Matsumoto for his valuable programming assistance. We also thank seminar participants at the EGDI-WIDER Conference in Helsinki, an anonymous referee, and especially to Elinor Ostrom, Amos Sawyer, and Lyn Squire for detailed comments and useful discussion.

'owned' in any formal sense but only in a very loose sense by their collective membership. Often, the voluntary contributions of time, in-kind goods and services, and money to these institutions by community members are the most important source of public goods production at the local level.

Yet, both casual observation, and the studies reported in the growing literature on local public goods production make it clear that the number and quality of activities provided by informal institutions may vary considerably across countries and communities, according to various community characteristics, such as size, level of development, degree of income inequality, and ethnic and religious diversity. Even more importantly, the magnitude and character of government or other formal sector participation (funds, personnel, maintenance, etc.) in these institutions may vary from one institution to another both within and between communities.

To accomplish the objective of this chapter, we attempt to identify (1) the magnitude and direction of the effects of both external interventions and various community, household, and individual characteristics, on the voluntary contributions of individuals to informal activities of the 'unlocking human potential' type, and (2) how the effective provision of human potential unlocking activities at the level of the local service provider, is affected by different forms of external support and supervision as well as by a variety of community level characteristics.

The benefits of private sector activities and the provision of government-supplied infrastructure and services for the well-being of different segments of the community will depend considerably on the nature of the relationships identified. If the provision of goods, services, and employment by the formal sector merely substitutes for those provided by informal institutions, the net benefits may be much smaller than when the activities are in fact complementary. Knowledge concerning the character of these relationships and how they are affected by community and other characteristics may go a long way towards designing optimal mechanisms for 'unlocking the human potential' through these linkages.

The chapter is organized as follows: Section 12.2 which follows provides a brief review of relevant literature on local public goods production and the role of informal activities. Section 12.3 defends the choice of both country (Indonesia) and informal service providers (posyandus) and describes the data set. Section 12.4 describes the methods. Section 12.5 presents the empirical results. Section 12.6 derives implications for theory and policy.

12.2 Brief Review of Relevant Literature

The importance of local public goods as a means of facilitating investments in human capital and the establishment of firms is generally appreciated. Indeed, many of the basic needs of human beings and especially the basic services to develop human capabilities are supplied in the form of public goods at the local level (Sen 1985). Basic education, health, protection of person and property, the supply and maintenance of water supply, local streets, and other infrastructure are in most countries supplied by the public or NGO sector at the local level.

Although many local public goods are not pure public goods, and hence are not fully jointly consumable and are non-excludable, they typically share these characteristics to some degree. This implies that their provision is inhibited by the incentive to 'freeride'. This of course undermines the efforts that local communities may make in providing the local public goods. Indeed, it is widely believed that, as a result, public goods production will be too low.

Much of the literature has been devoted to identifying various characteristics of groups that may be advantageous in helping to overcome the freerider problem and hence also the bias towards undersupply of public goods. While some of these group characteristics are generally agreed upon, such as small size, members' length of association, and commonality of backgrounds, others have been controversial. For example, Olson (1965) argued that income or wealth inequality might stimulate collective action whereas others like Bardhan (2000) have argued that it would weaken collective action. Similarly, some feel that ethnic or religious diversity would help the production of local public goods whereas others believe the opposite.

To the extent that exclusion of non-contributors is possible, the incentive to freeride may be weakened. Public goods in such situations are called 'club goods' and the underproduction problem controlled. As Wilson (1992) indicated in his study on the efficiency of public good production in Kenya by the Harambee Movement, efficiency is strengthened when the local population itself chooses the public good which is most needed, and individuals and institutions make their contributions contingent on the contributions of others. The underproduction of such public goods can also be mitigated by compensating people for their voluntary contributions, perhaps with non-monetary rewards, or by assigning penalties to those who do not contribute. The extent to which people are desirous or in need of the public good can also be a factor. For example, those who would especially benefit from the public good would have greater incentive to contribute than others.

Because the effects of income inequality, and ethnic and religious diversity have been especially controversial, much research has been devoted to these effects in recent years. Evidence provided by Alberto Alesina and various co-authors, especially Alesina *et al.* (1999) and Easterly and Levine (1997), show that some countries, and regions within countries, are considerably disadvantaged in the production of local public goods by virtue of considerable ethnic diversity. Swaminathan and Nugent (2003) and Nugent and Swaminathan (2005) demonstrate the existence of deleterious effects of income inequality on public goods production at the local level, specifically for Indonesia. These effects may be realized in several ways: (1) by making it more difficult to agree on the kind and quality of public goods to be produced and the ways to finance them, (2) by diverting expenditures away from development-related public goods towards incentive-reducing redistributive transfers (Alesina and Perotti 1996), (3) by the lack of altruism of those in other ethnic or income groups, and (4) by limiting the strength of social sanctions in penalizing those who do not contribute to their production (Miguel and Gugerty 2002). On the other hand, as indicated above, collective action theory can also lead to the opposite conclusion.

Another relevant literature for the determinants of voluntary activities and public goods production is that of behavioural economics. The fact that substantial percentages of the population in such countries have been engaged in voluntary activities has been used to suggest that behaviour is only boundedly selfish instead of purely selfish (Mullainathan and Thaler 2000). But, time spent in such activities can alternatively be explained by (1) tax laws discriminating against labour supply of secondary workers in the household ('the marriage tax'), (2) the direct consumption utility derived from participatory community activities (or even just to be seen participating with certain others they want to be associated with), and (3) the special needs that the volunteers may have for the goods produced.

12.3 Choice of Country, Posyandus, and the Indonesian Data Set

Indonesia is chosen as the country of study for several reasons, including its relatively low level of development, its economic and cultural diversity, and the diversity of its informal sector activities. To accomplish the aforementioned objectives, detailed data at the individual, household, and community levels on formal and informal sector activities as well as on the numerous factors that have to be controlled for are required. Fortunately, such data is available for Indonesia, thanks to the three waves of the Indonesian Family Life Survey (IFLS 1, 2, and 3). Table 12.1 presents a description of the variables and variable names used in the analysis.

One important feature of IFLS is the detailed information provided by the individual and household questionnaires concerning the time and money contributed voluntarily to each informal and formal sector activity by each of 19,800 individuals sampled from the 321 communities. In each community, information was collected from a sample of health facilities, both formal and informal. Taken together also, the various questionnaires provide the information that can be used as reference regarding community size, income inequality, ethnic diversity, employment opportunities, the level of development, and government-supplied infrastructure. Another strength of the data is the extremely low rates of attrition of households from the initial sample in the subsequent rounds of the survey.

For the informal sector to be studied we choose *posyandus* (impermanent integrated community health posts). The posyandus provide health services primarily to young children and family planning services to adults. These community health posts have played a very important role in Indonesia's public health strategy, success in lowering infant mortality, raising the country's health statistics, and human development index. Posyandus typically operate in a community only about once a month. Since they are staffed by volunteers, it is clear that without local volunteers there would be no services. Yet, especially in terms of quality, posyandus can benefit from supervision and visits from trained staff (including physicians and midwives) from the government-run health centres (*puskesmas*) and family planning clinics. Financial support for posyandus comes from several sources including the village budget and local community members. Many of the medical instruments and supplies used in the posyandus (such as weighing scales and pills) are provided by the health centres and are extremely low cost but effective. Organized at the community level by the Family Welfare Movement (PKK), Indonesia's posyandus have won awards from both WHO and UNICEF, for their success in volunteerism and health improvement.

By the mid 1980s posyandus became a critical feature of Indonesia's overall health improvement plans and, as a result, their presence spread rapidly. From 20,000 in 1985, the number of posyandus increased to about 200,000 in 1988 and became available in almost every village by the early

Table 12.1. Model specifications

Variables	Participation/ hours in Posyandu	No. of cadres in Posyandu	No. of visitors to Posyandu	Posyandu services to children	Child visit to Posyandu
YRSSCHOOL (education level of women in years)	x				x
AGE (age of woman)	x				x
AGE squared	x				x
Gini of YPC (community level gini of income)	x			x	x
DmMARRIED (married dummy)	x				x
KIDS0–5 (No. of kids between 0 and 5 years)	x				x
URBAN (urban dummy)	x	x	x		x
DIVLANG (diversity in language)	x	x	x		x
dmMJRLNG (dummy: own language is majority)	x				x
YPC (total household income)	x	x	x		x
CmYPC (mean community income)	x	x	x	x	x
CmPOP (population in community in 1997)		x	x		
CmYRSSCHOOL (avg. educ. level in community)		x	x		
AVGTINST (avg. no. of instruments per posyandu)	x				x
AVGPUSKV (avg. no. of annual puskesmas visits)	x				x
AVGFPVIS (avg. no. of annual family planning visits)	x				x
NUMBPOS (no. of Posyandus in community)	x				x
NUMBPUSK (no. of Puskesmas in community)	x				x
PUSKFUND (Posyandu funding from Puskesmas)		x	x		
VILBUD (Posyandu funding from village budget)		x	x		
TINST (no. of instruments in Posyandu)		x	x		
POSYREVIT (Posyandu revitalization)		x	x		
PUSKSTAFF (staff from Puskesmas when child visit)				x	
CHILDAGE (age of child)				x	
FRAC_VILBUD (fraction of Posyandus funding from village budget)				x	
FRAC_POSREVIT (fraction of Posyandus revitalized)				x	

Note:
x indicates that the variable was used in the model, while blanks indicate the variable was not used.

1990s. Especially given their voluntary character and the magnitude of the 1997–98 financial crisis, however, the quantity and quality of posyandu services have varied over time. Indeed, during the crisis, posyandu volunteerism and service quality deteriorated substantially. Table 12.2 shows that the proportion of women who participated in posyandus fell from 22 per cent in 1997 to 15 per cent in 2000. It also shows some decline in the average number of cadres in posyandus over the 1993 to 2000 period. Notably, there is also a sizable variance around the mean in any given year. It is this variability over both time and space that makes the posyandu experience over the three waves of IFLS so useful for a study such as ours. The deterioration in the quality of the posyandus was sufficiently great in 1997–98 that in 1998 a Posyandu Revitalization Programme was initiated, but only in certain communities. Table 12.3 shows that about 50 per cent of the posyandus in 2000 were part of the revitalization programme. This revitalization comprised cadre training, improving the incentives of the cadres, and improving the quality of the instruments in the posyandus.

Table 12.2. Variation in the dependent variables

Dependent variables	1993	1997	2000	Model	Estimation
Participation in posyandu by women		0.22	0.15	Logit: Random and conditional fixed effects	Maximum likelihood
Annual hours involved in posyandu activities		14.3 (16.6)	14.8 (17.1)	Tobit model: Random effects	Generalized least squares
No. of cadres	5.5 (3.3)	4.4 (2.6)	4.8 (2.4)	Poisson: Random and fixed effects	Maximum likelihood
Total no. of visitors in 3 months prior to survey	102.6 (50.9)	152.4 (122.9)	303.1 (236.1)	Linear model: Random and fixed effects	Generalized least squares
Child received service at posyandu: Vitamin A pill			0.55	Probit model estimated jointly with selection into posyandu visit	Maximum likelihood
Child received service at posyandu: Oral Rehydration Solution			0.12	Probit model estimated jointly with selection into posyandu visit	Maximum likelihood
Child received service at posyandu: Immunization			0.48	Probit model estimated jointly with selection into posyandu visit	Maximum likelihood
Child visited posyandu in 4 weeks prior to survey			0.13	Selection equation	Maximum likehood

In 1993 and 1997 there is information at the level of the posyandu about inputs from both formal and informal sectors. For example, among the former are the frequency of the supervision of the posyandu by the puskesmas. At the same time, for each posyandu, there is information on the quantity, quality and frequency of the services provided and the number of users. Finally, from the sampled adult women, there is information on both their participation and hours volunteered to the posyandus and the quality of services received by their children when visiting the posyandus.

Table 12.3 presents descriptive statistics for the main independent variables used in the analysis. However, the statistics in Table 12.3 mask the degree of change over time within a given community. While some communities did not exhibit change in the number of posyandus, there are quite a few that experienced either increases or decreases between 1997 and 2000. Similar variation is observed for two other 'formal' interventions: the average number of instruments in the posyandu, and the number of visits per year from the family planning clinic to the posyandu. The dependent variables exhibit variation as well (Table 12.2).

12.4 Methods

Our goal is to estimate the effect of formal interventions on participation in, and the quality of, involuntary institutions. We estimate models at two different levels: At the posyandu level, we estimate the determinants of two outcomes: (1) the number of cadres (volunteers), and (2) the number of visitors (services used). While the model is estimated in levels with controls for community population, an alternative would have been to estimate the model with the dependent variable, now expressed as a fraction of the population of children in the community. At the individual level, we estimate the determinants of two other outcomes: (3) participation of individual women in the posyandu as users of posyandu services, and (4) the quality of the posyandu as measured by the care individual children received. The formal intervention variables used include, supervision of posyandu activities by the staff of the puskesmas, funding of the posyandu from the village budget, the Posyandu Revitalization Programme, and other variables such as education, income, and income inequality. The description of covariates used in the models is presented in Table 12.1.

Table 12.3. Longitudinal and cross-sectional variation in important covariates and dependent variables

	1993	1997	2000
Community level			
FRAC_VILBUD	0.35	0.39	0.31
AVGFPVIS	1.39	7.78	5.81
	(0.85)	(3.89)	(3.92)
AVGTINST	7.25	7.47	5.56
	(1.5)	(2.06)	(2.00)
NUMBPOS	8.67	8.35	8.30
	(8.19)	(6.64)	(6.78)
Gini of YPC	0.70	0.5	0.5
	(0.11)	(0.09)	(0.09)
DIVLANG	x	0.18	0.19
		(0.22)	(0.23)
Posyandu level			
VILBUD	0.35	0.38	0.31
TINST	7.2	7.5	5.5
	(2.1)	(2.6)	(2.6)
POSREVIT	0	0	0.48
PUSKSTAFF	x	x	0.81
Other covariates used in analysis			
YRSSCHOOL			6.28
			(4.35)
AGE			37
			(16)
DmMARRIED			0.64
KIDS0–5			1.29
			(0.56)
URBAN			0.53
CHILDAGE			7.23
			(4.36)
CHILDMALE			0.50
YPC			1172762
			(1575827)
CmYPC			1189486
			(659605)

Notes:

x represents non-availability for that variable–year combination.

Standard deviations in parenthesis for continuous variables, but are not reported for discrete variables.

For outcomes (1), (2), and (3) above, we estimate two specifications that vary in the way the effect of formal intervention is identified. The general specification can be written as:

$$y_{jt} = \beta_0 + \beta_1 Interven_{jt} + \beta_2 X_{jt} + \delta_j + v_{jt} \tag{12.1}$$

In this model (*j*) indexes observation (either individual or posyandu), and (*t*) indexes time. The first specification is the random effects model that uses cross-sectional and longitudinal variation in $Interven_{jt}$ to identify β_2. The second specification is the fixed effects model that uses only variation in $Interven_{jt}$ over time to identify the model. The advantage of the fixed effects model is that it eliminates any bias caused by correlation between $Interven_{jt}$ and δ_j. This correlation might exist, for example, if formal interventions are more likely in areas where individuals have a lower propensity to participate in community activities. When the unit of observation is the posyandu, we cannot introduce fixed effects at the posyandu level, but do so at the community level. This is because posyandus are, by their very nature, informal institutions, and hence cannot be linked over time. Introducing community level fixed effects in the posyandu level model allows us to identify β_2 using both longitudinal and cross-sectional variation in $Interven_{jt}$ among posyandus' within a community.

Our final model (4), estimates the effect of formal intervention on the quality of healthcare provided to a child visiting the posyandu. Since comparable data is not available in the earlier waves of IFLS, to estimate this model we use data only from Wave 3 (2000). This model provides an estimate of the effect of formal intervention on the probability of receiving specific kinds of healthcare in the posyandu, namely, vitamin A pills, an immunization, and an oral rehydration solution for treating diarrhoea.

The model estimated here is:

$$q_{ij} = \gamma_{1j} Interven_i + \gamma_{2j} X_i + u_{ij} \tag{12.2}$$

where q_{ij} indicates whether service of type (j) has been provided to child (i), $Interven_i$ is the formal intervention, and X are other controls. One problem in unbiased estimation of equation (12.2) is that q is not observed for children that have not visited the posyandu in the four weeks prior to the survey. If those children that have visited the posyandu are a non-random subset of the entire sample of children, the estimates in equation (12.1) might be biased. To account for this potential non-random selection, we also jointly estimate the selection equation:

$$q_{i,not\ missing} = \alpha_1 Z_i + \alpha_2 X_i + v_i \tag{12.2$'$}$$

The correlation in the error terms in equations (12.2) and (12.2′) is identified using the instruments in the vector Z_i that includes variables such as the number of posyandus in the community, etc. Table 12.1

lists the covariates used in both the service (12.2) and selection (12.2′) equations. For each type of service, equations (12.2) and (12.2′) are estimated by maximum likelihood allowing for correlation in the error terms u and v.

12.5 Empirical Results

The results for volunteerism at the individual level are presented in Table 12.4. We estimate models for two different measures of posyandu participation, namely the decision to participate or not (DmPART) and the number of hours devoted to posyandu activities (HOURS). Since the former is a binary variable, it is estimated by Probit. Since the latter is continuous but bounded below at zero, it is estimated by Tobit.

Beginning with the characteristics of the individual woman, schooling has positive effects on both DmPART and HOURS. Age has a non-linear effect; being married and having children less than five years of age has positive effects on both. At the household level, income per capita has negative and significant effects, and speaking the same language as the majority in the community has a positive but not significant effect (except

Table 12.4. Participation in and hours supplied to Posyandu by women

Explanatory variable	Participation (DmPART)		Hours
	Random effects	Fixed effects	Random effects
YRSSCHOOL	0.0620***	0.1551***	0.8039***
AGE	0.0657***	0.1354***	0.6171***
AGE Squared	−0.0018***	−0.0025***	−0.0173***
Gini of YPC	0.3283	0.8420*	6.1452*
DmMARRIED	2.0998***	1.9158***	23.799***
KIDS0–5	0.7840***	0.3453**	8.2226***
URBAN	−0.0304		−0.4073
DIVLANG	−0.5044***	−0.4491	−4.5829**
dmMJRLNG	0.0730	−0.2861*	1.5829
YPC	−0.0001***	−0.0001**	−0.0010***
CmYPC	−0.0005***	−0.0006***	−0.0047***
AVGTINST	0.0199*	0.0358*	0.2581*
AVGPUSKV	0.0052	0.0057	0.0237
AVGFPVIS	0.0199***	0.0222**	0.1077
NUMBPOS	0.0314***	0.0542*	0.3762***
NUMBPUSK	0.0003	0.0032	−0.0859
CONSTANT	−4.2559***		−54.5386***
Log likelihood	−6780	−1771	−19611

Note:
***, **, and * indicate that the coefficient indicated is statistically significant at the 1, 5, and 10 per cent levels, respectively.

in the case of fixed effects in which case the effect on dmPART is negative and significant at the 10 per cent level). At the community level, both language diversity and average per capita income have negative and significant effects on both measures of participation in posyandus. As to the intervention variables, the average number of instruments in each posyandu (TINST), the number of annual visits from staff of the National Family Planning Board (FPLANV) and the number of posyandus in the community, have positive and significant effects on both dmPART and HOURS. Urban location, visits of puskesmas staff to the posyandus, and the total number of activities in the community have no significant influence on either measure of voluntary participation in posyundu activities.

The strength of the age and other demographic effects shows that voluntary participation by Indonesian women in posyandus is a life cycle phenomenon, triggered by marriage and having small children. This can also be interpreted as relative need for the services that posyandus provide, suggesting that such volunteerism is by no means selfless in nature. Since both household and community level per capita incomes have negative effects on posyandu participation, posyandus seem to cater primarily to poor people, also suggesting that individuals' with better labour market prospects (and hence higher household income) participate less in the voluntary activity. The positive effect of inequality in per capita income can be interpreted in a similar way since, for any given per capita income at the community level, greater inequality would imply a relatively larger proportion of poor people in the community. As suggested in the local public goods literature, ethnic diversity (reflected in language) reduces voluntary participation in posyandu activities.

As far as the effect of formal sector contributions on participation is concerned, several pieces of evidence suggest that these effects are positive. Education is a formal sector activity that has positive and significant effects on both measures of participation. Likewise, the following measures of formal sector contributions to and supervision of posyandu activities—AVGTINST, AVGFPVIS, and NUMBPOS—all have positive and significant effects on voluntary activities by individuals to posyandus. To assess the magnitude of these effects, we simulated the effect of changes in specified covariates. We find that increasing the number of visits of staff from the family planning clinic from once every 4 months to once every month increases the probability of participating in the posyandu by about 2 percentage points. Relative to the mean participation probability of about 0.18, this represents an increase of just over 10 per cent. Further, increasing the education level of women from primary (6 years) to junior high (10 years) increases the probability of participation by 2 percentage points.

Next, we turn to the results at the posyandu level given in Table 12.5. In this case, we use the number of cadres in a posyandu (CADRES) as a measure of volunteerism, and then the total number of visits to posyandus (VISITS) during the last three months as a measure of client participation, the latter reflecting, in part, the quality of services offered by the posyandu. The results for CADRES are more similar to the results for voluntary participation at the individual level in Table 12.4 than are those for VISITS. Similar to the results at the individual level, schooling and the inequality of per capita income, both have positive and significant effects on CADRES, while YPC has a negative, but insignificant effect. Of special interest, however, are the positive and significant effects for two measures of formal sector contribution to posyandus, that is, funding from the village budget and the number of instruments that the posyandu has (TINST). These results again demonstrate how voluntary activities can be induced by formal sector contributions and are unaffected by the choice between fixed and random effects estimates. TINST is an especially significant determinant of the number of cadres. Simulation results show that starting with covariate values at their respective means, increasing the number of instruments in the posyandu from 3 to 6 increases the number of cadres by about 10 per cent.

Table 12.5. Posyandu level participation by volunteers (cadres) and clients

Explanatory variable	No. of cadres in Posyandu		Total no. of visits to Posyandu during last 3 months	
	Random effects	Fixed effects	Random effects	Fixed effects
Health centre funding	0.0235	0.0365	7.3773	2.1995
Village budget funding	0.0472*	0.0661**	−8.5307	−0.9272
TINST	0.0188***	0.0151***	4.774***	3.5060**
POSYREVIT	0.0200	0.0193	140.1894***	143.9775***
GiniYPC	0.5514***	0.6200***	−277.1782***	−320.3041***
CmYPC (in millions of rupiah)	−0.003	−0.0054	0.0045***	0.0059***
CmYRSSCHOOL	0.0289***	−0.0239	−4.8472**	−21.7575***
CmPOP	0.0044***		0.0013***	
URBAN	0.1634***	0.0586	21.3402*	−2.5055
Log likelihood	−4341	−3237		
Within group R2			0.20	0.22

Note:
***, **, and * indicate that the coefficient indicated is statistically significant at the 1, 5, and 10 per cent levels, respectively.

From the results for VISITS given in the last two columns of the table, one can again see the positive effect of instruments (TINST). Having a Posyandu Revitalization Programme (POSYREVIT) also has a positive and significant influence on VISITS, the measure that presumably better reflects the quality and usefulness of the services. Note that in this case, YPC at the community level has a significant positive effect, and the inequality in YPC, a highly significant negative effect. The latter finding is consistent with our aforementioned earlier results (also for Indonesia, and based on the same data sets) showing that inequality was found to have a significant negative effect on health care utilization and educational investments at the individual level. Average schooling levels in this case have a negative and significant effect, possibly reflecting the fact that those communities with more education on an average would be expected to have more formal sector sources of health service provision, than would those with lower schooling levels. Simulation results reveal that increasing the posyandu's number of instruments from 3 to 6 increases the number of visitors by about 10 per cent, while having a revitalization programme increases the number of visitors by about 140.

While VISITS may be a reasonable proxy for quality of posyandu service provision, it is certainly a rather blunt measure. Clearly, the connection to service quality and health outcomes is at best, quite suggestive. In the final step of our analysis, we treat the visit to a posyandu (VISITPOS) as a selection equation (to test for the possibility of selection bias), and then attempt to explain variations in the delivery of each of three specific services—labelled VITAMIN, IMMUN, and ORALR, respectively—to these individuals. Once again, we introduce controls for various individual, household, and community characteristics, but place special emphasis on the effects on the posyandu of three types of formal sector contributions: (1) the presence at the time of delivery of the service of a staff member from the (formal sector) 'puskesmas', or public health clinic (PUSKSTAFF), (2) funding from the village budget (VILFUND), and (3) a Posyandu Revitalization Programme (POSYREVIT). Since both VISITPOS and each of the three service provision variables are (0, 1) dummy variables, the parameters of the jointly estimated selection and service equations are probit estimates. The results are presented in Table 12.6.

Turning first to the results for VITAMIN, we find that both VILFUND and POSYREVIT have positive effects on the probability that vitamin pills are provided when a child visits the posyandu. Of even greater relevance is the positive and significant coefficient of PUSKSTAFF. The selection equation (VISITPOS) results reveal no evidence of gender bias

Table 12.6. Provision of services at Posyandu (child level model)

	VITAMIN	ORALR	IMMUN
Service provision to child			
PUSKSTAFF	0.24**	0.73***	0.34***
CHILDAGE	0.21***	0.008	−0.42***
FRAC_VILFUND	0.18*	−0.06	0.11
FRAC_POSREVIT	0.19**	−0.03	−0.09
Gini of YPC	−0.17	0.33	0.08
Selection equation			
YRSSCHOOL	0.005	0.006	0.01*
AGE	−0.007	−0.006	−0.008
AGE Squared	0.00007	0.00005	0.00001
Gini of YPC	0.48*	0.53*	0.61*
DmMARRIED	−0.10	−0.09	−0.08
KIDS0–5	−0.02	−0.03	−0.02
URBAN	0.15**	0.17***	0.22***
DIVLANG	−0.48***	−0.48***	−0.40***
dmMJRLNG	0.07	0.07	0.09
YPC (in millions of rupiah)	−0.03	−0.04*	−0.01
CmYPC (in millions of rupiah)	−0.14**	−0.15***	−0.17***
AVG_TINST	−0.03**	−0.03**	−0.025**
AVG_PUSKV	−0.013**	−0.015**	−0.017***
AVG_FPLANV	0.004	0.001	0.001
NUMBPOS	0.03***	0.03***	0.027***
NUMBPUSK	0.01	0.01	0.014**
CHILDMALE	0.018	0.008	0.016
CHILDAGE	−0.37***	−0.36***	−0.37***
Rho (*u*,*v*)	−0.36	0.41*	0.80***
N	1055	1055	1055
Log Likelihood	−2484	−2149	−2435

Note:
***, **, and * indicate that the coefficient indicated is statistically significant at the 1, 5, and 10 per cent levels, respectively.

(CHILDMALE), but a very strong negative influence of CHILDAGE, positive effects of the number of posyandus in the community (NUMPOS) (a measure of proximity), and the income inequality measure GINIYPC. The fact that household income has a negative effect supports our earlier assessment that the posyandu is an informal institution primarily serving the poor.

The second set of results in the table is that for ORALR. Quite naturally, the results for the selection equation (VISITPOS) are virtually identical to those found in the selection equation for VITAMIN. Once again, the effect on the formal sector contribution measure PUSKSTAFF is positive and significant at the 1 per cent level. None of the other determinants have statistically significant influences on ORALR.

Finally, for immunization (IMMUN) we again find that having health centre staff present at the time of the posyandu visit, increases the likelihood of the child getting immunized. Not surprisingly, older children are less likely to be immunized when they visit the posyandu. None of the other formal sector variables affect the probability of immunization. Thus, the presence of a staff member from the puskesmas is significantly associated with provision of all three services. Simulation shows that the effect of having a pukesmas staff member present, conditional on the child visiting the posyandu, increases the conditional probability of the child receiving vitamin pills from 0.72 to 0.79, that of receiving ORALR from 0.13 to 0.37 and that of getting immunized from 0.03 to 0.08.

12.6 Conclusions

What kinds of implications can be drawn from this analysis for both theory and policy? First, from the descriptive statistics, we showed that there has been a considerable increase in participation in informal activity by Indonesian women from 1993 to 2000 despite some decline in the 1997–2000 period. To a large extent, their posyandu participation and hours of time provided are dictated by life cycle and demographic factors. Those married with young children are much more likely to participate than younger ones without young children. This suggests that voluntarism in local public goods production is partly motivated by self interest, in that the women who participate are those most in need of the services provided. Since use is negatively related to income both at the household and community levels, and positively related to income inequality at the community level, the primary beneficiaries would appear to be relatively poor people who can ill afford other alternatives.

Since the services produced by the posyandus are quasi-public goods, our results also have implications for the theory of collective action in general and local public goods in particular. Of particular relevance are the effects of income inequality and ethnic diversity. Ethnic diversity was shown to have a negative effect on voluntary participation in posyandus, while speaking the same language at home as the majority in the village has a positive effect. On the other hand, per capita income inequality affects participation negatively only in the case of our quality-related measure of posyandu activities (number of visits). Indeed, it has positive effects on participation in informal activities in some other cases, perhaps because income inequality for given average income implies that the poor may be relatively more numerous.

Finally, given our focus on the relevance of formal sector contributions and support for informal sector activity, the most important findings are the positive effects of several of the indicators of formal sector support for posyandus. The validity of our estimates is bolstered by the fact that several formal interventions are shown to be causally related to voluntary participation and service provision in posyandus, in both random and fixed effects specifications. An increase in the numbers of either instruments in the posyandu or visits from staff from the family planning board increases the probability that a woman will participate in the posyandu. Similarly, increasing the education levels also leads to higher participation. At the posyandu level, 140 more visits were observed in those posyandus that underwent a revitalization programme in 1998–99 than in those that did not. Taken as a whole, these results suggest a significant role for the formal sector in improving the quality of posyandu services based largely on voluntary participation.

While, as noted above, posyandus have received considerable acclaim for their low cost approach to improving health, especially of children and mothers, further research would be needed to quantify the special benefits on such health measures conferred by the qualitative improvements in posyandu services demonstrated in this chapter.

References

Alesina, A., R. Baqir, and W. Easterly (1999). 'Public Goods and Ethnic Divisions'. *Quarterly Journal of Economics*, 114(4): 1243–84.

Alesina, A. and R. Perotti (1996). 'Income Distribution, Political Instability and Growth'. *European Economic Review*, 40: 1203–28.

Bardhan, P. (2000). 'Understanding Underdevelopment: Challenges for Institutional Economics from the Point of View of Poor Countries'. *Journal of Institutional Economics*, 156: 216–35.

Easterly, W. and R. Levine (1997). 'Africa's Growth Tragedy: Policies and Ethnic Divisions'. *Quarterly Journal of Economics*, 112(4): 1203–50.

Miguel, E. and M. K. Gugerty (2002). 'Ethnic Diversity, Social Sanctions and Public Goods in Kenya'. Berkeley: University of California Working Paper.

Mullainathan, S. and R. Thaler (2000). 'Behavioral Economics'. Working Paper 7948. Cambridge, MA: NBER.

Nugent, J. and S. Swaminathan (2005). 'Household Investments in Education and Income Inequality at the Community Level: Evidence from Indonesia', in A. de Janvry and R. Kanbur (eds), *Poverty, Inequality and Development: Essays in Honor of Erik Thorbecke*. Boston: Kluwer.

Olson, M. (1965). *The Logic of Collective Action: Public Goods and the Theory of Groups*. Cambridge, MA: Harvard University Press.

Sen, A. K. (1985). *Commodities and Capabilities*. Amsterdam: North-Holland.

Swaminathan, S. and J. Nugent (2003). 'Income Inequality and Investments in Prenatal Care: Evidence from Indonesia'. Under review.

Wilson, L. S. (1992). 'The Harambee Movement and Efficient Public Good Provision in Kenya', *Journal of Public Economics*, 48(1), 1–19.

13

Social capital, survival strategies, and their potential for post-conflict governance in Liberia

*Amos Sawyer**

13.1 Introduction

The typical approach employed by the international community to assist countries in transition from violent conflicts involves inserting a peace-keeping force, establishing an interim government based on a power-sharing arrangement among antagonistic armed groups, and holding elections. Democratic governance is considered introduced by holding national elections, and post-conflict reconstruction planning commenced with needs-assessment surveys. While national elections are an important activity in the reconstitution of governing arrangements in post-conflict situations, they cannot yield systems of sustainable governance; neither can all the formal institutions and processes of government by themselves. The informal institutions through which people reach understandings among themselves, resolve conflicts, and undertake a variety of collective actions contribute to critical foundations of self-governance. Though assessment of needs for developing inventories of

* I gratefully acknowledge the support of the Workshop in Political Theory and Policy Analysis of Indiana University and the US Institute of Peace for the research on which this chapter is based and consultancy support of the EGDI-WIDER conference. This chapter has benefited from helpful comments of Michael McGinnis, Sheldon Gellar, and other members of the Africa Governance Working Group of the Third Quintannual Workshop on the Workshop held at Indiana University, 2–6 June 2004. I also thank Alfred Kulah, Tiawan Gongloe, Gediminar Flomo, and Michael Jebboe for their inputs and the editors of this volume and others who reviewed this chapter.

what is perceived to be lacking in local communities is important, such assessments do not always tell the full story because they do not always assess available capabilities such as the stocks of social capital of local communities.

This chapter shows that informal institutions were critical to the survival of local people during state collapse and violent conflicts in Liberia as they are in many other conflict situations. It argues that if used to buttress formal institutions, many of these informal institutions can become important building blocks in the reconstitution of post-conflict governance arrangements. Prevailing post-conflict reconstruction strategies focus typically on identifying and repairing formal organizations and physical infrastructures and tend to ignore the informal arrangements that sustain people over years of state failure. While there have been many disastrous formal and informal organizational arrangements in Liberia, there are still some very healthy informal arrangements that have not been well recognized. Failure to recognize these has frequently led to the presumption of a social capital deficit and, therefore, the need to look outside for such resource. This chapter, therefore, argues that unlocking such capital is important in enabling people to make transitions from short-term survival strategies to more productive long-term arrangements. First, I briefly discuss the toll of conflict as a legacy of a failed, over-centralized, and predatory government in Liberia and then turn to equally brief discussions of how, during years of violent conflicts, informal institutions and networks were used by local people to ensure their security, resolve conflicts, and provide other public goods. I conclude by stressing the importance of informal institutions as building blocks in the constitution of self-governing orders in post-conflict situations as Liberia.

13.2 Violent Conflict as a Legacy of the Over-centralized and Predatory Governance

Liberia's political order emerged as an over-centralized and predatory order that turned increasingly repressive as pressures for inclusion intensified over the years. Despite formal laws that established a legislature and a judiciary as independent and co-equal bodies, Liberia's political order evolved for a century with powers concentrated in the hands of the president. It ultimately collapsed under such pressures as external support declined with the ending of the Cold War. In 1980, a group of noncommissioned officers of the Liberian military staged a *coup d'etat* and established a military government that rapidly degenerated into a brutal dictatorship. In 1985, rigged elections and an attempted coup triggered a protracted violent conflict that engulfed the country and in 14 years made Liberia the centre of a wider system of violent conflicts in the Mano basin area of Liberia, Sierra Leone, and the forest region of Guinea. About 200,000 or six per cent of Liberia's population was killed; 700,000 sought refuge abroad at one time or another and more than a million were internally displaced in villages, towns, and cities around the country. Leaders of armed groups turned young children into fighters, young girls into 'war wives', and killed and demeaned elders. Millions of dollars of property was destroyed or stolen. As the conflict raged on, armed groups plundered the resources of the country and sold them on international markets. Ordinary people stood vulnerable to such predators and were left to rely upon external humanitarian assistance where available and their own resourcefulness. By seeking to understand what kinds of survival strategies were available to local people, we broaden our understanding of how social capital enables collective action and constitutes foundations for human survival.

13.3 Social Capital and Collective Action

Understanding how social capital is created and utilized in society is critically important in assessing capacity for self-reliant development. Elinor Ostrom's (1990) argument, that understanding how people craft or adapt institutions of collective action provides clues regarding their possibilities for self-governance, can be extended to embrace situations of governance failure and violent conflict where survival is at stake. Studies of how local people survive in situations of violent conflicts focus typically on how behaviour of belligerent parties affecting local people are constrained by the intervention of national and external actors. Creation of 'zones of peace' and demarcation of 'security corridors' for the delivery of emergency assistance by international humanitarian organizations are among strategies often analysed. Conflict resolution strategies are also typically analysed with respect to the initiatives of third-party mediation and facilitation (Hartzell 1999; Walter 1999). Important as these external interventions are, they do not exhaust the efforts that enable local people to survive amid such hostilities and resolve conflicts among themselves. External intervention alone cannot provide lasting solutions to security and governance dilemmas within a society, thus, understanding social capital among local people may offer insights for building self-governing capabilities. How did local people survive amid the plunder and carnage that characterize internal wars in African countries? How do they constitute or adapt mechanisms for the resolution of conflicts among themselves? What potentials do these forms of social capital have for post-conflict reconstruction? This chapter explores these questions in the case of Liberia.

13.3.1 *Social Capital and Survival Strategies*

There is hardly a more auspicious opportunity to observe how people build and use social capital than that which is offered in circumstances where people are confronted with grave insecurities and uncertainties. In situations of violent conflict when the rule of law breaks down, people are left largely to find recourse in norms, relationships, and institutional arrangements which they create themselves or have inherited over the years through customs and traditions. In such situations when people take advantage of lulls between firefights to find food and other goods, an enterprising young man may identify an opportunity to organize a group, using wheelbarrows to provide a service transporting goods for local people, where, due to a shortage of gasoline and commandeering of vehicles by armed groups, automobiles are unavailable or in short supply. Entrepreneurial skills, establishing trusting relationships beyond one's immediate family and associates, and crafting and effectively implementing appropriate rules are all important elements in building stocks of social capital. But social capital can also be used for harmful purposes. For example, in Rwanda, Sierra Leone, Sarajevo, as well as in Liberia, there were horrific stories of how networks of armed individuals constituted marauding gangs that committed atrocities.[1] Yet, the use of social capital can have harmful externalities for some and constructive outcomes for others. Understanding externalities and developing the ability to internalize negative externalities are crucial in using social capital for collective action (Ostrom and Ahn 2003; Ostrom 2005). In some cases, governing institutions of larger scales are required to

[1] Richard Lloyd Parry's (1998) graphic description of the horrors of communal violence between the Dayaks and Madurese of Indonesia is also a tragic example of the harmful use of social capital.

successfully address or avoid the negative externalities that can result from the use of social capital.[2]

13.3.2 *The Availability of International Humanitarian Assistance*

Hundreds of thousands of Liberians, victims of the decade and a half of conflict, owe their survival to the humanitarian assistance provided by the international community. In 1990, West African peacekeepers who arrived in Monrovia met a society so desperate for food that soldiers had to share their rations with local people. Although there are no comprehensive estimates of humanitarian assistance to Liberia, anecdotal estimates run high. Between 1990 and 1995, the United States is said to have provided US$381 million in humanitarian assistance. In 1997, the World Food Programme targeted its food assistance programme to 1.05 million people, three-quarters of whom were internally displaced. Numerous international humanitarian organizations contributed emergency relief during the period of violent conflict. And yet, all those needing assistance could not receive assistance or could not survive solely on the assistance received. Several challenges confronted the dispensing of humanitarian assistance. In some cases, logistical difficulties reduced access to humanitarian assistance. This was frequently the case in the rainy season when roads became impassable and bridges were swept away. In other cases, armed bands held groups of people hostage as a means of seizing humanitarian rations provided to vulnerable groups. There were situations in which limited assistance would be provided after long intervals, clearly leaving local people to their own devices. Many communities could not be reached at all. In 1997, the United Nations Office for the Coordination of Humanitarian Assistance (UNOCHA) reported that several areas in Liberia had not been accessed by international relief agencies in seven years. While international relief organizations were able to assist hundreds of thousands of people, there remained a significant gap between the survival needs of local people and the humanitarian assistance delivered to them. Large numbers of local people still had to rely partially or wholly on their own resourcefulness. In

[2] Krishna (2002) has stressed the importance of 'bridging' social capital in engendering cooperation among diversed communities. Moreover, this is why the establishment of multiple levels of nested organizations is critical to addressing many social dilemmas that are characterized by heterogeneous preferences (see E. Ostrom 2005: ch. 9). For example, in some situations, local prejudices can run so deep that they do lead to the crafting of rules of exclusion that work against the interest of minority groups. In such situations, rules crafted at provincial or national levels of governance are often needed to ensure inclusion of such groups.

the next three sections, I describe how under circumstances of violent assault by armed bands, local communities struggled to provide for their security, resolved community-based conflicts and, where possible, engaged in community development undertakings.

13.4 Security Strategies and Mechanisms

13.4.1 *Coping with Insecurity*

Domination of local communities by the central state has been a defining feature and the most enduring characteristic of autocracy in Liberia as is the case elsewhere in Africa (Wunsch and Oluwo 1990). Control by the presidency over the process of selecting chiefs and local leaders, and their manipulation by that office, is a strategy of domination and predation inherent in the nature of autocratic rule in Liberia (Liebenow 1969; Dunn and Tarr 1988; Sawyer 1992). State-sponsored violence has always been one of the instruments that ensured control. However, during the years of military rule, such violence became the main instrument of control.[3] Local officials were routinely harassed, violently intimidated, and capriciously hired and dismissed. Such practices were intensified when the civil war broke out in 1989. For most of the period of violent conflict, every town and village in Liberia was not only affected by violence but also ruled by an armed commander or an individual associated with an armed group. Young ex-combatants and their associates constituted the largest number of village and township heads. This pattern remained unchanged until 2003 when an interim government was established as part of the peace settlement. Although responses of villagers and townspeople to their new rulers varied, in almost every case, local communities sought recourse in traditional institutions in order to cope with the security dilemmas they faced. Examples from northwestern and southeastern Liberia reveal variability in forms of community responses to the problem of physical security posed by armed groups.

[3] The period of military rule in Liberia began with the military takeover of 1980. Although in 1986, the military leader Samuel Doe was elected in rigged elections, the pattern of post-elections rule did not differ substantially from the preceding five years. Threat and use of military force, decrees, and strongman arbitrariness were as much the dominant features of post-elections rule as they were earlier. Thus, except where otherwise stated, the entire period of control by Doe (from 1980 to 1989) is referred to as the period of military rule.

13.4.2 *Poro* Authority and Armed Rule at the Village Level

In many parts of northern and northwestern Liberia, villagers adapted to the rule of their new armed leaders through *Poro* solidarity. *Poro* has been the foundation pan-ethnic social institution embracing the collective social and historical experiences of most Mel and Mande-speaking groups in Liberia, Sierra Leone, and Guinea. It is considered to be of a deeper order of legitimacy than any group of secular rulers and commands a wider pool of resources than those available to any single ethnic community. With deep roots in vast sections of the rainforest, *Poro* institutions have been embedded in social organization from the level of the village to higher levels of authority. With hierarchical and gerontocratic principles central to its operations, *Poro* was a source of stability in the rain forest prior to the spread of Islam or the establishment of European colonial control (Little 1966). Despite commitment to its principles, *Poro* organization has seemed flexible when necessary and provided scope to accommodate opportunistic behaviour in adapting to change (d'Azevedo 1962).

One way in which *Poro* authority sought to protect rural dwellers during the violent conflict was to co-opt the young armed leaders. In several towns, local people clothed their 'armed chiefs' with the traditional chieftain authority and quickly constituted advisory councils in accordance with traditional practices.[4] These councils sought to constrain the actions of armed fighter-chiefs. In other situations, *Poro* authority constituted a parallel but unobtrusive authority structure that supported some of the actions of the new armed leaders where considered appropriate, while artfully and quietly organizing resistance where necessary and feasible, to protect the interest of local people. Historically, the dynamics of co-optation between central government and *Poro* has worked both ways: Liberian government officials have often co-opted *Poro* symbols and *Poro* authority has often adapted opportunistic behaviour vis-à-vis the government. More widely understood is how the president and his senior officials have over the years attempted to influence *Poro* authority. In the last 25 years, both presidents Doe and Taylor imposed themselves on *Poro* as its highest authority. What has now become evident is how in recent times, *Poro* authority and local communities have also adopted strategies of manipulation and accommodation to ensure their survival.[5] Thus, by co-opting the new leaders, *Poro* authorities of villages

[4] Author's interview with informant.

[5] D'Azevedo (1969–71) saw the offer of Gola girls as wives to settler leaders and government officials, a practice that existed since the mid-1800s, as elements of Gola strategy for accommodation with the Liberian state.

and towns sought to restrain the actions and behaviours of armed men who operated with hardly any supervision and owed loyalty only to a warlord.[6]

13.4.3 *Community Retreat and the Formation of Auxiliary Forces*

In southeastern Liberia where the *Poro* does not exist and where communities are acephalous, some communities tended to respond to the imposition of the rule of armed bands by retreating from their towns and villages to smaller hamlets located deeper in the rainforest. Households retreated as a unit. Although most forest communities sought sanctuary in the forest at one time or the other, members of southeastern communities were on the run more frequently between 1990 and 1998 and constrained to abandon their towns and villages for longer periods of time. *Kwee* is a social institution that exists across many clans and in many ethnic groups of southeastern Liberia; however, unlike *Poro* in northern and western Liberia, *Kwee*'s authority is circumscribed and its scope of operation limited.[7] In coastal southeastern areas that were not forested, a common strategy used widely was to mobilize local men in age-set units for defence of local communities. These units operated in association with the occupying armed group. Local elders negotiated with the occupying armed group to have such local militia units accepted as part of the occupying armed group. In this way, local communities were often tentatively spared the ravages of armed bands. However, violence always flared up when another armed group sought to dislodge an occupying band. Suspicions ran high between local forces and occupying groups and arrangements of cooperation often broke down. Thus, what we see are patterns of responses to security threats adapted to the ecology of the area and rooted largely in the nature of the indigenous social organization extant in an area. Local people found recourse in indigenous and local institutions to cope with their security dilemmas.

[6] Informants from Kpelle and Loma ethnic communities of central and northwestern Liberia observed this security strategy in many Kpelle and Loma communities. However, further research is needed to enhance understanding of the extent, effectiveness, and conditions under which this strategy was used more generally among Mande and Mel-speaking communities of Liberia and Sierra Leone.

[7] Humanitarian relief workers and other informants have noted the prolonged absence (frequently for years) of southeasterners, especially in Sinoe and Grand Gedeh, from their unattended villages as contrasted to the early return of people of Lofa to their villages and towns despite intermittent violent assaults and plunder by armed groups. For example, the people of the Gbunde clan near Voinjama are known to have repeatedly returned to their towns and villages within weeks after armed assaults, carried on *Poro* rites, and resumed livelihood activities including farming.

13.5 Local Institutions and Conflict Resolution

13.5.1 Poro *Authority and Inter-Ethnic Conflict Resolution in Northwestern Liberia*

Poro authority has also been a force for ending violence and managing and resolving inter-ethnic conflicts. The case of violent clashes between Mandingo and Loma communities in Zorzor is illustrative and deserves discussion. Mandingo and Loma have lived together in the same villages and towns in the area of Zorzor district on Liberia's border with Guinea even before the founding of Liberia. Both communities are part of larger ethnic communities that extend into Guinea. Mandingo are largely Moslems while Loma are Christians, Moslems, and adherents to forms of traditional worship. *Poro* is an important institution in Loma society but not in Mandingo; nonetheless, Mandingo have always respected *Poro* authority. The two ethnic communities have been closely linked through inter-marriage (more often Loma women to Mandingo men), shared mythologies, and history.[8] Joint mechanisms of conflict resolution evolved between the two communities typically, at the level of the village or town, include processes through which elders of the various *quarters* constitute a court, whose decisions are supported by the chief and council, and enforced ultimately (if necessary) by *Poro* authority in the case of the Loma and Quranic authority in the case of the Mandingo. Since the consolidation of the Liberian state, state-based conflict resolution processes intervened and imposed a higher level of authority through the interior bureaucracy and the judiciary. Under strains of violent conflicts in recent times, both sides accused each other of breaking the age-old covenant that had bonded them. Both communities have been seething with bitterness and suspicion against each other.

Reconciliation between the two groups has become one of the most important post-conflict challenges. As government's mediation interventions amounted to nothing more than efforts to win the support of both sides, actions of government's security operatives tended to exacerbate the problem (Sawyer *et al.* 2000a). Non-governmental organizations (NGOs) serving as facilitators were better able to get both sides to begin a dialogue.[9] As dialogue progressed, *Poro* leaders from Loma communities in Guinea were said to have been indispensable in initiating a process of

[8] See Sawyer *et al.* (2000a).

[9] The Center for Democratic Empowerment, the Catholic Peace and Justice Commission, and the Lutheran World Federation are among the NGOs that have played facilitation roles.

re-covenanting. Pan-Poro solidarity provided a context for security and a framework for problem-solving among the Loma. Loma *Poro* objects looted by Mandingo youth were retrieved through pan-Poro channels that involved the intervention of Guinean Loma communities with their Mandingo compatriots. Appropriate rites of restoration were performed, and with due respect accorded by the Mandingo, the basis for reconciliation was established. The Mandingo received assistance from Loma communities in the construction or renovation of mosques allegedly burned down by Loma youth, and both communities were subsequently engaged in establishing joint mechanisms for early warning and for dispute settlement. Such mechanisms operated with the endorsement of both *Poro* and Quranic authority and within the framework of Mandingo and Loma cross-border ethnic-based jurisdictions of larger scales.[10]

13.5.2 *'External Elite' as Conflict Resolution Catalysts in Southeastern Liberia*

In southeastern Liberia, reconciliation among ethnic groups proceeded differently. As stated above, there is hardly a single indigenous institution whose legitimacy cuts across all communities of these acephalous groups. As a result, Kru and Sarpo elite living in Monrovia have been the prime initiators of reconciliation between the two groups. Local people have relied on the lead and advice of their educated sons in Monrovia.[11] Such an 'externally-driven' approach to conflict resolution has not been without noticeable consequences. First, up to the ending of hostilities generally in 2003, rifts between communities did not seem to be healing as fast as they appeared to be between the Loma and Mandingo of northwestern Liberia. Second, these Monrovia-based processes of reconciliation were more easily manipulated by president Charles Taylor up to the time of his downfall and expulsion. Rival Monrovia-based elites could hardly avoid the temptation of turning to the Ministry of Internal Affairs for some form of intervention. Third, solutions evolved from such government-driven reconciliation processes seemed designed to redress perceived ethnic-based imbalances in appointments to county-level positions in government rather than to heal wounds between people who had committed egregious breaches against each other. As a result, when differences among such elites about job placements proved irreconcilable, demands for the creation of new political

[10] There is no sense of *Sharia* legal application in these matters. Mandingo Islamic clerics operate in conjunction with Mandingo elders, many of whom are of mixed parentage.

[11] See Sawyer *et al.* (2000b).

jurisdictions such as new statutory districts or townships have been heightened.[12]

The case of ethnic conflict between the Krahn and Grebo also of the southeast was even more illuminating with respect to the creation of new political jurisdiction as a strategy for the resolution of ethnic-based conflict. The military takeover of 1980 catapulted the Krahn to national leadership as well as local leadership in their southeastern home county of Grand Gedeh which they shared with the Grebo. Until then, Grebo dominance in local government and professional positions was due largely to their superior educational achievements.[13] Krahn and Grebo leaders were unable to arrive at a common understanding of their differences and an approach to their resolution. Massive Grebo support for anti-government forces during the early years of the conflict was attributed in part to their desire to end Krahn domination and control of their jointly shared home-county. Becoming more dominant in Charles Taylor's government, Grebo leaders used their newfound influence to press for the carving out of a new county from what was Grand Gedeh County. The creation of Grebo-dominated River Gee County has ended the competition for government allocated positions which has been a major bone of contention between Grebo and Krahn elites over the years.

What we have seen here is that, deeply affected by violent disruptions, local communities found recourse for conflict resolution in their own indigenous institutional patterns where such institutions were available, and appropriate, or otherwise strategically involved state authorities as mediators. *Poro* authority interacted with Quranic authority to provide a basis for co-existence and gradual cooperation between the Loma and Mandingo of northwestern Liberia. In southeastern Liberia, among the Kru and Sarpo, the role of elites of the two ethnic communities resident in Monrovia seemed pronounced, and where reconciliation has proved difficult due to lack of appropriate institutions, as is also the case between the Grebo and Krahn, local elites have opted for the creation of new political jurisdictions. Thus, the nature of community social organization has played a major role in determining prevailing responses to conflict. Needless to say, these patterns remain under pressure and in various states of adaptation.

[12] The creation of the statutory district of Tarjaurzon out of Juarzon is a more recent example.

[13] Grebo communities extend from the Atlantic coast into the interior; as such they were among the first ethnic groups to have access to schools first established along the coast by missionaries and later, the Liberian state. Located entirely inland, the Krahn lived largely in hunting and gathering communities well into the early decades of the twentieth century. See Schroder and Seibel (1974).

13.6 Collective Action and Associational Life under Adverse Circumstances

In many instances, society's resilience can be observed in the nature and quality of associational life that makes survival possible in spite of state predation and collapse. By associational life, I refer to the full array of collective action situations organized by individuals and communities in pursuit of a full range of desired outcomes.[14] These include formal and informal groups, networks and associations, established on the basis of a variety of membership rules for collective action for the provision, production, and use of collective goods (Ostrom 1990; 1992). Many of these organizations and networks have members who live outside Liberia. I briefly highlight some examples of how in situations of state predation, repression and violent conflicts, local people in both rural and urban communities have still been able to engage in collective action to provide some of the public goods and services essential to their lives. Clan and community-based organizations have been the principal institutional arrangements for collective action in such situations.

13.6.1 *Clan-Based Institutions of Collective Action*

The most enduring form of collective action that ensured community survival despite violent conflicts, was undertaken by networks and organizations whose membership is based on clan-related identity. These are genuinely self-reliant and demand-driven groups. Typically, they are referred to as 'development' associations and have numerous voluntary groups nested within them. Organizations such as the Dugbe River Union in Sinoe County are well known for their multiple roles as safety nets, conflict resolution mechanisms, and for the social and physical infrastructure development activities they undertake independent of the state and often, despite state predation. In northern Liberia, among the Mano and Gio, the accomplishments of clan-based organizations have been indispensable to the welfare of local communities. *Seletorwaa*, the development association of Mensonnoh Clan and Zao Development

[14] Discussion about associational life in Africa frequently becomes central to the debate about what constitutes civil society in Africa. That debate largely centres on the potential of civil society to advance democracy in Africa. See Harbeson *et al.* (1994); Hutchful (1997); Kasfir (1998); Orvis (2001). Although critical, this debate is not central to the concern of this chapter. My focus is on how individuals and communities organize themselves for collective action to meet the variety of dilemmas they confront in the circumstance of state predation, collapse, and violence.

Association of the Zao, for example, have been extraordinary in their development initiatives. They have built schools, clinics, and roads and have organized scholarship schemes to assist promising young men and women to go to college. *Seletorwaa* began in the early 1980s by members of the Mehnsonnoh clan resident in Monrovia. It was a response to the military takeover and its consequences on Nimba County. Among the numerous projects it has undertaken over the years is a clinic built in Guotowin, and several scholarships to the young people of the clan to pursue studies at technical schools and institutions of higher learning in Liberia.[15] Women's clubs within the development association have catered to the needs of the sick and disabled, and have often organized for increased production of food to ensure food security. As self-reliant entities, clan development associations are largely supported by the resources of their individual and constituent community members, through labour quotas and through taxation of individual production. The role of clan members in Monrovia and abroad is critical in resource mobilization. Many such organizations receive regular contributions from members now resident in the United States. More recently, members of *Seletowaa* in the United States have been providing equipment and supplies for elementary schools in the clan.[16] Clan-based development associations are often able to tap into external resources mobilized through international entities; yet their strength is in their self-reliance. They must be seen as significant local capabilities for the reconstitution of post-conflict governing order in Liberia.

13.7 Informal Institutions as Building Blocks for Constructing Post-conflict Self-governing Orders

Survival strategies used by local people faced with violent conflict perpetrated by armed groups, range from complicity and accommodation with the perpetrators to resistance. While some of these strategies, especially those that involved complicity with armed groups to harm others, pose serious hurdles to post-conflict reconciliation, many others can appropriately serve as building blocks of a new post-conflict order. For example,

[15] Interviews with members of *Seletorwaa*.

[16] The amalgamated initiatives of clan-based organizations that sustain inter-clan development projects, must not be confused with such countywide development associations that are organized by the central state through the Ministry of Internal Affairs. The former are the result of local initiatives; the latter are top-down government-driven structures that seem to become very active on special occasions such as a pending visit of the president.

the entrepreneurship of clan-based organizations, remittance flows of diasporic groups, and the self-organized deliberative forums of leaders of trans-boundary ethnic communities offer a rich pool of 'informal' institutional resources for conflict resolution, community development, and foundations for self-governance. A fundamental mistake is made when post-conflict reconstruction initiatives begin with an assessment of needs of local communities, unaccompanied by a corresponding assessment of capabilities such as these. The *Joint Needs Assessment* undertaken by the Liberian government, the World Bank, and United Nations Development Programme (UNDP) has ignored the fact that even before the collapse of the state, local clan-based and community-based associations supported by members and alumni associations abroad, were the prime supporters of schools and road repair projects in several parts of Liberia.[17] By failing to reflect the capabilities of local people and their extensions abroad, needs-assessment surveys have the potential of reorganizing local communities for dependency and not for self-reliant development.

The challenge of attaining lasting peace in post-conflict situations such as Liberia can best be met by constituting self-governing institutional arrangements rather than reconstituting the over-centralized state. Self-governing orders are constituted on foundations rooted in local communities; they draw upon the capabilities of individuals and local communities rather than smother or destroy them. They provide possibilities for building from the bottom up, and of doing so in variable patterns that link communities in horizontal and vertical arrangements for provision of public goods. For example, a local community may build and run an elementary school, while several working together and assisted by their diasporic members may build and run a secondary school. The variable principles of organization and patterns of aggregation to be found in local communities in Liberia as in other countries make for potentially robust systems of polycentric governance (Ostrom 1999). Moreover, in the case of Liberia, capabilities provided by sub-national trans-boundary institutions such as pan-ethnic conflict resolution mechanisms, can add resilience to governance arrangements and nest them in the larger Mano basin subregion that includes Sierra Leone and Guinea, such that subregional levels of governance rooted in interactions among communities and not only in interactions among unitary states can be imagined. For a subregion that is awash in arms as a result of 14 years of violent conflict,

[17] See National Transitional Government of Liberia, United Nations, and World Bank (2004).

there is no better way of sustaining efforts to ensure a secure environment than by establishing early warning and early response mechanisms that draw upon the self-organized initiatives of local peoples throughout the Mano basin area (see Sawyer 2004).

What all of this means, is that understanding and use of appropriate locally-based social capital can unlock human potential, and add to the resource pool from which a society draws to constitute self-governing orders that can further enhance human capabilities to transcend destructive conflicts.

References

d'Azevedo, W. L. (1962). 'Some Historical Problems in the Delineation of a Central West African Region'. *Annals of the New York Academy of Sciences*, 96: 512–38.

d'Azevedo, W. L. (1969–1971). 'A Tribal Reaction to Nationalism'. Parts 1–4. *Liberian Studies Journal*, 1 (Spring 1969): 1–21; 2 (1969): 43–63; 3 (1970): 99–115; 4 (1970–71): 1–19.

Dunn, D. E. and S. B. Tarr (1988). *Liberia: A National Polity in Transition*. New Jersey: Metuchen, and London: The Scarecrow Press, Inc.

Harbeson, J. W., D. Rothschild, and N. Chazen (eds) (1994). *Civil Society and the State in Africa*. Boulder, CO: Lynne Rienner.

Hartzell, C. (1999). 'Explaining the Stability of Negotiated Settlements to Intrastate Wars'. *Journal of Conflict Resolution*, 42(1): 3–22.

Hutchful, E. (1997). 'Political Parties and Civil Societies in Sub-Saharan Africa: Conflicting Objectives?', in M. Ottaway (ed.), *Democracy in Africa: The Hard Road Ahead*. Boulder, CO: Lynne Rienner, pp. 43–64.

Kasfir, N. (ed.) (1998). *Civil Society and Democracy in Africa: Critical Perspectives*. London: Frank Cass.

Krishna, A. (2002). *Active Social Capital: Tracing the Roots of Development and Democracy*. New York: Columbia University Press.

Liebenow, J. G. (1969). *Liberia: The Evolution of Privilege*. Ithaca: Cornell University Press.

Little, K. L. (1966). *The Mende of Sierra Leone: A West African People in Transition*. Revised edn, London: Routledge and Kegan Paul, and New York: Humanities.

National Transitional Government of Liberia, United Nations, and World Bank (2004). *Liberia: Joint Needs Assessment*. February.

Orvis, S. (2001). 'Civil Society in Africa or African Civil Society'. *Journal of Asian and African Studies*, 36(1): 17–38.

Ostrom, E. (1990). *Governing the Commons: The Evolution of Institutions for Collective Action*. New York: Cambridge University Press.

Ostrom, E. (1992). *Crafting Institutions for Self-Governing Irrigation Systems*. San Francisco, CA: Institute for Contemporary Studies Press.

Ostrom, E. (2005). *Understanding Institutional Diversity*. Princeton, NJ: Princeton University Press.

Ostrom, E. and T. K. Ahn (eds) (2003). 'Introduction', in E. Ostrom and T. K. Ahn (eds), *Foundations of Social Capital*. Cheltenham and Northampton, MA: Edward Elgar, pp. xi–xxxix.

Ostrom, V. (1999). 'Polycentricity' (parts 1 and 2), in M. D. McGinnis (ed.), *Polycentricity and Local Public Economies: Readings from the Workshop in Political Theory and Policy Analysis*. Ann Arbor, MI: University of Michigan Press, pp. 75–103.

Parry, R. L. (1998). 'What Young Men Do'. *Granta*, 61: 84–123.

Sawyer, A. (1992). *The Emergence of Autocracy in Liberia: Tragedy and Challenge*. San Francisco, CA: Institute for Contemporary Studies Press.

Sawyer, A. (2004). 'Violent Conflicts and Governance Challenges in West Africa: The Case of the Mano River Basin Area'. *Journal of Modern African Studies*, 42(3): 437–63.

Sawyer, A., C. Wesseh, and S. Ajavon, Jr. (2000a). *Sharing the Kola Nut: Understanding Ethnic Conflict and Building Peace in Liberia—Experiences from Lofa and Nimba*. Monrovia: Center for Democratic Empowerment, Sabanoh Printing Press.

Sawyer, A., C. Wesseh, R. Panton, and T. Synyenlentu (2000b). 'Ethnic-Based Conflict in Sinoe: Challenge and Opportunities for Conflict Management and Reconciliation—A Report from Research and Reconciliation Interventions'. (Center for Democratic Empowerment) Monrovia. Unpublished manuscript.

Schroder, G. and D. Seibel (1974). *Ethnographic Survey of Southeastern Liberia: the Liberian Kran and the Sapo*. Newark: Department of Anthropology, University of Delaware.

United Nations Office for the Coordination of Humanitarian Assistance (UNOCHA) (1997). *Consolidated Inter-Agency Appeal 1997*.

Walter, B. (1999). 'Designing Transitions from Civil War: Demobilization, Democratization, and Commitment to Peace'. *International Security*, 24(1): 127–55.

Wunsch, J. S. and D. Olowu (eds) (1990 [1995]). *The Failure of the Centralized State: Institutions and Self-Governance in Africa*. San Franscisco, CA: Institute for Contemporary Studies Press.

14

Enforcement and compliance in Lima's street markets: the origins and consequences of policy incoherence towards informal traders

Sally Roever

Almost 20 years ago researchers from the Institute for Liberty and Democracy in Peru identified a key source of poor people's decisions to work outside the bounds of the formal legal system: 'bad laws' that impose disproportionate costs on those who choose formality. The source of bad laws, they argue, is a tradition of rent-seeking whereby interest groups aim to extract favourable regulatory concessions from lawmakers at the expense of economic efficiency (de Soto 2002: 190). The resulting 'infinity of regulations' prevents informal workers from using their assets productively.

How can we explain unsuccessful efforts to integrate informal workers into the formal legal system two decades later? This chapter argues that while a multitude of conflicting regulations still precludes effective governance of informal commerce in Lima, the sources of those conflicts are more diverse—though perhaps more tractable—than they might have been 20 years ago. The first part of the chapter identifies two sources of policy incoherence toward street traders, perhaps the most visible segment of the informal sector: (1) a lack of definitional clarity in national and metropolitan level policy,[1] and (2) contradictory legal provisions concerning municipalities' right to charge fees for street vendors' use of

[1] To be sure, academic definitions of the informal sector also frequently lack clarity. See reviews from Peattie (1987); Carbonetto *et al.* (1988); Portes and Schauffler (1993); Portes (1994); Roberts (1994); and Cross (1998).

public space. The second part of the chapter discusses the consequences of this policy incoherence. In particular, it shows how policy at the municipal level oscillates dramatically over time as municipal governments experiment with different ways to implement the contradictory policies created by national and metropolitan level laws. The constant improvisation at the municipal level precludes stable and effective governance of informal trade.

The evidence presented here calls into question two alternative explanations of ineffective governance of street trade in Lima. The first is that 'redistributive combines'—the term de Soto *et al.* use to refer to interest groups that pressure policymakers into making laws on their behalf—are directly responsible for bad laws. Specifically, they identify organizations of street vendors, which were strong politically and organizationally in the mid 1980s, as the primary culprits of bad policy. However, these organizations became extraordinarily weak in the 1990s, losing their capacity for effective lobbying and their credibility among politicians across the ideological spectrum. Yet bad policy persisted throughout the 1990s, long after these groups disappeared as relevant political actors.

The second alternative explanation is that policymakers simply favour the status quo. Street vending provides an outlet for thousands of workers who would otherwise be unemployed in Peru's depressed economy,[2] and tolerating it may provide policymakers with a low-cost solution to the country's economic woes. Yet national, metropolitan, and local level officials have repeatedly invested time and money into efforts to solve the problems associated with street vending, citing an urgent need to bring order to the city's chaotic and largely ungoverned streets. Were the status quo preferable, policymakers would not treat street vending as such an urgent problem.

14.1 The Origins of Policy Incoherence

Major national and metropolitan level policies intended to govern street commerce in the past 20 years can be divided into three general policy periods (see Table 14.1). During the first period (1984–91), two landmark measures provided the framework for the governance of street commerce: the 1984 Law of Municipalities (Law No. 23853), and 1985 Metropolitan

[2] The best available estimate of the total number of street vendors in Lima as of 2002 is approximately 360,000 (Roever 2005).

Table 14.1. Policy periods, 1984–2002

Policy period	Relevant policies	Date passed	Date published[a]
1984–91	Law of Municipalities (Law No.23853)	28 May 1984	9 June 1984
	Metropolitan Ordinance 002	2 April 1985	17 April 1985
	Supreme Decree 005–91	25 January 1991	26 January 1991
1991–93	Ministerial Resolution 022–91	6 February 1991	7 February 1991
	Law of Microenterprises (Legislative Decree 705)	5 November 1991	8 November 1991
	Law of Employment Promotion (Legislative Decree 728)	8 November 1991	12 November 1991
1993–2002	Law of Municipal Taxation (Legislative Decree 776)	30 December 1993	31 December 1993

Note:
[a] Laws, Decrees, Resolutions, and Metropolitan Ordinances generally go into effect one day after being published in the country's official gazette, *El Peruano*.

Ordinance 002. While these measures formed the cornerstone of street vending policy in the Peruvian capital, they also created the backdrop for ongoing disputes over their applicability.

The Law of Municipalities was the primary law governing the rights and responsibilities of municipal governments, and it clearly gave them jurisdiction over regulating and controlling street commerce.[3] It also authorized them to administer two kinds of fees that in theory could be applied to street vendors: licensing fees and entitlement fees.

The law established that licensing fees could be charged for obtaining authorization for specific activities that should be regulated and controlled for reasons of public interest, including the occupation of public space. It also stated that the administration of licences was subject to regulations established by the government of Metropolitan Lima. Thus, municipal governments could charge street vendors for a licence to use public space, as long as they did so in conformity with metropolitan level ordinances.

The provisions outlining entitlement fees were slightly more ambiguous. The law stated that municipalities could charge entitlement fees, or *derechos*, 'in exchange for an administrative service that the Municipality provides for the use or exploitation of public or municipal goods'. The law further stated that entitlement fees should be based on the cost of the service provided. Street traders clearly use public space, and if public space counts as a public good, then municipalities could in theory charge

[3] Title III, Chapter II, Article 68, paragraph 3 (*El Peruano*, 9 June 1984: 26248). All translations of policy language in this chapter are my own. I use the term 'street vendors' and 'street traders' interchangeably throughout.

vendors for this use. At the same time, the unambiguous intent of the law is to generate the funds necessary to cover the administrative costs of allowing citizens to use a public good. Thus, a municipal government could charge street traders for their use of public space, but they would need to provide some administrative service in return.

The Law of Municipalities therefore provided a clear jurisdictional mandate for municipal governments to regulate street commerce, though it did not offer a definition of street commerce or street vendors. It also established a fee structure that in theory could be used to charge vendors for their use of public space, without making that link explicit.

One year after the passage of the Law of Municipalities, the metropolitan government under Mayor Alfonso Barrantes passed a landmark policy called Metropolitan Ordinance 002. Ordinance 002 was a comprehensive measure designed to govern nearly all aspects of street vending in the metropolitan area. It defined street commerce as an 'economic activity developed in *campos feriales*[4] or regulated areas of public space that provides services and/or sales of prepared, manufactured or natural products in direct form and on a small scale'. It then defined street vendors as 'workers whose capital does not exceed two UIT (*unidades impositivas tributarias*)[5] and who, lacking any labour relation with their suppliers, exercise street commerce individually in direct form and on a small scale'.[6] Based on these two definitions, then, street vendors are those who (1) work in regulated public spaces, (2) have less than two UIT of capital, (3) sell directly to consumers,[7] and (4) vend on a small (though undefined) scale.

Ordinance 002 further entitled street vendors to certain privileges, and imposed on them certain responsibilities. The measure granted street vendors three significant privileges: legal recognition; participation in a Mixed Technical Commission (CTMCA) designed to work out problems associated with street commerce at the local level; and access to a Vendors' Assistance Fund (FOMA) intended to deliver services and benefits to licensed street vendors. These concessions to street vendors represented a major political and legal advance on vendors' behalf, as they called on municipalities not only to recognize and tolerate the existence of street

[4] *Campos feriales* are a sort of fairgrounds, typically open-air markets, that are set up on government-owned property (such as the medians of large avenues) for the specific purpose of street vending.

[5] Income units that are used to calculate taxes and fees of various kinds.

[6] Title I, Article 3, paragraphs (a) and (b) (*El Peruano*, 17 April 1985: 34118).

[7] That is, they are not wholesalers, and they are not employees of wholesalers.

vending, but also to negotiate with vendors through the CTMCA and deliver services to them through the FOMA.

In return, Ordinance 002 outlined a host of responsibilities and requirements for street vendors to meet. The most important of these was the payment of a daily entitlement fee, called the *sisa*, in exchange for the right to use public space. Fifty per cent of the revenue generated through the *sisa* was to be used to fund the FOMA. Vendors were also required to maintain the appearance of their posts, wear uniforms, obtain health certificates if they were selling food, provide proof of origin of their merchandise, and vend in authorized spaces.

The normalization of the *sisa* had positive consequences for both sides. The fee generated substantial income for municipal governments, and by paying it, vendors gained legal protection against arbitrary expulsions by the police, at least in theory. Yet Ordinance 002 in its totality proved difficult for local governments to implement. The working definition of street vendors in the policy excluded hordes of vendors who worked in unauthorized space or earned more than 2 UIT annually.[8] The meaning of 'small scale' was left open to interpretation. And local governments' administrative capacity was insufficient to identify, classify, and authorize all individuals who sold merchandise in public spaces within district territory. Without an adequate administrative infrastructure to issue and deny authorizations to those entering, exiting, or maintaining street vending as an occupation, the remainder of the rights and responsibilities became difficult to enforce.

Moreover, many municipal administrations either selectively enforced certain elements of Ordinance 002, or simply ignored it altogether.[9] This non-enforcement on the part of municipal governments infuriated vendors, who in turn sometimes refused to comply with the ordinance's restrictions, on the basis that the government was not holding up its end of the bargain. In particular, vendors had a good case for refusing to conform to sanctions for non-compliance that were not developed with the participation of the CTMCA. Likewise, municipal governments in some cases charged vendors for the *sisa* without delivering any services in return, on the basis that vendors did not comply with all of the restrictions outlined in the ordinance.

[8] In any case, there was no system in place for tracking and verifying vendors' income to measure against this threshold.

[9] According to Vildoso (2000: 3), the metropolitan government only has normative jurisdiction over municipal districts, so that metropolitan ordinances are recommendations rather than binding policies.

14.1.1 *The Second Policy Period: More Definitions, Less Coherence*

After the 1990 election of Alberto Fujimori to the Peruvian presidency, the administration used its power to issue a variety of executive decrees that further destabilized the policy regime that had begun to develop after 1985. These measures were part of broader efforts to implement market-oriented reforms, but their hasty formulation complicated the efforts of district governments and created a set of conflicting incentives that increased non-compliance among vendors.

The first was Supreme Decree 005 of 1991. This decree was likely designed as a political appeal to street vendors, who were thought to have supported Fujimori in large numbers in the 1990 presidential election. The measure's stated purpose was to recognize the juridical quality of what it called 'autonomous ambulatory workers' (TAAs), though it provided no definition of that term. The decree implies that autonomous ambulatory workers are the same thing as street vendors by referring to a national Law of Street Commerce that the administration had apparently planned to pass, but such a law never materialized. A Ministerial Resolution (No. 022) issued as a follow-up to Supreme Decree 005 then defined 'autonomous ambulatory workers' as those with a maximum level of working capital to be determined by each municipality, rather than the two UIT limit established in Ordinance 002.

Because the Peruvian constitution states that laws issued at a higher level of government take precedence over lower level laws, it could be assumed that municipalities thereafter were to determine their own income ceilings for 'autonomous ambulatory workers' rather than following the limit established by Ordinance 002. Nonetheless, Supreme Decree 005 and Ministerial Resolution 022 provided no concrete policy measures for local governments to take street vendors with; they merely recognized vendors' legal status. Yet, the rhetorical appeal of these measures to the legal status of street vendors emboldened them to resist municipal efforts to expel them from unauthorized spaces.

Nine months after issuing Supreme Decree 005, the Fujimori administration passed two additional laws that would contribute to the definitional ambiguities already present. The first was the Law of Microenterprises. This law introduced the term 'PYMES'—the Spanish acronym for 'small and microenterprises'—into the country's legal lexicon. It defined PYMES as firms with any organizational or administrative structure that engage in any kind of productive, commercial, or service activity, in which (1) the proprietor is also a worker; (2) the total number of workers and employees does not exceed 10 persons (for a microenterprise) or twenty persons (for a small enterprise); and (3) the total annual value of sales does not exceed 12 UIT (microenterprise) or 25 UIT (small enterprise). Because it does not specify whether PYMES must operate in private space rather than public space, in theory any individual who qualifies as a street vendor under Ordinance 002, or as an autonomous ambulatory worker under Supreme Decree 005, could also be considered a PYME under the Law of Microenterprises, as long as that individual does not have more than twenty employees or make more than 25 UIT—an unlikely scenario for virtually all street vendors.

The Law of Employment Promotion, passed three days later, called on the Ministry of Labour and Social Promotion to create programmes aimed at productively converting 'informal sector firms' to formal sector firms by increasing their levels of productivity and their capacity to create additional jobs. 'Informal activities' were defined as those that 'develop independently in the range of small and microenterprises ... and that engage mostly in commerce, services, small industry, construction and the manufacture of basic goods destined for the internal market'. The law added that the boundary for maximum income levels should be set by the government agency CENIP, rather than municipalities. Again, this definition of the 'informal sector' could encompass street vendors, as defined by Ordinance 002; autonomous ambulatory workers, as labelled by Supreme Decree 005; and PYMES, as defined by the Law of Microenterprises.

Above and beyond the definitional issues, the Law of Microenterprises and the Law of Employment Promotion further complicated the picture by granting PYMES and informal sector workers access to state programmes, at least in theory. The former called on appropriate government ministries to provide entrepreneurial training and legal assistance, free of charge to all those who qualified as PYMES—which again could be interpreted to include street vendors. In addition, it prohibited municipal governments from requiring operating licences or authorizations other than a particular kind of licence established by national law, and required PYMES to keep accurate books. Thus, by not distinguishing between PYMES and street vendors, the law in theory granted street vendors access to free training without requiring them to formalize, and implied that municipal governments could no longer charge street vendors the licensing fee established by the 1984 Law of Municipalities. The effect of the second policy period was therefore to embolden street vendors, confuse the distinction between street vendors and small enterprises, and create a conflicting set of incentives for street vendors to interpret.

14.1.2 *The Third Policy Period: New Taxes, Old Controversies*

The Law of Municipal Taxation, passed in December 1993, dramatically changed the regime governing municipal taxation. This legislative decree redefined municipal governments' ability to levy taxes and nullified the articles of the Law of Municipalities that established the licensing and entitlement fees described above. In their place, Legislative Decree 776 authorized the use of *tasas*, or valuation fees, in exchange for the private use of municipal property. The decree further stated that *tasas* charged for the use of municipal property should not exceed the cost of administering the service that allows citizens to use that property, and that income generated through the fee should be used exclusively to cover those costs.[10]

Having eliminated municipal governments' ability to levy entitlement fees such as the *sisa*, the Law of Municipal Taxation seemed to grant them the ability to establish a fee that would serve the same purpose through the establishment of *tasas*. However, the law also contained several mechanisms designed to eliminate barriers to free trade within the country, part of the Fujimori administration's broader market-oriented reform strategy. For example, Article 61 stated that municipalities were prohibited from charging *tasas* for the use of streets, bridges and other infrastructure, and that they could not levy fees that would 'impede free access to markets and free commercialization within national territory'. This article therefore created an important ambiguity with regard to street vendors. On the one hand, local governments seemed to have the authority to charge vendors, *tasas* for their use of public space. On the other hand, it was not clear whether Article 61's prohibition of such fees for the 'use of streets' applied to street vending, or whether charging such a fee would impede free access to markets.

Moreover, without the authorization to charge the *sisa*, it became unclear whether municipal governments were still obligated to enforce the parts of Ordinance 002 that relied on the income the *sisa* was supposed to generate, most importantly the FOMA. At the same time, many municipal governments continued to charge vendors the *sisa* even after the Law of Municipal Taxation revoked their authority to do so. The *sisa* thus became a central source of conflict between vendors and municipal governments; vendors argued that they need not pay it if the municipality failed to deliver any services in return, and municipal governments argued that vendors shall have to pay it regardless of their use of public space.

[10] Title III, Chapter II, Articles 68, 69, and 70.

Faced with the inconsistent application of Ordinance 002 and the Law of Municipal Taxation, street vendors attempted to use the legal system to settle the *sisa* issue in 1994. On 23 August of that year, the United Front of Informal Workers of the District of Pueblo Libre (FEDITAPUL) presented a denunciation to the National Institute for the Defense of Competition and Protection of Intellectual Property, or INDECOPI, against the City Council of Pueblo Libre[11] for violating Legislative Decree 776.[12] One of INDECOPI's responsibilities was to rule on charges brought against state actors for interfering with free competition. The authors of the denunciation argued that charging the *sisa* and establishing a costly fee for a health certificate violated the principles of free and open competition, as established in the Law of Municipal Taxation. INDECOPI, which had not previously ruled on either issue, accepted the case.

The resolution issued by INDECOPI the next year seemed to deliver a victory to street vendors by declaring the *sisa* illegal.[13] The resolution stated that the collection of the *sisa* in the district in question took place without any sort of municipal service delivery, which violated the Law of Municipal Taxation's definition of *tasas*. INDECOPI further ruled that charging people to exercise rights (in this case, the constitutional right to work) constituted a clear violation of the new tax law. Although the Law of Municipalities did grant municipalities the power to regulate areas in which street commerce exists, INDECOPI argued, 'at no point does it signal that this power includes the right to levy charges of any kind'.

In theory, the INDECOPI resolution should have brought to an end the practice of charging the *sisa* for the right to use public space. In practice, it did not. Although INDECOPI's rulings are distributed to the relevant national level institutions for enforcement, the practice of charging the *sisa* continued in many jurisdictions after 1995.

National and metropolitan level measures intended to govern street commerce between 1984 and 1994 thus produced a conflicting and confusing body of policy. First, the major policy measures issued during this period used inconsistent labels and incomplete or conflicting definitional attributes to refer to essentially the same type of worker: someone who, in one way or another, sells things individually on a small scale (see Table 14.2). Moreover, many workers on the ground exhibit some, but not all, of the definitional attributes presented in Table 14.2. Take a hypothetical worker, for example, who fits all of the characteristics of a street vendor

[11] Pueblo Libre is a small municipal district in central Lima.

[12] The information presented here is based on INDECOPI Case File No. 121–94/CLC.

[13] INDECOPI Resolution No. 027–95 was passed on 26 July 1995.

Table 14.2. Policy definitions of small scale traders

Policy	Term	Attributes				
		A	B	C	D	E
Ordinance 002	Street vendor	2 UIT	Regulated public space	No employer	Small	*
Supreme Decree 005	TAA	*	*	*	*	*
Ministerial Resolution 022	TAA	Municipality-defined maximum	*	*	*	*
Law of Microenterprises	PYME	12 UIT / 25 UIT	*	Maximum of 10/20 employees	*	*
Law of Employment Promotion	Informal sector	CENIP-defined maximum	*	*	*	Internal

Note:
A = Maximum income; B = Workplace; C = Labour Relations; D = Scale of Enterprise; E = Market; * = not specified in policy.

but does not work in an authorized, regulated area. If the policy definitions above were applied strictly, that worker would be considered a PYME (i.e. the income ceiling and has fewer than ten employees) but not a street vendor (i.e. works on an unregulated street). This classification, however, would fly in the face of these policies' intent; PYMES are considered 'more formal' than street vendors, and the motivation for passing the Law of Microenterprises was to stimulate the growth of PYMES, not unauthorized street vendors. Another hypothetical worker could vend on regulated streets but make 3 UIT annually; this worker would likewise qualify as a PYME but not a street vendor, even though vending in an authorized area.

The body of law that developed between 1984 and 1994 also complicated the relationship between vendors' constitutional right to work and municipal governments' authority to levy fees for the use of public space. Municipal governments were put in the difficult position of deciding which workers belonged to what category; maintaining order on the streets, in accordance with the Law of Municipalities; developing a fee structure in accordance with the Law of Municipal Taxation; and responding to vendors' accusations of abuses of their constitutional rights. Street vendors, meanwhile, argued among themselves as to whether or not they should pay the *tasa* deemed illegal by INDECOPI anyway for the sake of securing their right to occupy public space. As a consequence of these dilemmas, specific portions of these policies were selectively enforced in most jurisdictions, and some street vendors complied with them while others disobeyed. A difficult cycle of partial enforcement and partial compliance has resulted.

14.2 The Consequences of Policy Incoherence

These difficulties with enforcement and compliance are clearly illustrated in the improvisational approach that many municipalities take toward street vending. To demonstrate, the following discussion explores policy instability in one district, La Victoria, over the course of three administrations (1992–2002). La Victoria is a large, poor, centrally located district that houses the city's largest wholesale and retail markets, along with its vibrant garment district, Gamarra. As such, it has a densely concentrated commercial zone with thousands of street vendors and micro-entrepreneurs. While it is not representative of all districts in Lima, its policy problems are emblematic of other large, centrally located districts.[14]

In the 10 years beginning in 1992, this district passed no fewer than seventy-four new policies related to street vending (see Table 14A.1).[15] The sheer volume of regulations attempting to govern street trade during this time period is emblematic of policymakers' desire to address problems associated with street commerce, rather than opting for simple negligence or maintenance of the status quo. This high volume is also indicative of several practical problems in implementing incoherent policies.

First, the difficulties with implementing Ordinance 002 are evident in the body of policies summarized in Table 14A.1. The fundamental problem in this district was that the ordinance relied on the effective collection of the *sisa* to fund services for street vendors. Without the proper administration of *sisa* funds, the ordinance could not work. Yet, attempts by both municipal officials and vendor leaders to administer those funds resulted in endless controversy. Local officials first contracted with private citizens to collect the fees shifted responsibility for collection to the directors of the FOMA, and then assigned the responsibility to a municipal office, after accusations over the mismanagement of *sisa* funds began to surface. A lack of proper oversight provided an opportunity for those who handled *sisa* income to line their own pockets, and the constant shifting

[14] For more on Gamarra, see Ponce Monteza (1994), Gamero (2001), and Sulmont Haak (1999).

[15] The actual number of policies passed during this period is undoubtedly higher. Appendix Table 14A.1 shows the results of a search for policies conducted during fieldwork in 2001 and 2002; for the sake of presentation, some of the less relevant policies were omitted from the table. Informants (including leaders of street vending organizations and municipal officials) were asked to identify policies related to street vending during each of the three administrations, and a search for the text of each policy mentioned was undertaken. However, some municipal policies are never published in *El Peruano*, and the municipality does not keep complete records of the policies it passes. Without such an archive, it was impossible to determine the exact number of policies issued during this period.

of responsibility for *sisa* collection in local legislation reflects suspicion on each side that the other managed funds improperly. The bitter struggle over who would collect *sisa* revenues and who would oversee their disbursement eroded the ability and desire of street vending leaders and local officials to cooperate with one another.

Second, the municipal government lacked a thorough registry of vendors. The CTMCA directors conducted the first census of the district's street vendors in 1994, but the district lacked the capacity to maintain its accuracy over time. This led to disputes over which vendors qualified for licences, which vendors were allowed access to FOMA benefits, and which vendors were allowed to vend in what spaces. Both the municipality and the CTMCA directors faced an impossible task of keeping unlicensed vendors out of unauthorized areas, adequately distinguishing between complying and non-complying vendors, and punishing the latter effectively.

Perhaps most fundamentally, the particular actors involved could not iron out the details of implementing the policy in order to make it work. While in principle none of these controversies *had* to derail the effort to implement Ordinance 002, the policy left a great deal of negotiation and improvisation up to the actors involved. Once it became clear that the ordinance in its entirety would not be adequately enforced, actors on both sides had little incentive to faithfully adhere to the rules. The lack of compliance on both sides quickly soured the relationship between vendor leaders and local officials.

Furthermore, many of the policies listed in Table 14A.1 are quite particularistic and ad hoc. Examples of particularistic policies include measures that declare street vending illegal on individual streets, grant legal recognition to individual associations of street vendors, establish rules only for vendors of certain products, and call for the eradication or relocation of a single stand, oftentimes in response to a complaint from a resident or shopkeeper. Thus, they are not regulations designed to impose order on the sector as a whole; rather, they respond to individual problems as they arise.

This hodge-podge of particularistic policies has a couple of important consequences. First, vendors who are negatively affected by these policies—for instance, a policy prohibiting them to vend in front of a particular house or store—can simply move to another street, creating the same problem in a different place. While they may be merely shifting the same problem to another location, in doing so these vendors are paradoxically in full compliance with the policy that caused them to leave.

Second, some of these policies grant important benefits to individual vendors or associations of vendors. For example, Ordinance 050 of July 2000 grants special authorizations to shoe shiners and vendors of quinoa, sodas and candy, herbal drinks, and magazines and newspapers. Leaders of vending associations in these product categories considered the ordinance an important political victory, and as a result distanced themselves from other associations in the district that did not enjoy the same privileges. This policy therefore had a divisive effect on vendors who otherwise would share a common interest in beneficial legislation for the whole district. Party politics and improper influence may also play a role in the bargaining process between individual groups of vendors and the local officials responsible for issuing authorizations, furthering division within the sector. Furthermore, formal shopkeepers and real estate proprietors with a large financial stake in the garment district's success, have pressured local officials to enact regulations that emphasize order and control over the social benefits and policy participation outlined in Ordinance 002, which in turn has exacerbated the difficulties with implementing a stable governance regime in the district.

Moreover, many of these regulations are not published, making their diffusion difficult in practice. Those that are published in *El Peruano* sometimes do not appear until up to a year after they are passed. Few street vendors regularly purchase and read the country's official gazette to check for new regulations; rather, they are dependent on leaders of vending organizations to present and explain the content of new policies. These difficulties are exacerbated when new policies are issued on average, once every seven weeks. It is not surprising, then, that many street vendors do not adapt their behaviour to the frequently changing rules of the game. Passing law after law hardly helps to create a policy framework that gives vendors clear incentives for becoming formal.

The broader consequence of this tangle of national, metropolitan, and municipal laws is that vendors and policymakers remain locked in a perpetual cycle of negotiating the terms of formalization. While ordinance 002 explicitly defined the key mechanisms for formalization—most importantly, the *sisa*, the FOMA, the CTMCA, and municipal licences—subsequent laws created several layers of ambiguity in terms of how those mechanisms should be implemented. The controversies resulting from that ambiguity have created a perpetual cycle of conflict between vendors and governments; the result is that the sector is no more formalized than it was 20 years ago. Rather, individual groups of vendors are left to negotiate the terms of their formalization with local authorities, resulting in a chaotic governance regime for the sector as a whole.

14.3 Conclusion

The evidence presented here suggests that although the problem of 'bad laws' still plagues the informal sector in Peru, its sources may be more tractable than they were 20 years ago, when rent-seeking pressure groups were much stronger. Existing laws governing street commerce use conflicting and ambiguous definitions that do not adequately capture the range of conditions found on Lima's streets. These ambiguities in turn produce a dizzying array of conflicting incentives for those who may seek to formalize their work. They also provide the groundwork for a host of conflicts once actors attempt to implement these policies on the ground; without an adequate legal foundation, actors on both sides can argue indefinitely about who should have to comply with what law. Municipal governments' *ad hoc* efforts to respond to these conflicts reduce trust between government officials and leaders of vending organizations, which in turn generates cynicism toward the formal political system among street traders. These conditions produce a difficult cycle of non-enforcement and non-compliance.

Certainly the problem of bad laws may be partially rooted in the country's history of corruption and rent-seeking behaviour, but Peru is not alone in having an insufficient policy framework toward street commerce. The problem of harnessing the entrepreneurial potential of informal workers for the sake of economic development remains urgent enough to warrant a more serious consideration of specific institutional sources of policy incoherence. Appropriate interventions by formal sector actors can generate positive effects within the informal sector (see Nugent and Swaminathan, chapter 12, this volume), and more coherent policy could reduce the incentives for remaining informal.

Appendix

Table 14A.1. Street vending policies in La Victoria, 1992–2000

Policy number	Date	Summary
A.C. 001-92-CM	2 March 1992	Prohibits vending on certain streets
R.A. 1307-92-ALC	25 August 1992	Negates pact with vending associations on three streets; calls for vendors' immediate eradication
D.A. 015-93-ALC	10 May 1993	Prohibits vending on certain streets
Edicto 001-93	20 May 1993	Creates new tax to fund security force
R.A. 0253-93-ALC	25 May 1993	Calls for relocation of one kiosk
D.A. 023-93-ALC	4 June 1993	Calls for restructuring of CTMCA
Ord. 005-93-LV	8 June 1993	Prohibits vending on certain streets
A.C. 020-93	9 August 1993	Prohibits sale of certain foods on streets of La Victoria
R.A. 1060-93-ALC	25 August 1993	Recognizes individual vending association
D.A. 092-93-ALC	10 September 1993	Establishes FOMA and *sisa*
D.A. 093-93-ALC	10 September 1993	Sets contribution levels for *sisa*; restricts size of posts
D.A. 102-93-ALC	28 September 1993	Establishes *sisa* for kiosks
Ord. 009-93-LV	12 October 1993	Authorizes sale of food in tents
R.A. 1238-93-ALC	9 November 1993	Names *sisa* collectors and establishes commissions
R.A. 1239-93-ALC	*	Names new *sisa* collectors and changes commissions
R.A. 1459-93-ALC	*	Recognizes individual vending association
*	*	Names new *sisa* collectors and changes commissions
R.A. 0041-94-ALC	13 January 1994	Calls for immediate eradication of 4 kiosks
D.A. 004-94-ALC	9 February 1994	Shifts responsibility for collecting *sisa* to FOMA
*	10 June 1994	Approves new regulations for FOMA; negates D.A. 092-93
A.C. 020-94	9 August 1994	Suspends payment of salaries to FOMA members
A.C. 021-94	9 August 1994	Shifts responsibility for collecting *sisa* to Municipal Treasury
A.C. 022-94	9 August 1994	Calls on FOMA representatives to return paid salary
A.C. 023-94	9 August 1994	Establishes Evaluation Commission to investigate FOMA
R.A. 2205-94-ALC	15 August 1994	Calls for immediate eradication of vendors at one location
R.A. 1663-94-ALC	6 October 1994	Authorizes one company to install kiosks around district
D.A. 0033-94-ALC	7 December 1994	Raises level of *sisa* contributions and reduces commissions
D.A. 0045-94-ALC	23 December 1994	Authorizes FOMA to enact cleaning campaign
D.A. 0046-94-ALC	23 December 1994	Calls for reordering of street commerce by eradicating vendors without current licenses
D.A. 0047-94-ALC	26 December 1994	Approves new regulations for FOMA
D.A. 0048-94-ALC	26 December 1994	Approves new regulations for CTMCA
*	*	Calls on CTMCA to conduct registration campaign
R.A. 0274-95-ALC	28 February 1995	Recognizes representatives of one vending federation
R.A. 0275-95-ALC	28 February 1995	Recognizes representatives of one vending federation
D.A. 0020-95-ALC	15 March 1995	Suspends payment of *sisa*

Table 14A.1. *(Continued)*

Policy number	Date	Summary
D.A. 0046-95-ALC	22 May 1995	Prohibits vending near Parque Canepa; authorizes only vendors deemed indispensable to district
R.A. 0427-95-ALC	31 July 1995	Calls for immediate eradication of various kiosk and cart owners
R.A. 1737-95-ALC	28 August 1995	Calls for expulsion of vendors occupying storefront garden
A.C. 006-96	19 January 1996	Establishes new commission to investigate FOMA and CTMCA
A.C. 029-96	9 May 1996	Calls for new regulations of FOMA and external audit; shifts responsibility for collecting *sisa* to complete municipal control
A.C. 034-96	20 May 1996	Calls on CTMCA to develop new vending regulations
A.C. 045-96	22 May 1996	Rejects complaint filed by vendors regarding A.C. 029
Ord. 001-96	22 August 1996	Creates new *tasa* to be charged to vendors; negates *sisa*
A.C. 065-96	22 August 1996	Approves new regulations for street vending throughout district
Ord. 003-96-MDLV	22 August 1996	Outlines new regulations for street vending
R.A. 0904-96-MDLV	15 November 1996	Outlines administrative reorganization of municipal government
Edicto 001-96	23 December 1996	Establishes new organizational structure of municipality
A.C. 106-96	31 December 1996	Recommends disbanding FOMA in light of elimination of *sisa*
D.A. 033	16 April 1997	Creates special municipal commission to devise new strategy for formalizing vendors
D.A. 048	18 June 1997	Prohibits vending on certain streets
A.C. 039-97	23 June 1997	Prohibits vending on certain streets
D.A. 004-97-ALC	2 October 1997	Declares beginning of new project to reorder Jiron Gamarra, including expulsion of street vendors
Ord. 002-99-MDLV	6 January 1999	Redefines municipal tax regime; negates all previous *tasas*
Ord. 004-99-MDLV	6 January 1999	Establishes framework for funding security force; duties include collection of daily payment from street vendors
Ord. 005-99-MDLV	6 January 1999	Redefines time frame for charging operating licences
Ord. 014-99-MDLV	28 January 1999	Approves new regulations for issuing operating licences
Ord. 015-99-MDLV	28 January 1999	'Formalizes' street commerce in the district
Edicto 001-99-MDLV	28 January 1999	Creates new municipal office to oversee street vending issues
A.C. 016-99-MDLV	19 March 1999	Declares urgent situation in area of wholesale and retail markets
Ord. 018-99-MDLV	19 March 1999	Establishes tax incentive for vendors who formalize
Ord. 028-99-MDLV	23 July 1999	Establishes sanctions and fees for various acts of non-compliance
Ord. 033-99-MDLV	15 October 1999	Establishes rules for applying above sanctions
Ord. 035-99-MDLV	23 November 1999	Names special zone around wholesale and retail markets; prohibits occupation of public space in that zone

Table 14A.1. (*Continued*)

Policy number	Date	Summary
R.A. 0578-00-ALC	21 June 2000	Authorizes vendors on sidewalks around one commercial center
Ord. 047-00-MDLV	22 June 2000	Approves new comprehensive regulations for area around wholesale and retail markets
Ord. 045-00-MDLV	22 June 2000	Approves formal legal text for above regulations
Ord. 050-00-MDLV	14 July 2000	Grants special authorization to vendors of certain products
Ord. 054-00-MDLV	30 November 2000	Approves new regulations for authorized vendors

Note:
* In some cases only drafts of policies missing policy numbers and dates were available.

References

Carbonetto, D., J. Hoyle, and M. Tueros. (1988). *Lima: Sector Informal*. Lima: CEDEP.

Cross, J. C. (1998). *Informal Politics: Street Vendors and the State in Mexico City*. Stanford: Stanford University Press.

de Soto, Hernando, with the Instituto Libertad y Democracia (2002 [1989]). *The Other Path: The Economic Answer to Terrorism*. New York: Basic Books.

Gamero, J. (2001). *Redes de la Informalidad en Gamarra*. Lima: Universidad Ricardo Palma.

Peattie, L. (1987). 'An Idea in Good Currency and How it Grew: The Informal Sector'. *World Development*, 15(7): 851–60.

Ponce Monteza, C. R. (1994). *Gamarra: Formación, Estructura y Perspectivas*. Lima: Fundación Friedrich Ebert.

Portes, A. (1994). 'The Informal Economy and Its Paradoxes', in N. J. Smelser and R. Swedberg (eds), *The Handbook of Economic Sociology*. Princeton: Princeton University Press, pp. 426–49.

Portes, A. and R. Schauffler (1993). 'Competing Perspectives on the Latin American Informal Sector'. *Population and Development Review*, 19(1) (March): 33–60.

Roberts, B. (1994). 'Informal Economy and Family Strategies'. *International Journal of Urban and Regional Research*, 18(1): 6–23.

Roever, S. (2005). 'Negotiating Formality: Informal Sector, Market, and State in Peru'. Ph.D. Dissertation, Department of Political Science, University of California at Berkeley.

Sulmont Haak, D. (1999). 'Del "Jirón" al "Boulevard Gamarra": Estrategies políticas y gobierno local en La Victoria-Lima', in M. Tanaka (ed.), *El Poder Visto Desde Abajo: Democracia, Educación y Ciudadanía en Espacios Locales*. Lima: Instituto de Estudios Peruanos.

Vildoso, C. (2000). 'Street Vendors: Challenges and Strategies for Survival'. *Women and Microenterprise Series* No. 2 (October), New York: International Coalition on Women and Credit.

15

Formalizing the informal: is there a way to safely unlock human potential through land entitlement? A review of changing land administration in Africa

Liz Alden Wily

15.1 Introduction

It is well-established orthodoxy that the most important material capital of agrarian populations is their land, around which twentieth-century colonial and post-colonial land policies in Africa were built. Contradictory ambitions existed from the outset. On the one hand, these have sought (as phrased by the East African Royal Commission on Land Tenure in 1955) 'to ensure the power of progressive farmers to buy out the less progressive' while on the other promoting peasant security against such threats of transformation and to provide a basis upon which poor peasant farmers could themselves capitalize their farms. The instrument for both objectives was formal entitlement. The argument ran that a flourishing market in land, credit to invest in the tools needed to expand production, and mortgages to obtain the credit were all dependent upon the holding of statutory title deeds. The underpinning assumption was that customary tenure forms did not amount to private rights and could not be traded in the marketplace. The conversion of customary interests into individualized European forms such as freeholds or leaseholds thus became an early plank of formalization. Programmes of adjudicated individualization, titling, and registration followed, usually founded upon formal land surveys. On paper at least, land registration (or privatization, as it has been known) has, since the 1950s in sub-Saharan Africa, consistently been posed as one of the essential conduits to unlocking economic and social potential in agrarian societies, and in which millions of dollars have been invested.

As with so much development process, the reality is somewhat different. Progress has been limited. Less than 1 per cent of the land area of sub-Saharan Africa is today covered by cadastral survey and entitlement and most of this is within South Africa (Augustinus 2003). Well over 90 per cent of Africans continue to own their houses, farms, and shares in common properties under customary means. Failure in the reach of systematic titling programmes is variously attributed to its complexity, cost (for both government and client), time-consuming nature, and belated recognition that informal mechanisms continue to provide significant security of occupancy within the local community. Demand for farm mortgages has also fallen well below expectations, due largely to the practical difficulties in markedly raising small farm productivity beyond that already achieved, in the absence of new technological advances, water availability, and market infrastructure.[1] As elsewhere in the world, African banks have proven, in any event, reluctant to lend on the basis of property alone, and are particularly adverse to mortgage farms where foreclosure would render a peasant family homeless and without means of survival. Meanwhile, microcredit opportunities in a range of forms (including, for example, repayment of purebred milk cows by progeny) have steadily increased since the 1970s and are perceived as less risky and manageable than mortgages (Bruce and Migot-Adholla 1994; Carter *et al.* 1994; Platteau 2000; Alden Wily 2003a; Deininger 2003; Hunt 2005).

Nor is the security argument of converting customary rights to European-derived entitlements necessarily holding up; as the Kenyan Government itself has acknowledged for some years, most people still have not collected their title deeds even when these were issued 30 years past (Government of Kenya 1994). The continued existence of customary assurance of intra-community security clearly plays a part. Owners in one part of Kenya, for example, recently explained that they did not need to collect their deeds as they were 'satisfied that their rights over land had been validated by the adjudication process itself' (Hunt 2005). Travel, time, and fee costs of collection are other disincentives (Okoth-Ogendo

[1] This contrasts with the case in Thailand, Vietnam, China, Honduras, and Paraguay where titling programmes demonstrate positive impact upon investment and agricultural productivity, given greater opportunities for intensification (World Bank 2003).

1999). Having launched perhaps the most determined titling programme in black Africa, the Kenyan experience is most commonly examined but with similar impacts reported in Ghana, Senegal, Somalia, and Uganda (Bruce and Migot-Adholla 1994; Platteau 2000; El-Ghonemy 2003; FAO 2003b). In Kenya, mass rural registration began in the 1950s and continues until today, but with still well-under-half of the total land area covered, enormous costs incurred, and political recognition that classical titling does not easily apply in dry areas where such a high proportion of resources are community pastures and like communal domains (Okoth-Ogendo 1999). Even in fertile highland areas, it was evident by the 1980s that rural titling had *not* stimulated credit availability or its uptake, had *not* stimulated a rural market in land, and had *not* provided the promised indisputable system of evidence of ownership and transaction (Carter *et al.* 1994; Migot-Adholla *et al.* 1994; Alden Wily and Mbaya 2001; KLC 2003). Although farm investment has increased, this has often been in the form of on-farm planting, designed to offset loss of access to common property resources during the entitlement process (Hunt 2005). The promised sanctity of the register and title deeds has been widely disproven with malfeasance and corruption rife, rendering title deeds unreliable (Okoth-Ogendo 1999; KLC 2003). Disputes over titled land have sharply risen, not fallen (Government of Kenya 1994). Sustaining accurate title is proving difficult, with required offices too remote and costs too high, resulting in a high proportion of out-of-date registry records. Nor are expensively arrived-at boundary coordinates proving useful for small farmers, who need to hire surveyors to know where the boundary officially described in coordinates on the entitlement actually lie on the ground, and who routinely revert to customary verification methods (Alden Wily and Mbaya 2001).

The social soundness of classical entitlement has also come under attack. Throughout sub-Saharan Africa the process has routinely altered, rather than simply converted and entrenched, the rights that exist (Toulmin and Quan 2000). Family title, for example, is routinely lost with the narrowing down of ownership to (male) household heads. This alone has generated significant intra-family disputes, as custom and related responsibilities battle with the 'facts' on title deeds. Nor have invaluable secondary rights been widely accounted for, with longstanding tenancies and seasonal access rights of pastoralists routinely undermined (Platteau 2000). In the absence of acknowledgement of common property as a private property right, vast swathes of pasture, forest, and swampland have been lost to communities, either subdivided at registration, often to community members with means, or transferred to state organs, to the detriment of whole communities and especially the poor (Alden Wily and Mbaya 2001). Indeed, a good half-century after the first land security programmes were mooted, insecurity is arguably more, not less, of an issue for the majority poor. Rural landlessness is on the rise and less acceptable as an inevitable cost of modernization, given limited commercialization in the sector or off-farm employment opportunities (Deininger 2003). Wanton land grabbing of customary property continues, not least by the hand of governments and their officials, often supported by legal norms which still render unregistered landholders mere tenants of state, vulnerable to lawful eviction at any time and compensated only for the loss of crops. As of old, common properties have proven most vulnerable, given their historical and legal treatment as *de facto* public lands (Alden Wily and Mbaya 2001).

Recognition that reform is needed in the land tenure and administration sector has slowly gathered pace since around 1990. Aided by wider democratizing trends, legal paradigms and procedural norms are beginning to change, with majority rights better catered to. Often however, the driving force towards this is less benign concern for the rights of the poor than renewed interest to make more land available for investors, including foreigners, much encouraged by the current wave of so-called economic liberalization. For this, formalization of title is still seen as key. The upshot has been a plethora of national (and international policies such as illustrated by the World Bank) which promote improved approaches to titling, and within which pro-poor livelihood objectives are an (often awkward) adjunct to the retained classical objective—to bring more land into the market place for growth (World Bank 2003).[2]

Upwards of half of Africa's 56 mainland and island states are now involved in this reformism (Alden Wily 2003a). Original triggers and strategies (such as political change and subsequent restitution policies in southern African states) are appropriately distinctive to each state.[3] Among the mixed intentions and developments, two trends do however suggest departures, and which could, if fully carried through, genuinely enhance majority land security in ways not seen over the last century. Without such basic change, aspirations of 'turning sand into gold' or

[2] Most recently, this latter objective has been firmly concretized in the establishment of a new UN High Commission for the Legal Empowerment of the Poor, mandated to put into effect Hernando de Soto's (2000) vision of turning the dead capital of the poor into live capital.

[3] For reviews of current land reform in Africa, refer to Toulmin and Quan (2000); Alden Wily and Mbaya (2001); FAO (2003a); and Deininger (2003).

'dead' capital into 'live' capital will remain irrelevant. Both developments are examined below; first, in the still inchoate trend towards devolving land administration authority to landholders themselves, and second, in changing treatment of customary land rights, with the promise of a radical shift in the basis upon which informal rights are formalized and protected in law. In combination, it is posited, these have the potential to sharply and surprisingly, quickly limit rising tenure insecurity and halt the attrition of the land capital of the poor. Moreover, it is suggested, these changes could at the same time open up much-needed new routes through which the poor may capitalize upon their properties, through collateralization or otherwise. Such objectives must remain, however, entirely secondary to the primary requirement for the enhancement of mass tenure security and perhaps best treated distinctly. Thus far, collateralization as a justification for registration of rights has shown itself somewhat of a red herring, and this could still remain the case.

15.2 Decentralization: Unlocking Voices and Capabilities

A word on ideal improvements to tenure administration is in order. Common sense suggests that the nearer to the landholder, the more accessible, cheaper, speedier, ultimately efficient—and used—the system is likely to be. In matters of recordation, the ultimate test of efficacy is the proportion of transactions actually registered, and owners will not bother to do this if distances, costs, or complexity are too great. Localization of machinery and simplification of procedures (including land survey) are prerequisites of voluntary and sustainable mass uptake.

Modern land administration also needs to meet the demands of good governance, in this instance meaning less extending the reach of the bureaucratic arm to the majority, than empowering them wherever possible to design and implement relevant procedures and decision-making themselves, albeit with appropriate technical guidance and monitoring as necessary. Land is, after all, the primary and often only capital asset of the rural majority, and control over which is ill-advisedly fully surrendered. A minimal requirement is that even localized administrations are as accountable downwards to client right-holders as upwards to remote state agencies. Opportunities for rent-seeking, corruption, and land grabbing by economic or political elites are no more acceptable at the community level than at higher levels, and as the history of land administration on the continent thus far shows, needs clear and workable preventative and remedial measures from inception onwards.

15.2.1 *More Deconcentration than Devolution*

Countries which eschew decentralization altogether are few (e.g. Zambia and Mozambique) with most sub-Saharan states sharing policy commitment to decentralized land administration.[4] This manifests in practice more often as deconcentration of state authority than devolution of power to either elected local governments or communities, Eritrea and Rwanda being good examples. Quite often, administration is being formally decentralized for only customary rights whilst those arising out of national statutes (e.g. freeholds and leaseholds) remain under national control (e.g. Burkina Faso, Tanzania). Or, rights may be permissively regulated by local leaders as in the past but with formal functions centrally retained, and with conversionary processes still the norm (e.g. Côte d'Ivoire, Ghana, Zambia).

Even where new and localized regimes are proposed, these are frequently to be operated at multiple levels. Thus in Namibia, traditional authorities regulate local access and approve leases issued by new regional Communal Land Boards (Government of Namibia 2002). This is also broadly the case throughout Francophone Africa where chiefs remain involved but in ways subordinate to Land Commissions or other bodies created at district/commune level, most clearly the case in Niger (Lund 2000).

The real measure of devolution is in the extent of powers granted. The well-established District Land Boards of Botswana, the new District Land Boards of Uganda, the Communal Land Boards of Namibia, the Regional Land Authorities in Ethiopia, and the District Land Commissions of Niger are among those legally proclaimed autonomous. In practice, none of these bodies are free from central government dictate. This extends beyond ministerial powers to regulate or provisions, providing useful checks and balances into significant roles in decision-making. As expected, the more sophisticated the land administration services, the greater the state intervention. For example, in Botswana, government provides each Land Board with land use planners, surveyors, and the powerful Land

[4] This section is based upon a detailed review of decentralizing land administration in twenty African states in Alden Wily (2003a) and where full documentation may be found.

Board Secretary and who may be fired only by central government. This model is being replicated in Namibia and to an extent in Uganda.

A more radical devolution of land authority to community level is nonetheless gathering pace as a favoured strategy. The most developed case is Tanzania, where new land legislation endows each of the already operating 11,400 elected village governments as the Land Manager of their respective village areas—domains which often include substantial commons alongside individually owned farm and house plots (Alden Wily 2003b). Land plans in Côte d'Ivoire, Burkina Faso, Lesotho, Swaziland, and the Ethiopian States of Tigray and Amhara provide similar but less empowered arrangements (Stamm 2000; Alden Wily 2003a; ORGUT 2004). Community-level bodies are also legally provided for (or proposed) in Uganda, Niger, Benin, Mali, Malawi, and Swaziland, but largely instituted thus far to provide consultative and permissive inputs (Alden Wily 2003a). Insufficient devolution is currently a cause of debate around Angola's new Land Bill (Marongwe and Palmer 2004).

15.2.2 *Making Land Administration Locally Accountable*

The relationship of local land institutions with formal local government is worth observing. Where new land institutions are created at district or higher level, the common strategy has been to keep these agencies separate from local government (e.g. Botswana, Namibia, Niger, and Uganda). Moreover, the new land agencies are rarely elected bodies at this level. For example, only five of twelve members of land boards are elected in Botswana, and not through private ballot (Government of Botswana 1993). Nor do supporting regulations of district-level institutions require decision-makers to even report problems and progress to constituent landholders; most new local land administration bodies are accountable to their appointees, departmental heads, commissioners, or ministers.

The closer the authority centre is to the community, the more logical it appears to integrate general governance and natural resource governance functions, particularly where these bodies are elected—the case in Lesotho, Mali, Senegal, and Tanzania. By virtue of local government law, if not the land laws, measures for the public accountability of elected officials are increasingly evident. Many flaws nonetheless exist; in Burkina Faso, for example, elected village governments administer land alongside newer village land use management committees, generating functional overlap and conflict, exacerbated by the uncertain status of customary authorities (Ouedraogo 2002). On the whole, powers of chiefs are being curtailed, or at least located within a wider context of their representation on otherwise elected bodies. In Eritrea, Ethiopia, Rwanda, Tanzania, and Uganda, they are excluded in new localized land administration altogether. New land policy and programming in Ghana expansively acknowledges the particularly well-entrenched authority of chiefs over 80 per cent of the land area, but nonetheless refrains from devolving registration powers to them (Government of Ghana 1999; World Bank and MLF 2003). On the other hand, those reforms do not require chiefs to be more accountable to their communities, an issue of concern, where most claim to be more landlords than trustees over customary lands and collect substantial transaction fees accordingly (Alden Wily and Hammond 2001). Such rent-seeking on the part of traditional leaders is quite widely observed elsewhere in West Africa and to a lesser extent elsewhere (e.g. Lund 2000 on Niger; Norfolk and Liversage 2002 on Mozambique).

Limitation against such tendencies has been a purpose in the Malawi reforms, and where chiefs may legally administer land only in conjunction with three locally-elected advisers, thus combining traditional and modern regimes (Government of Malawi 2002), a model similar to that proposed in Swaziland (Government of Swaziland 1999). Under local government law (1997), up to two traditional leaders may have places on Lesotho's otherwise elected village councils, now like Tanzania's village governments, mandated to manage land matters (Marongwe and Palmer 2004). An important exception to the trend is South Africa, where the Communal Lands Reform Act 2004, as an allegedly pre-election bid to secure their support, effectively handed over control over the properties of 13 million Africans in the ex-homelands to traditional leaders rather than to elected bodies as originally intended (Marongwe and Palmer 2004). Registration itself remains a central government function.

15.2.3 *Simplifying Procedures and Keeping Costs Down*

Efforts to simplify requirements for mass use are also very mixed. Registration of rights clearly remains the *raison dêtre* of formal land administration services. How far new land policies genuinely seek to support smallholder rights remains an open question. Often, steps enabling the rural poor to register ownership derive not from pro-poor commitments but interest to make their land more freely available in the land market—the catalyst to even recent reforms in countries as far apart as Angola, Eritrea, Ghana, Mozambique, and Uganda. This may blunt equity aspects of encouraged formalization of local land rights. In Mozambique, for example, local consultation exercises were introduced into the Land Law 1997 to enable communities to indicate where a proposed land concession to a non-local person or foreigner will interfere with their own occupation and use. In practice, documented community consultations have taken place in a minority of cases (Norfolk and Liversage 2002). Moreover, there is nothing in the law that requires government to *not* allocate the land if it is found to be occupied or used by communities. Procedures have since been introduced to enable communities to at least delimit the areas they do not want interfered with, so far undertaken only with external facilitation and financial support, given the high costs of formal survey and demarcation still required (Norfolk and Liversage 2002).

Keeping requirements to the minimum, costs down, and uptake high, is of necessity better catered for where community-based land administration is being fostered. In Tanzania, for example, no financial support is promised to the 11,400 new formal land managers (village councils) and which will establish village registers and registration regimes in accordance with detailed guidelines, and receive technical support on an *ad hoc* demand status (Alden Wily 2003b). The salary of their single administrative employee, the Village Executive Officer, now also to serve as the Village Land Registrar, is already usually covered by community-raised taxes. Recordation costs associated with land administration are to be met through community levies and fees, set by regulation at low levels (Government of Tanzania 1999). Village Councils may use village taxes to cover adjudication costs where they decide to systematically pursue this, thus making it 'free and fair' for all villagers. The main cost to be covered will be sitting allowances to members of the Village Adjudication Committee and the external Adjudication Adviser whom the community selects to advise it.

Nor will registration of homes and farms be any longer dependent upon time-consuming formal survey and mapping, but upon community agreement as to the accuracy of the general boundary description provided and adjudicated—a strategy also being considered in Tigray, Ethiopia, and in Lesotho (Kingdom of Lesotho 2001; Marongwe and Palmer 2004; ORGUT 2004). Reluctance to abandon cadastral survey more broadly remains. In Ghana, Mozambique, and South Africa, private sector survey work is encouraged and suggests strong bias to the better-off. The Malawi National Land Policy is unusual in pledging subsidies for the poor to offset this (Government of Malawi 2002).

Where, overall, do changes in land administration systems stand? They are clearly mixed, with relatively few countries thus far genuinely devolving authority and to sufficiently local levels where land administrators must directly face and be accountable to the landholders they are supposed to serve. Nonetheless, the fact that this democratization and localization of tenure governance is taking place at all is a positive step, more so given that each year is seeing another State adopt the strategy.

15.3 Improving the Status of Customary Rights: Unlocking Rights for Development

A main driver to devolving governance of land relations and formalization of rights within this is the underlying change in the legal position of customary land rights themselves. Quite simply, if customary rights are to be registrable, then customary or at least community-based procedures are logically the foundation for this. These countries now permit customary land interests to be directly registered without conversion into non-customary forms like freehold or leasehold rights: Botswana, Ghana, Mozambique, Namibia, Niger, Tanzania, Uganda; and proposed in Lesotho, Malawi, and Swaziland (Alden Wily 2003a). In Uganda and Tanzania, for example, these entitlements are respectively known as a Certificate of Customary Ownership and a Customary Right of Occupancy, and broadly have all the incidents of freehold and/or as customarily agreed, and may be roughly translated as 'customary freeholds'. In most cases, registration is to be undertaken by a decentralized body at district or even community level (Ghana and Mozambique being main exceptions). Six other states accept informal rights for registration but as of old, in the process transform these into new forms: a Lifetime Usufruct in Eritrea, a Holding Right in Ethiopia, a Right of Private Ownership in South Africa, a Concession in Rwanda, and a Land Title in Côte d'Ivoire (Alden Wily 2003a).

15.3.1 *Recognizing Common Property as Private Property*

Perhaps more radical is the growing number of cases (but not Botswana, Ghana, Namibia, or Tigray) where these entitlements may apply not only to individually held estates like farms, shops, or houses, but to common properties such as pastures, forests, marshes, hilltops, or local public spaces. Families, clans, groups, or whole communities in Tanzania, Uganda, Niger, and Côte d'Ivoire, among others, may thereby become the private registered landholder of estates conceived as private group-owned land, owned in undivided shares by all members of the group.

It is this change that most represents innovation in the current land administration reforms in the continent. It opens the way for many millions of hectares of highly vulnerable property, previously held to be *de facto* un-owned land, to be properly secured as the private property of the community or group, and moreover registered formally as such. The properties affected are highly significant. They include, for example, around 300 million hectares of off-reserve forests and woodlands in sub-Saharan Africa. These are but the residue from as many millions of better quality forest already drawn out of local control as government reserves and parks, and an even greater number of hectares lost to rampant land grabbing and/or urbanization. These land losses have been effected with due support of law, laws which acknowledged occupancy if not ownership of customary lands used for farming or settlement, but which could not conceive of communal tenure as having the incidents of private property. Such a position was self-evidently notoriously helpful to land-greedy governments and their agents. As *terres sans maitre*, these lands may be reallocated at will—and were—throughout many sub-Saharan states. Perhaps the most currently topical example is Sudan, where persistent refusal to acknowledge pastures or woodlands as owned by African communities has enabled many millions of (African-held) common properties to be reallocated to (non-African, and often non-national) entrepreneurs, needless to say, one of the drivers to the long north–south war (Manger 2003).

New recognition of customary rights as private land rights and accordingly registrable in their diverse forms, turns the tide on such losses. Not least of this is the reality that as private property, properties customarily held in common are in these environments now due the same level of compensation if acquired for public purpose, as other more obviously private (individually-held) properties (Alden Wily and Mbaya 2001).

It is unfortunate, therefore, that the constructions through which common property registration may be effected are still often awkwardly formed, if evolving. Collective titles in Mozambique and Côte d'Ivoire have the disadvantage of including common and individual properties, and have more accurately less entitlement than confirmation of community jurisdiction. In South Africa, the first country to provide for common property registration, the title itself is more refined, but achievable only through expensive and complicated creation of a Communal Property Association resulting in limited uptake (Mostert and Pienaar 2004). The Communal Land Reform Act 2004 introduced a simpler mechanism, based primarily on the registration of rules for the property by the co-owners. This is pragmatic in targeting the issue that most distinguishes individual and common properties; the need for there to be fair and inclusive means through which any change in its status or use is a shared decision by all shareholders.

The most straightforward mechanism to date has been to make blanket provision for land to be held 'by a person, a family unit or a group of persons recognized in the community as capable of being a landholder' (Government of Tanzania 1999a) and providing for registration of this as a single process, irrespective of the nature of the owner. This route exists in the new land laws of Uganda, Amhara in Ethiopia, Tanzania, and potentially in the laws of Lesotho, Malawi, and Swaziland. In addition, these laws meet the problem noted above by requiring the community to agree and record at the same time how the common property will be accessed, used and transacted in the form of a simple management plan (Alden Wily 2003a). The Tanzanian law is particularly mindful of the centrality of common estates to the livelihood of the poor, and the need to limit wanton subdivision that may be prompted through entitlement opportunities. The Village Land Act 1999 accordingly disallows the adjudication and titling of *individual* holdings until the community has identified and registered its shared properties.

Family title is also emerging in stronger registrable form. This is most distinctly provided for in Ethiopia and Malawi (Government of the Federal Republic of Ethiopia 1997; TRS 1997; ARS 2000a, b). Adoption of procedures which limit transfers of family land without the full support of family members, but which do not unduly inhibit transactions, has preoccupied several states (e.g. Malawi, Uganda) and is likely to preoccupy Lesotho, Rwanda, and Swaziland where family title and spousal co-ownership entitlements are also provided for or proposed (Kingdom of Lesotho 2001; Government of Rwanda 2003).

Despite these important developments, few states as yet endow registered customary interests unequivocal equivalency with tenure forms. An exception is Tanzania, where not only is declamatory statement made to this effect (Land Act 1999), but the incidents of a registered customary right are superior to those of a granted right from the state to the extent that its term is unlimited (Village Land Act 1999). In Uganda, the benefits of stated equivalency are undermined by, as clear encouragement to convert a Customary Certificate into a freehold entitlement, also available in Ghana and Lesotho. Some other new laws make no attempt at equivalency; in Côte d'Ivoire, an Ownership Certificate is not held to be full ownership, but may be registered subsequently and converted into a

European form of tenure in the process (Stamm 2000). Côte d'Ivoire is additionally one of the few countries not to offer legal protection to unregistered customary rights after a few years hence (Stamm 2000). Elsewhere, registration of customary interests is strictly voluntary, at least as such time as systematic-assisted registration is launched.

15.4 Conclusion

There is little doubt that some important changes are afoot in the evolving land reform movement in the African continent, and those reviewed here do suggest potential removal of long-standing constraints affecting majority rural populations in this sphere. Customary rights have enjoyed subordinate status, as merely permissive rights up until this current period of change, pending what have ultimately proven broadly unsuccessful attempts at their transformation. What is new today, is the opportunity to register customary rights 'as is', without necessary conversion or loss of customary incidents (such as if and how the property may be sold or in whom the property is vested; one, two, or more persons). Even without formalization possibilities, the current reform movement enhances customary security, after a century of what now seems like entirely unnecessary subordination. Moreover, in the more adventurous paradigms, mechanisms are being put in place to enable communities (or more exactly, their representatives) to administer these rights themselves, building upon existing inchoate regimes in combination with more modern norms. Both rights and improved land tenure governance are well served, important triggers, to unlocking socioeconomic potential.

Limitations clearly abound. One of these is that despite the inclusion of common properties as private, and registrable estates, formalization strategies visibly still focus upon the family farm and house. This is problematic for two reasons: first, it is the commons of Africa—the pastures, forests, swamps, hills, and other shared land resources—that are most at risk of loss through unplanned expansion, wrongful occupation, unregulated market forces, and co-option by state agencies. Forests and pastures are enormously valuable assets to communities even without development, and a stronger effort to assist communities to formalize their rights over these resources is long overdue—and in which the community forestry sector, rather than the land sector, has thus far been the leader in the creation of community-owned and managed forest reserves (Alden Wily and Mbaya 2001).

Second, failure to promote and facilitate the registration of these group-owned properties represents a lost opportunity for one realm of land-based capitalization in agrarian states. It has been shown above how mortgaging of the family farm or house does not appear to have resonated with local aspirations and/or been readily achievable. Reasons for this have been suggested, including market-related and other limitations beyond the control of the individual mortgagor. It could well be the case that the larger and often more virgin common estates possess potentials which are less vulnerable to such constraints, and of which emergent eco-tourism, hunting, and logging enterprises are early tasters. The above example of central Sudan suggests another potential where communities, rather than the state, should benefit substantially through simply leasing out parts of their substantial common resources to entrepreneur farmers. Even securing the substantial harvesting fees currently earned by government for the collection of gum arabica in these common properties would restore significant revenue to rightful owners (Alden Wily forthcoming).

There is another dimension of note. The harsh realities of under-serviced rural Africa and the extremely limited assets of individual families mean that working together as communities to secure change or services has proved a logical and essential *modus operandi* in much of sub-Saharan Africa. Whether to establish schools, hire teachers, build roads, protect a forest, or other activities, thousands of African communities routinely demonstrate the advantages of community-based initiative. Tapping into this rare capacity opens opportunities for investment founded upon the mortgage of sometimes vast common estates (or parts thereof). Moreover, these could deliver local-level developments or revenue sources of benefit to whole communities, and in a manner that could be a good deal more viable than individual enterprise and much safer than focusing the family field. In addition, as equal shareholders in the ownership of the capital, the poor could be better targeted as beneficiaries or, at least for once, not easily excluded. Obviously, the good governance requirements outlined above would need to be applied to ensure this is realized.

Such developments are premised, however, upon local communities securing these resources as their own private property in the first instance, and this, with or without possible collateralization, must remain the primary rationale for any form of titling. In the current wave of reforms, we may see that enhancement of tenure security really could become a reality, now that the objective is more clearly to entrench existing rights in law rather than transform these. Ironically, the route towards this remains the same as in the past—registration and entitlement, or formalization of informal rights in ways which the law must uphold—the very route which once weakened communal interests but now acknowledges and strengthens these. It is this shifting ground upon which this procedure operates, and related shifts in the balance of controlling authority over land rights from centre to periphery that holds most promise for the majority poor, and makes the current reform initiatives worth watching. It could even—incidentally—be that new and more useful forms of land mortgaging in time eventuate.

References

Alden Wily, L. (2003a). 'Governance and Land Relations'. A Review of Decentralization of Land Administration and Management in Africa. London: IIED.

Alden Wily, L. (2003b). 'Community Based Land Tenure Management. Questions and Answers About Tanzania's New Village Land Act 1999'. *Drylands Issues Paper* 120. London: IIED.

Alden Wily, L. (forthcoming). 'The Role of Customary Property Rights in the Legal Disempowerment and Empowerment of the Poor A Case Study from Sudan'. Paper to be presented to an International Symposium: At The Frontier of Land Issues: Social Embeddedness of Rights and Public Policy ENSAM-INRA Campus, Montpelier, 17–19 May 2006.

Alden Wily, L. and D. Hammond (2001). 'Land Security and the Poor in Ghana. Is There a Way Forward?'. A Land Sector Scoping Study. London: DFID.

Alden Wily, L. and S. Mbaya (2001). 'Land, People and Forests in Eastern and Southern Africa at the Beginning of the 21st Century. The Impact of Land Relations of the Role of Communities in Forest Future'. Nairobi: The World Conservation Union.

Augustinus, C. (2003). 'Comparative Analysis of Land Administration Systems: African Review with special reference to Mozambique, Uganda, Namibia, Ghana, South Africa'. Washington, DC: World Bank.

Bruce, J. and S. Migot-Adholla (eds) (1994). *Searching for Land Tenure Security in Africa*. Dubuque, IA: Kendall/Hunt.

Carter, M., K. Wiebe, and B. Blarel (1994). 'Tenure Security for Whom? Differential Effects of Land Policy in Kenya', in J. Bruce and S. Migot-Adholla (eds) *Searching for Land Tenure Security in Africa*. Dubuque, IA: Kendall/Hunt, chapter 7.

Deininger, K. (2003). *Land Policies for Growth and Poverty Reduction* (World Bank Policy Research Report). New York: Oxford University Press.

de Soto, H. (2000). *The Mystery of Capital Why Capitalism Triumphs in the West and Fails Everywhere Else*. London: Black Swan Books.

El-Ghonemy, M. (2003). 'Land Reform Development Challenges of 1963–2003 Continue into the Twenty-First Century', in FAO (2003a) 'Land Reform, Land Settlement and Cooperatives', FAO: Rome, pp. 32–42.

FAO (2003a). 'Land Reform, Land Settlement and Cooperatives'. Issue 2 of 2003. Rome.

FAO (2003b). 'Land Reform, Land Settlement and Cooperatives'. Issue 3 of 2003. Rome.

Government of Kenya (1994). National Development Plan 1994–1996. Nairobi.

Hunt, D. (2005). 'Some Outstanding Issues in the Debate on External Promotion on Land Privatisation'. *Development Policy Review* 23(2): 199–231.

Kenya Land Commission KLC (2003). Report of the Presidential Commission of Inquiry into Land Matters.

Kingdom of Lesotho (2001). Draft National Land Policy of Lesotho.

Lund, C. (2000). 'Seeking Certainty and Aggravating Ambiguity: On Property, Paper and Authority in Niger'. Paper presented at seminar on Institutions and Uncertainty held at IDS Sussex, Brighton on 6–8 November.

Manger, L. (2003). 'The Issue of Land in the Nuba Mountains'. A Desk Study Prepared for UNDP, Sudan (unpublished).

Marongwe, N. and R. Palmer (eds) (2004). 'Land Reform Highlights in Southern Africa 2003–4'. Harare: Independent Land Newsletter.

Migot-Adholla, S., Fr. Place, and W. Oluoch-Kosura (1994). 'Land, Security of Tenure and Productivity in Kenya', in J. Bruce and S. Migot-Adholla (eds), *Searching for Land Tenure Security in Africa*. Dubuque, IA: Kendall/Hunt, chapter 6.

Mostert, H. and J. Pienaar (2004). 'Communal Land Title: An Assessment of the Efficacy of Legislative Intervention for Tenure Security and Access to Land', (unpublished).

Norfolk, S. and H. Liversage (2002). 'Land Reform and Poverty Alleviation in Mozambique'. Paper for the Southern African Regional Poverty Network, Human Sciences Research Council.

Okoth-Ogendo, H. (1999). 'Land Issues in Kenya. Agenda Items from the 20th Century'. Department for International Development, Nairobi.

ORGUT (2004). *Evaluation of the Pilot Land Administration Scheme in Amhara National Regional State*. Stockholm: ORGUT.

Ouedraogo, M. (2002). 'Land Tenure and Rural Development in Burkina Faso: Issues and Strategies'. *Issue Paper* No. 112. Drylands Programme, IIED.

Platteau, J.-P. (2000). 'Does Africa Need Land Reform?', in C. Toulmin and J. Quan (eds), *Evolving Land Rights, Policy and Tenure in Africa*, London: IIED Bookshop, pp. 51–73.

Stamm, V. (2000). 'The Rural Land Plan: An Innovative Approach from Côte d'Ivoire'. *Issue Paper* No. 91. Drylands Programme, IIED.

Toulmin, C. and J. Quan (eds) (2000). *Evolving Land Rights, Policy and Tenure in Africa*. London: DFID/IIED/NRI.

TRS (Tigray Regional State) (1997). Proclamation No. 23 of 1997. Rural Land Proclamation.

World Bank (2003) Agricultural Investment Source Book, Draft, 2 September.

World Bank and MLF (Ministry of Land and Forestry) (2003). Ghana Land Administration Project.

Acts and Legislation

Amhara Regional State (ARS) (2000a). Proclamation No. 46/2000 Issued to Determine the Administration and Use of The Rural Land in the Amhara National Region.

Amhara Regional State (ARS) (2000b). Proclamation No. 47/2000 on Environmental Protection, Land Administration and Use Authority Establishment.

Government of Botswana
(1993) Tribal Land (Amendment) Act to Tribal Land Act Cap 32: 02

Government of Eritrea
(1994) Land Proclamation No. 58/1994
(1997) Proclamation to Provide for the Registration of Land and Other Immovable Property No. 95/1997

Government of the Federal Republic of Ethiopia
(1997) Proclamation No. 89/1997. Rural Land Administration Proclamation

Government of Ghana
(1999) National Land Policy. Ministry of Land and Forestry

Government of Malawi
(2002) Malawi National Land Policy

Government of Mozambique
(1997) Land Law with Technical Annex
(2000) Regulations 1998 with Technical Annex to Regulations 1999

Government of Namibia
(2002) Communal Land Reform Act 2002

Government of Rwanda
(2003) Draft Rwanda Land Law Act

Government of Swaziland
(1999) Draft National Land Policy

Government of South Africa
(1996) Communal Property Associations Act
(1997) National Land Policy
(2004) Communal Land Reform Act

Government of Tanzania
(1999) The Village Land Act and Regulations 2001
(1999) The Land Act and Regulations 2001

Government of Uganda
(1998) The Land Act

Government of Zambia
(1999) Draft National Land Policy

INDEX